The Politics of Constitutional Reform in North America

Politikwissenschaftliche Paperbacks

Studien und Texte
zu den politischen Problemfeldern
und Wandlungstendenzen
westlicher Industriegesellschaften

Herausgegeben von

Dieter Nohlen
Rainer-Olaf Schultze
Wichard Woyke

Band 30

Rainer-Olaf Schultze/Roland Sturm (Eds.)
in collaboration with Steffen Schneider

The Politics of Constitutional Reform in North America

Coping with New Challenges

Springer Fachmedien Wiesbaden GmbH 2000

We gratefully acknowledge the financial support of the Bavarian American Academy, the Association for Canadian Studies in German-Speaking Countries, and the Canadian Embassy, Berlin.

Gedruckt auf säurefreiem und alterungsbeständigem Papier.

Die Deutsche Bibliothek – CIP-Einheitsaufnahme
Ein Titeldatensatz für diese Publikation ist bei Der Deutschen Bibliothek erhältlich

ISBN 978-3-663-11630-1 **ISBN 978-3-663-11628-8 (eBook)**
DOI 10.1007/978-3-663-11628-8

Ursprünglich erschienin bei Leske + Budrich, Opladen in 2000

Preface

In October 1999, some fifteen academic experts and government practitioners from Germany and North America gathered for two days at the University of Augsburg to discuss the topic of "Constitutional Reform and Constitutional Jurisprudence in Canada and the United States." The present volume documents the results of that conference, a collaborative effort of the Department of Political Science, University of Erlangen-Nuremberg, and the Institute for Canadian Studies, University of Augsburg.

In organizing this workshop, we were guided by two basic sets of ideas and assumptions: First, all "established" democracies are regularly confronted with the need to adjust their constitutional order to changes in their environment lest democratic stability be transformed into rigidity; in many western nations, including Canada and the United States, developments such as the crisis of the Keynesian welfare-state or the emergence of increasingly heterogeneous, postmodern societies have ushered in an era of heightened, yet not always successful constitutional reform activity. Secondly, however, there is no unique path towards, or model of, an "optimal" constitutional order, however defined; rather, constitutional reform processes, their underlying normative principles and their outcomes are strongly path and context-dependent.

Therefore, the participants of the workshop and authors of this volume were asked to examine the specific preconditions, context, nature and impact of recent constitutional reform processes in the United States and Canada. Five broad and crucial areas of constitutional reform were discussed: changes in the legislative and executive branches, trends in federalism and intergovernmental relations, the politics of budgeting and minorities, and the role of constitutional jurisprudence in reform processes.

We are confident that the thirteen papers included in this volume illustrate the considerable range and scope, as well as the relevance, of constitutional reform activity in the two North American polities. We also hope that they underline the value of an historically and empirically oriented, context-sensitive approach to the study of constitutional reform processes, and hence represent a meaningful contribution to the (scarce) comparative literature on this important topic.

The editors would like to thank the individuals and institutions whose cooperation and support facilitated the organization of the October conference and the swift publication of the proceedings: first, the participants who made their contributions available for this volume and revised their papers under severe time restrictions (unfortunately, not all papers were available or received in time, as a glance at the conference program in the appendix shows); secondly, Steffen Schneider who assisted us in organizing the conference and in editing the proceedings; and finally, the board of the Bavarian American Academy with its chairman, Prof. Dr. Helmbrecht Breinig, the Association for Canadian Studies in the German-speaking Countries, and the Canadian Embassy, Berlin, who extended generous financial support to us.

Augsburg/Erlangen, June 2000

Rainer-Olaf Schultze
Roland Sturm

Contents

I. Constitutional Reform – Theoretical and Comparative Perspectives

Constitutional Reform as Process

Rainer-Olaf Schultze

Constitutional politics as a research field is currently marked by a peculiar contradiction:[1] On the one hand, processes of constitution-making and constitutional reform have abounded on a global scale at least since the post-1989 upheavals (von Beyme/Offe 1995; Merkel 1996; Merkel et al. 1996). On the other hand, there is a considerable dearth of solid empirical and comparative work on these processes, even though constitution-making and constitutional engineering are genuine subfields of political science. The verdict made by German constitutional-law scholar and Federal Supreme Court Justice Dieter Grimm in 1978, according to which German political science had not contributed much to the research on constitutional politics and reform up to that point, is still largely valid today, minor exceptions notwithstanding (Grimm 1994: 338ff.). Although a series of monographs, the bulk of which examine the so-called unification reforms, has been published in the meantime, there is no systematically comparative elaboration of the topic to date (Benz 1993; Batt 1996). From an international perspective, the state of research is strikingly similar. Jon Elster, for instance, just recently (1993: 174) observed that

> "[t]he comparative study of ordinary law making is a central field of political science. The comparative study of revolutions has a long history. But to my knowledge there is not a single book or even article discussing the process of constitution-making in a general comparative perspective. The gap is puzzling, but it appears to be undeniable."

Giovanni Sartori's study on *Comparative Constitutional Engineering: An Inquiry into Structures, Incentives and Outcomes* (1994) was published against this background. In discussing Sartori's approach, this chapter presents some analytical reflections on the politics of constitutional reform in established democracies.[2]

---

1 This chapter is the revised English version of a paper first published in German, "Verfassungsreform als Prozess," in: *Zeitschrift für Parlamentsfragen* 28, 3 (1997), 502-520. Translated into English by Ulrike Rausch and Steffen Schneider.

2 The paper is primarily concerned with processes of constitutional reform in established democracies rather than constitution-making in the context of system transformations. Considering the state of research, it will only be possible to explore the field, not to present detailed results. The term "established democracies" (also labeled "stable" or "old

I. Constitutional Engineering – A Critique of Sartori's Propositions

Sartori is particularly concerned with the impact of electoral systems and further analyzes the working conditions of presidential, parliamentary, and semi-presidential systems in an attempt to develop suggestions for constitution-making and institution-building: (a) In recommending the French electoral system – i.e., majority runoff elections –, he takes a stand that clearly differs from the conventional wisdom dominating international research on electoral systems. His view also contradicts the trend that emerges from an empirical analysis of recent electoral system reforms, which tend to aim at improving the proportionality of existing systems or at introducing PR altogether (Lijphart/Grofman 1984; Lijphart 1994; Nohlen 2000; Nohlen/Kasapovic 1996). (b) As type of government, Sartori embraces semi-presidentialism – i.e., the institutions of the French Fifth Republic –, which he considers best in terms of functionality. Here again, he contradicts leading scholars of comparative government (Nohlen 1992).

1. Concepts and Methods

Sartori claims that his conclusions are based on inductive research methods and empirical evidence. He is concerned with the "conditions under which specific constitutional reforms – including major ones – are likely 'to cause' (or not) the intended effects" (1994: 201). He further states "that there is no getting away from context" (1994: 135). Taking these words at face value, one should expect the following elements from a study entitled *Comparative Constitutional Engineering*: (a) an historically precise analysis along neo-institutional lines of reasoning that examines, in a detailed way, the connection between institutional arrangements and their context across time and space; (b) a comparative analysis focusing on specific reform processes; and (c) an actor-centered analysis that (i) concentrates on the interests and goals underpinning the behavior of political and social actors in the process of constitutional engineering, (ii) outlines their reform options and constraints, and hence (iii) provides policy consultants with a realistic view of the preconditions and context of constitutional reform.

However, Sartori's epistemological credo and theoretical position lead him in exactly the opposite direction. Sartori develops his epistemological points of reference in debating the theoretical counter-position of Jon Elster,

democracies") refers to Robert A. Dahl (1996: 177) who uses it for political systems that have been steadily governed in a democratic way for several generations – i.e., at least since the end of World War Two.

as well as the historically and empirically grounded counter-arguments of Dieter Nohlen (Sartori 1994: 27ff.). In his contributions to the international discussion on electoral systems, Nohlen has repeatedly stated over the last couple of years that the maneuvering space of electoral reformers is dependent on context and thus extremely limited (Nohlen 1984, 2000). Based on rational-choice theory, Jon Elster has convincingly argued that it is impossible to make reliable predictions about the results and impact of constitutional reform processes (Elster 1988a, 1988b). Sartori, by contrast, puts things in a different light: According to him, purposeful constitutional engineering is possible, although he does not waste much time reflecting on this proposition. In his view, the social scientist assumes the role of an engineer who enables politicians to conduct proper reforms by pointing out the relevant causal structures and sociological laws to them. Still according to Sartori, electoral experts have so far not taken on this task. On the contrary,

"[t]he truth is, I submit, that our alleged electoral experts have largely failed to develop the expertise that is required of them, and that much of their current counseling is poor or plainly wrong." (Sartori 1994: 29)

This is the starting point for Sartori's own argument: "As I propose to show – beginning with showing (contrary to the prevailing wisdom) that the effects of electoral systems can be adequately predicted and determined" (Sartori 1994: 29). However, Sartori's research is rooted in a narrow understanding of political institutions and constitutions. This fact is illustrated by the introductory motto borrowed from John Plamenatz: "The proper study of politics is not man but institutions" (Sartori 1994: ix). Sartori's work only deals with government institutions, including the rules of electoral systems. He conceptualizes institutions as independent variables that have a lasting effect on the stability and efficiency of political systems. Constitutions are understood as mere organizational frameworks for state institutions – as "machines" that have to go like a clockwork in order to produce desirable political results. Thus for Sartori, just like for the American founding fathers Alexander Hamilton and James Madison, a bill of fundamental rights is no necessary component of a constitution (Sartori 1994: 198). The fact that the Bill of Rights was added to the U.S. Constitution in the first ten amendments for a good reason is acknowledged in a passing remark only. For Sartori, constitutions are just synonyms for the procedures that are needed to control power. It is of course true that constitutions have to fulfill this function, too; but Sartori errs if he concludes that "constitutions are, and must be, 'content-neutral'" (Sartori 1994: 202). For constitutions and the institutional arrangements they sustain always reflect historically specific constellations of power in society and politics.

Sartori's understanding of politics itself is equally flawed and biased towards stability and efficiency considerations. He is not interested in the process of constitutional and institutional change. Not surprisingly, his study does not take into account the interests of actors in the reform processes. Yet only the comparative study of these processes will yield systematic evidence on patterns of behavior and the multiple social and political, structural and historically contingent limits to reform. Such a view of reform processes would at the same time reveal how restricted the predictive abilities of constitutional experts are in any given reform situation.

2. *Reform Suggestions*

Democratic politics is characterized by conflict and competition, uncertainty and openness (Przeworski 1988, 1991). It is further determined by the inherent tension between the requirement of citizen participation and political accountability on the one hand, the need for an effective (and socially equitable) policy output on the other hand. Sartori touches upon this basic aspect of democracy by considering problems of representation. He correctly points to the different meanings of the term "responsible government:"

> "On the one hand responsible implies 'responsiveness'; but on the other hand it implies independent responsibility, the kind of behavior that consists of 'acting responsibly', with all the competence, prudence and ability that any representative is required to muster *vis-à-vis* those represented." (Sartori 1994: 73)

And he rightly adds that these two components cannot be separated from each other: Both aspects are as unlikely to be resolved one-sidedly as the tension between inclusion and efficiency. With regard to electoral systems, this logic has two consequences: First, it means that the design of electoral rules can neither be exclusively oriented towards the principle of proportional representation – mirroring the exact make-up of society – nor solely geared towards the functional objective of generating majorities. Hence pure types of electoral systems, such as first-past-the-post elections or unfettered PR, cannot be considered viable options. Instead, an attempt at reconciling both goals of representation should be made. Secondly, electoral systems are context-bound combinations of different components; thus the extent to which the two different meanings of representation are built into them is influenced by social demands, traditions of political culture, and the reform opportunities provided by institutional arrangements.

In his reform suggestions with regard to electoral systems, Sartori himself does ultimately *not* follow these conclusions, which are nevertheless implied in his thinking. He *does* favor electoral systems that combine elements of both principles of representation to pure types, thus arguing less dogmatically than in the past. And yet PR systems that incorporate functional components such as thresholds or small electoral district sizes do not fare well in his analysis. Even the personalized PR system used in Germany, which has been hailed as a model by international electoral experts precisely because it couples PR with a legal threshold in a meaningful and successful way (Nohlen 2000), is included in this negative evaluation.

Since 1976, Sartori has based the measurement of two-party systems on a single variable: the existence of one-party government, majority or minority (Sartori 1976). Only this questionable conceptual simplification allows him to identify empirical examples of two-party systems (Schultze 1985, 1996). Sartori's infatuation with stability and effectiveness as indicators for his notion of "good government" explains why electoral rules, as well as the structure of parties and party systems, play such a crucial role in his work. What he calls the localism of parties and politics is seen as a major obstacle in this respect:

"The issue then becomes whether the localistic development of the single-member district system is somewhat natural and inevitable, or can instead be resisted. [...]. As we know, the 'sine qua non' condition of a two-party polity is a structured (strong) nation-wide party system; and this implies the district-centered politics and a two-party polity are incompatibles: if localism affirms itself, a two-party state purely and simply breaks down. In England and in the Commonwealth countries localism is resisted and counteracted, then, by the strength and the very self-preserving logic of the party system." (Sartori 1994: 58)

Regardless of the empirical fact that there are hardly any Commonwealth countries left that function as two-party systems, this reasoning follows a peculiar circular logic that depicts a strong and nationally defined two-party system both as precondition and result. With majority runoff elections, Sartori believes to have found a powerful counterforce against localistic trends. Unfortunately, no convincing evidence for this claim is offered. In order to prove this point, detailed empirical analysis showing why some countries have a localistic party system, and others do not, would be necessary. Particularly lacking is a detailed elaboration on the development of parties and the party system in the French Fifth Republic. It would reveal that while two different party camps have indeed developed there, the electoral system has not weakened the localistic orientation of French party politics – one just has to keep in mind the great many mayors and local dignitaries who are at the same time leading members of the French National Assembly (Converse/Pierce 1986). Sartori's expectations regarding majority elections with a double ballot cannot be substantiated with evidence from France. In addition, it would remain to be seen if the formation of blocs within the party system can be really traced causally to the effects of the electoral system.

Sartori's pledge for semi-presidentialism is equally unsubstantiated. It largely stems from his uneasiness with the inflexibility of U.S. presidentialism and the confrontational relationship between President and Congress, especially when "divided government" threatens to impair the efficiency of the policy output (Cox/Kernell 1991; Fiorina 1996). Still, it is hardly convincing to consider semi-presidentialism with its double executive – especially in the context of *cohabitation* as experienced in France – as escape from the dilemma posed by "divided government."

3. Preconditions for Constitutional Engineering

A considerably more thoughtful analysis of the preconditions for democratic constitutional politics has been proposed by Robert Dahl in an essay published almost simultaneously with Sartori's book. In 16 theses, Dahl develops a truly empirically based argument regarding the value of constitutions and institutional arrangements for the stability of democracies. In several ways, his conclusions offer a convincing alternative to Sartori's work:

(1) Dahl correctly refers to the importance of social context: "For developing and maintaining democratic political institutions, constitutional arrangements are less important than the existence of certain favorable conditions" (Dahl 1996: 178). These favorable conditions include: (a) the concentration of power in the hands of the democratic state and its representatives; (b) the organization of a society along the lines of modernity, dynamic pluralism, and market orientation; (c) the cultural homogeneity of a society or the existence of consociational arrangements in heterogeneous societies; (d) a participatory political culture together with a high degree of support for the institutions of polyarchy.

(2) Where these conditions are favorable for democracy, the institutional arrangements defined by a constitution do, according to Dahl, not play a crucial role in securing stability. This even holds true for the choice between presidential and parliamentary government, or majoritarian and PR electoral systems.

(3) Things look different in political systems where these favorable conditions lack entirely, or where they exist only to a limited extent. Here, political institutions gain in importance. In order to foster the much-needed inclusion and consensus-building in such a context, Dahl opts for parliamentary government, consociational arrangements and PR.

(4) As a general rule, the elements of democratic constitutions come in a multitude of possible variations and permutations; "every country's constitutional arrangements are unique" (Dahl 1993: 188), and hence "all general judgements about constitutional arrangements should always be tempered by the need to adapt constitutional arrangements to the special conditions of a country" (Dahl 1993: 195).

A comparison between both positions reveals the reasons for Sartori's misinterpretation. They have to be seen, first, in his unreflected concept of institutionalism which neither considers institutions as dependent variables, basically leaving aside their societal context, nor takes into account the fact that institutional arrangements such as electoral systems are the result of complex processes of decision-making. Therefore, institutional arrangements have to be seen as dependent variables, too, especially if the focus of the analysis is on policy consulting. Secondly, Sartori has to be criticized for his purely institutionalist concept of constitutions, neglecting their multifunctionality.

Policy consultants have to realize (1) that there is no universally accepted matrix of democratic institutions (Merkel et al. 1996: 32), and (2) that proper institutional arrangements cannot be designed without context-sensitive analysis. It is essential to ensure that political institutions are compatible with the cleavage structure of a society (Nohlen 1994). This, in turn, means that considerations regarding the transfer of constitutions and institutional arrangements have to be made with care; instead of an outright transfer, constitutional models have to be adapted to the social context of a country, its political culture and its already existing political institutions. Thus institution-building cannot be considered a science, but rather has to be pursued as an art, since there are no ways of reliably predicting the consequences of constitutional reform measures and processes of constitution-making (Lehmbruch 1985; Banting/Simeon 1985).

Sartori does not reflect on any of these issues in his study. On the contrary, together with a discussion of the context of constitutional engineering, he also omits the actors involved in reform processes, as well as their diverging interests. And he neither reflects on the function nor on the options of experts. In short, Sartori is not aware of the fact that processes of constitution-making and constitutional reform are always contingent compromises between competing interests which require a maximum of legitimacy and consensus, and hence generally have to be backed up formally by qualified majorities. Thus he misses the most central issues related to his topic: How, when, by whom, and with what kind of content and goals are reform processes initiated and reforms implemented? Which reforms are possible, and which are not?

II. Constitutional Reform as Process

1. Criteria

As we all know, constitutions regulate the relationships among citizens, between citizens and the state, and among government institutions. They are instruments that bind the Self and the Other, as well as means of organizing government and of conflict management. Furthermore, constitutions are instruments of a basic consensus-building which, in most cases, takes the form of normatively set human and civil rights, as well as fundamental constitutional principles. Finally, constitutions are legal norms of the highest priority, superior to all other norms.

(1) According to social choice and contract theory, constitutions are justified by the necessity to limit the freedom of the individual in order to preserve it (Holmes 1988). The argument of "autopaternalism" solves the inherent paradox of constitutional democracy, and hence justifies the necessity of binding the Self and the Other, of checks and balances, and of constitutional principles of control and restraint (Elster 1993: 174f.). Nevertheless, openness needs to be guaranteed, and this primarily implies a prohibition of self-enslavement. In addition, a binding commitment is only justified if "rather than merely foreclosing options, it makes available possibilities which would otherwise lie beyond reach" (Holmes 1988: 226). Accordingly, constitutions tend to have a conservative, i.e. status quo-oriented, and negative, i.e. protection-oriented, bias. And yet, they also have to provide for openness, as well as for opportunities of learning and change. Obviously, this has an impact on any process of "constitutional engineering:" Reforms that run against these and other basic principles of collective action have only limited chances to be implemented successfully, or (should one have managed to implement them) to be accepted in the long run.

(2) Constitutions provide the organizational framework for the political system and its institutions. They regulate the relations between government institutions, the distribution of jurisdictions, the separation of powers, and the system of checks and balances. Among the core items of constitutions are, by necessity, rules for their amendment (Loewenstein 1961; McWhinney 1981). Constitutions determine the patterns of decision-making and conflict resolution by defining residual powers and norms of judicial review. However, a distinction has to be made between two different prototypes of (written) constitutions which can be derived from an ensemble of four types listed by Daniel Elazar. He distinguishes between (a) constitution as frame of government, (b) constitution as code, (c) constitution as revolutionary manifest, and (d) constitution as political ideal (Elazar 1985: 233). The first two types are especially relevant for stable democracies: (a) Constitutions as codes, in the continental European legal tradition, define the institutional relations within the political system as comprehensively and exactly as possible. (b) As frames of government, in the Anglo-Saxon constitutional tradition, they simply determine the basic structures of government. This is why in these countries, constitutional change – as in the example of the U.S. – mostly happens below the level of formal constitutional amendment and primarily by way of judicial review. These differences have important consequences for the forms, arenas, styles, and contents of constitutional (reform) politics.

(3) Besides the organization of government, constitutions reflect the basic consensus in a society. They define issues that are not subject to the democratic contest by setting norms and granting fundamental rights – negative and positive, individual and collective –, by defining due process, and by establishing constitutional principles. Fundamental rights have, just like constitutions, experienced a materialist turn, as has been pointed out by Dieter Grimm (1994: 318). As a consequence, constitutions also become political manifestos, which in turn makes them not only more controversial, but also more complex and detailed. Thus, constitutional reform becomes similar to processes of normal politics, especially since there is a close relationship between the precision of a constitution and its need to be amended (Grimm 1994: 333f.). Hence there can be no fixed set of norms, and the shaping of fundamental rights is highly context-dependent. While the historical interpretation of Thomas Marshall remains largely accurate, his threefold typology of individual rights of freedom, rights of political participation and social welfare rights has to be complemented by new elements. Whereas in the past the functions of constitutions changed fundamentally as a result of the rise of the welfare state, recent processes of constitutional change in established democracies have evolved around cultural minority and ecological rights (Marshall 1992; von Beyme 1995: 26f.). This fact is neglected by a narrow institutional view of constitutional engineering.

(4) In addition to the above-mentioned basic functions, one can distinguish at least four additional key functions of constitutions (Dahl 1996: 179f.). They are further expected to promote or protect: (a) legitimacy and due process, i.e. procedural neutrality, transparency and comprehensibility; (b) inclusion, i.e. fair representation, comprehensive integration of interests and consensus-building; (c) efficiency and effectiveness, especially in terms of decision-making within the political system; and (d) a balance of stability and openness – i.e., stable democratic institutions combined with flexibility and adaptability.

There is a clear tension between these various functions. Their specific configuration varies with the development level of a society, its political culture, and its constitutional tradition. Furthermore, some functions and institutional arrangements are likely to gain higher priority than others in particular contexts and situations; some constitutional means are then more likely to be used in reform processes than others, and this in turn affects the design of the reform processes themselves, as well as the behavior of the relevant actors.

2. *Reform Types*

The politics of constitutional reform may take different forms: revolutionary act, constitution-making in the context of system transformations, result of normal politics, legislation by elected or appointed constituent assemblies, etc. There is no ideal path for constitution-making or constitutional revision, although the mode of reform may affect its content, acceptance and legitimacy, and may thus determine the development of "constitutional patriotism" (Sternberger).[3]

In comparing processes of constitutional reform, typological differentiations are indispensable. One has to distinguish between (a) processes of constitution-making versus constitutional revision; (b) constitution-making in the context of revolutions/system transformations versus constitutional reform in established democracies; (c) processes of reform where the basic normative patterns of a society are subject to change versus those where they are maintained; (c) total versus partial constitutional revision. These kinds of differentiations are seldom made because they seem trivial. They are nevertheless important with respect to the nature of such processes, the involvement of the relevant actors, and procedural legitimacy. Two examples should suffice to make the point:

(1) In cases of system change the very act of constitution-making itself is a potentially conflictual issue. As a consequence, reform processes are determined not only by controversies about their content, within a given constitutional framework, but the formation of the democratic constitutional state as such is at stake. Thus, constitution-making in situations of system change differs from reform processes in established democracies with regard to context, actors involved, and the nature of consensus-building.

(2) A detailed modernization of the relationship between the federal level (*Bund*) and the regional subunits (*Länder*) in German federalism can be expected to differ from the incorporation of new fundamental principles regarding the initiation of reform processes, actors involved, and forms of decision-making. Reform processes such as these should follow different formats, as they entail strongly different legitimacy requirements.

---

3 However, it would be too simple to suggest a direct (positive or negative) causal relationship between the form of transition and the consolidation of democracy – e.c., by elevating the democratic ideal of constitution-making to the status of a precondition for a stable and successful democratic order. The very opposite has often been the case (Merkel et al. 1996: 15f., 23f.).

With regard to the institutions that play a role in these processes, it makes sense to distinguish various types of reform: (a) In democracies, constitutional reform can take place within the framework of normal politics. In this case, it is initiated and implemented like any other piece of legislation by the responsible institutions, yet may require qualified majorities. (b) Alternatively, the reform is prepared by a special ad hoc committee whose members are appointed to reflect the established sociological and cultural structures of normal politics. (c) The process of decision-making can also be preceded by opportunities for citizen and interest group participation through informal gatherings, hearings, etc. Decision-making and ratification can then conform to the standard legislative procedures, yet may once again require qualified majorities. (d) In another possible variation, the reform is worked out by an appointed constitutional advisory council, including politicians, interest group representatives and experts, which submits a reform proposal that is subsequently ratified either on the basis of standard procedures (with qualified majorities) or by referendum. (e) Finally, the reform may be prepared by an elected constituent assembly that either passes its proposal directly (with qualified majorities) or seeks ratification by the public via referendum.

3. *The Legitimacy of Reform Processes and Outcomes*

Public acceptance of constitutional reform obviously has a substantial and a procedural component. Jon Elster has demonstrated that, from a strictly rational point of view and based on the facts alone, there is no justification for public consent to any reform, for one would have to be able to predict its outcome in order to make an informed, utility-maximizing choice. This, however, cannot be expected under conditions of uncertainty. Even a process of trial and error would not solve the dilemma, since the legitimacy of social and political institutions – and this is particularly true for constitutions – depends on their long-term validity, or at least their continuity.[4] Public consent thus depends on additional factors. Citizens will accept reform proposals that promise further, and positive, side-effects. This is reminiscent of Tocqueville's famous argument according to which the side-effects of democratic participation in society make up for the obvious disadvantages of democratic government in terms of efficiency, and hence account for the superiority of democracy.[5] Alternatively, citizens will accept reform proposals that are

4 This argument follows Jon Elster whose elaboration cannot be laid out in detail here (Elster 1988a, 1988b).

5 See Tocqueville 1945: 246ff. and Elster 1988b for an interpretation of his remarks. This basic condition could be illustrated with many specific examples of reform. One good recent example is represented by the electoral system change from majority voting to PR in New Zealand in 1992/93, since the voters' decision in the referendum was greatly influenced by a highly divergent range of additional expectations.

considered fair and just, and thus guaranteeing impartial treatment and equal influence for everybody (Elster 1988a: 316ff.).

4. Reform Actors

Besides these procedural requirements, the prospects of constitutional reform further depend on the perceived legitimacy of the participating (individual as well as collective) political and social actors. Their behavior is primarily determined by their respective, often diverging, interests and preferences: (a) the personal interests of actors; (b) their perception of the interests their party or organization, its members, supporters or voters stand for (in general, decisions made by actors are more likely to be determined by the presumed interests of their clients than by their personal interests); and (c) the interests embodied in political institutions that are directly or indirectly involved in, or concerned by, reform processes. Finally, the behavior of actors will be determined by the necessity to work out compromises, for public demands with regard to legitimacy and consensus-building will be considerably higher than in normal politics, and special requirements for approval have to be met. Logrolling as a typical strategy of tackling these challenges is, however, likely to result in the expansion or even overburdening of the reform agenda.

Both aspects suggest that reforms should indeed be pursued outside the institutions of normal politics; special assemblies (Benz 1993) should be convened, and as much transparency and accountability as possible should be ensured throughout the process of consultation (Elster 1993: 181ff.). As specifically appointed constitutional conventions tend to broaden the interest base of reform initiatives and the know-how available in them, one can expect more independence from the interests embodied in institutions, and particularly from bureaucratic rationality. As a consequence, the various dependencies of the actors will be diminished, since interaction within the framework of these conventions is necessarily time and content-limited, and decision-making processes are less likely to be burdened by logrolling if they are independent from the institutions and processes of normal politics. However, some compromises cannot be expected to obtain through public consultation, since it is almost impossible to publicly withdraw from positions previously taken. In addition, there is a risk in trying to camouflage particular interests with arguments of general welfare, justice, stability or efficiency. But these disadvantages can be more than made up, since too obvious forms of shady horse trading are not possible in public. Thus, the "civilizing force of hypocrisy" speaks in favor of a process of public consultation (Elster 1993: 183); it leads the actors to moderation and keeps them oriented towards the general welfare, or at least towards consensus. A maximum degree of transparency is also required in order to avoid problems of authenticity between actors and their respective supporters. But this will be possible only if the supporters have a chance to critically observe how their leaders go through learning processes, so that leaders and supporters can reach joint interpretations of a situation and joint evaluation criteria (Scharpf 1993). Only under these circumstances will there be a real chance that the contents of reform are considered just, and the process of reform legitimate, by a sufficient majority of citizens.

5. *Reform Contents*

Reform processes are either initiated top-down, by politicians and bureaucrats, or bottom-up, by society. The initiation of processes, their formats and key players largely depend on the reform objectives. Without unduly reducing the multitude and complexity of such processes in established democracies, their main objectives can be reduced to two basic types (Lehmbruch 1985; Banting/Simeon 1985): first, constitutional reforms that seek to improve the efficiency and effectiveness of government; second, constitutional reforms that focus on problems of inclusion.

(1) Efficiency-related reforms result primarily from the structural differentiation of society – especially from an increasing differentiation of regional/local and functional tasks –, from the expansion of state activity, etc. The political system reacts to these problems through the constitutional entrenchment of administrative reforms such as organizational deconcentration (not federal decentralization) or through the improvement of coordinating and bargaining mechanisms. Modernizations of this kind are typically initiated top-down, are accompanied by a low degree of political mobilization, and are carried out within the framework of normal politics.
(2) Inclusion-related reforms concern conflicts between rising and declining social groups and classes; the issue here is the representation and integration of new social interests, ethno-cultural minorities, divergent lifestyles, etc. Conflicts surrounding reforms of this kind normally develop within society, are initiated in a bottom-up approach, and are strongly politicized. In any event, social forces and movements, interest groups, the public and the media will be strongly involved in the reform process and its different stages: formulating goals and objectives, elaborating programs and proposals, participating in consultation, decision-making and ratification (Banting/Simeon 1985: 18f.). Two different subtypes of inclusive reform can be distinguished on the basis of the tools that are used: (a) institutional reforms that pertain to electoral rules, federalization/decentralization, referenda, or the involvement of NGOs and citizens' action groups in normal political decision-making – e.c., via

roundtables; (b) reforms concerning fundamental rights and the judicialization of politics in cases where institutional reforms are considered unfeasible or insufficient. These reforms are implemented by way of new or redefined fundamental rights that change or broaden the basic consensus in a society; they are an attempt to integrate primarily those conflicting interests that cannot be organized along territorial and functional lines.

6. *Reform Outcomes*

Constitutional reform within a democratic framework is subject to a formal and a factual conservative bias (Elster 1988a: 305ff.). Technically, reforms are – for good reasons – made difficult by specific requirements of consent which foster the maintenance of the status quo in constitutional politics, for rationally acting individuals will hesitate to get involved in any process of reform as long as its outcome is highly uncertain and cannot be anticipated. As a consequence, the status quo is preferred to uncertainty unless incentives to act differently are provided. However, *if* actors and citizens are prepared to follow the uncertain path of reform, the high hurdles for consent impede the negotiation of an agreement. This cycle results in a contradiction that is typical for processes of constitutional reform: On the one hand, the very fact that a consensus is either entirely lacking and/or hard to achieve makes constitutional changes necessary and urgent; on the other hand, it means that successful changes are rare. Failed reform plans and reform impasses are the rule (Elster 1988a: 305ff.). This is particularly true for inclusion-oriented reforms. While normal processes of bargaining between political actors can provide a base for successful consensus-building in the case of efficiency-oriented reforms, inclusion-oriented reforms pose additional problems. In order to enhance their chances of implementation, the following preconditions must be met: (1) reforms have to promise additional side-effects that are considered overwhelmingly positive; (2) they have to be rooted in the basic social consensus; and (3) they have to be considered fair and just.

III. Prototypes

Constitutional politics in Germany most certainly provides a prototype for efficiency-oriented reforms, while the procedural character, chances and risks, successes and failures of inclusion-oriented reforms can be studied with Canadian constitutional politics as an example.

1. Constitutional Politics in Germany: Efficiency-oriented

Gerhard Lehmbruch (1985) has demonstrated how efficiency-oriented constitutional politics works in Germany by analyzing the changes to the Basic Law during the Grand Coalition era, 1966-1969. Fiscal federalism, joint federal-state tasks, so-called framework legislation in the field of higher education, as well as many other reforms of this era, aimed at broadening the range of state acitivities and at improving government efficiency by way of constitutionally entrenched forms of interlocking government. The same is true for changes to the Basic Law in the wake of reunification and the Maastricht Treaty. From the outset, the body of consultation – an advisory council –, its standing orders, and the decision-making process had been set up in such a way as to reflect the traditional structures and power relationships of German politics (Batt 1996). In addition, ratification followed standard legislative procedures. Contrary to some public demands, the reform process was restricted to "securing existing achievements" and the "necessary modifications" (Dieter Grimm, quoted in Batt 1996: 146). The Joint Constitutional Committee of *Bundestag* and *Bundesrat* contented itself with minor adaptive reforms. Although Helge Lothar Batt is correct in stating that a comprehensive modernization of government organization has not taken place in terms of territorial reorganization, re-federalization, the reform of fiscal federalism, etc. (Batt 1996), the reforms that were actually passed were nevertheless focused exclusively on modernization and adaptation, and hence aimed at improving the efficiency and effectiveness of government. This can be shown, for example, with regard to the revised Article 23, Basic Law, or with respect to the reform of federal-state responsibilities in Articles 72-80 (Schultze 1993).

Recent constitutional politics at the *Länder* level shows a different picture (Jung 1995). In the processes of constitution-making that took place in the years 1992/93, the new *Länder* opted for inclusion-oriented reforms, as did some of the old ones (e.c., Schleswig-Holstein), when reforming their constitutions: All of them incorporated elements of direct democracy, as well as social and environmental rights. However, one should not overestimate the scope of these innovations, since the constitutional position of the *Länder* is clearly subordinate.

Even many of the changes to the fundamental rights enumerated in the Basic Law were primarily motivated by the search for government efficiency in the past; examples reach from the so-called emergency legislation to the curtailing of refugee rights. The fundamental constitutional principles that were added in the context of reunification – such as the change of Article 3, Basic Law, on gender equality, or the introduction of Article 20, on the protection of the natural foundations of life – cannot be considered as more than dilatory compromises (Batt 1996: 164f.).

Inclusion-oriented reforms of the Basic Law have either never been tried in the Federal Republic, or they were blocked. Even after reunification, no broad constitutional reform discourse has emerged. Voices demanding a constituent assembly have been marginalized, as have proposals for substantial institutional reform seeking to broaden the basis of representation. In conclusion, German constitutional reforms offer a telling example of just how extremely difficult it is – in light of the tremendous degree of coordination in German politics and an *étatiste* political culture – to get processes of constitutional reform started from below.

2. *Constitutional Politics in Canada: Inclusion-oriented*

In order to illustrate the problems of inclusion-oriented reforms, it suffices to highlight some aspects of Canadian reform politics since the 1970s (Schultze 1996; Schultze/Schneider 1997).

(1) Changes to the institutional arrangements of Canadian federalism are marked by continuous decentralization and a shift of responsibilities in favor of the provinces. The key words in this respect are asymmetric federalism and opting out. Reforms, which were partly implemented through constitutional change and partly carried out below that level, were not – or at least not primarily – motivated by the goal of increased efficiency. They were triggered by the participatory deficits and shifting power balances of major societal interests, and sought to mediate and integrate them into a political process largely determined by the British Westminster model.

(2) The patriation of the Canadian constitution in 1981/82 gave Canadians, by way of the Charter of Rights and Freedoms, one of the most modern catalogues of fundamental rights, although its impacts have been contradictory (Thunert 1991). The Charter combines classical citizen and protective rights with social rights. It does not only guarantee individual rights, but also collective rights for a host of different communities in Canadian society. However, the Liberal federal government under Pierre Elliott Trudeau had originally had different intentions. Trudeau's concern was to achieve individual equality of opportunity and similar living standards throughout the country. He further hoped to bring an end to the power shifts in favor of the provinces by using the centralizing force of the Charter of Rights and Freedoms as a counterweight. The ensuing judicialization of politics brought about major political changes; additional channels of influence and new possibilities of interest articulation, of which postmaterialist and other interests took advantage, were created. These had hardly been represented in the political system, its institutions and decision-making processes before (Schultze 1996).

(3) Later on, in the Meech Lake and Charlottetown processes, the people were involved in a more comprehensive way. Interests that had not sufficiently been taken into consideration so far were now included in the reform discourse, as was the case with experts who participated at various stages – defining goals, formulating proposals, and offering/gathering advice. Finally, the Charlottetown Constitutional Accord was submitted to the people for ratification. Without open consultation and decision-making processes, inclusion-oriented constitutional reforms cannot be pursued anymore. Nevertheless, both constitutional reform packages eventually failed. This enables us to point ex negativo to some crucial preconditions that must be met if these kinds of reforms are to succeed: (a) Although the reform processes had indeed been opened up, decision-making ultimately returned to the traditional framework of federal-provincial diplomacy between the political and administrative elites of the federal and provincial levels (Pal/Seidle 1993). Once again, extensive logrolling processes, a considerable broadening of the agenda and "mega-constitutional politics" (Russell 1993) ensued. (b) The failure of the Meech Lake and the Charlottetown packages further proves how difficult, but important, it is to reach a common understanding of the situation and reform criteria between governing elites and citizens. (c) If such inclusion-oriented reforms are submitted to the people by way of a referendum, justified expectations as to positive side-effects (which were entirely lacking in Canada during the 1980s and 1990s) are required, or else the proposed reforms have to be considered fair and just by a qualified majority. Otherwise, under the conditions of postmodern pluralism, "minoritarianism" (Cairns 1990) – i.e., negative coalition-building – will be the likely outcome. This effect occurred in the course of the Canadian reform processes. Various societal groups gained the impression that their particular objectives had been taken into consideration insufficiently whereas the demands of others had received too much attention. Thus in rejecting the negotiated reform packages, social groups found together which did not have much in common besides their opposition against the reform proposals. The more extensive the structure of bargaining processes and the content of reform packages, the more imminent the danger of negative coalition-building becomes.

IV. Constitutional Reform as a Field of Comparative Research

The preceding considerations explored constitutional reform as a field of comparative research. Five conclusions are particularly important:

(1) Comparisons that fail to distinguish between processes of constitution-making – especially in the context of system transformations – and instances of constitutional reform do not hold much promise, as the context, procedural character, expectations and patterns of behavior involved in these two forms of constitutional politics are too different.
(2) It therefore makes sense to focus on reform processes in established democracies. The analysis should include failed reform attempts and their causes to a larger extent than in the past. This is particularly true for studies that are supposed to underpin policy consulting efforts.
(3) The analysis should concentrate – and our critique of Sartori's contribution should have exemplified why – on historically grounded and comparative case studies; only this approach allows to take the context and procedural character of reforms into account properly.
(4) Furthermore, a broad definition of constitutions, based on a neo-institutional framework, is definitely needed.
(5) In addition, the distinction between efficiency-oriented and inclusion-oriented reforms appears to be quite promising. Such a distinction sharpens the awareness for the procedural character of constitutional reform, its context dependency, the different actors and interests involved, the varying forms of decision-making and ratification; most of all it allows to draw conclusions about the respective political cultures and the flexibility of constitutions.

References

Banting, Keith/Simeon, Richard (eds.) 1985: *Redesigning the State. The Politics of Constitutional Change*, Toronto: University of Toronto Press.

Batt, Helge Lothar 1996: *Die Grundgesetzreform nach der deutschen Einheit*, Opladen: Leske & Budrich.

Benz, Arthur 1993: "Verfassungsreform als politischer Prozess. Politikwissenschaftliche Anmerkungen zur aktuellen Reform des Grundgesetzes," in: *DÖV* 46, 881-889.

Beyme, Klaus von 1995: "Theorie der Politik im Zeitalter der Transformation," in: von Beyme/Offe (eds.), 9-29.

——/Offe, Claus (eds.) 1995: *Politische Theorien in der Ära der Transformation*, Opladen: Westdeutscher Verlag.

Cairns, Alan C. 1990: "Constitutional Minoritarianism in Canada," in: Ronald L. Watts/Douglas M. Brown (eds.), *Canada: The State of the Federation 1990*, Kingston: Institute of Intergovernmental Relations, 71-97.

Converse, Philip E./Pierce, Roy 1986: *Political Representation in France*, Cambridge, MA: Belknap Press.

Cox, Gary W./Kernell, Samuel 1991: *The Politics of Divided Government*, Boulder: Westview Press.

Dahl, Robert A. 1996: "Thinking about Democratic Constitutions: Conclusions from Democratic Experience," in: Ian Shapiro/Russell Hardin (eds.), *Political Order* (*Nomos* 38), New York: New York UP, 175-206.

Elazar, Daniel J. 1985: "Constitution-making: The Pre-eminently Political Act," in: Banting/Simeon (eds.), 232-248.

Elster, Jon 1988a: "Arguments for Constitutional Choice: Reflections on the Transition to Socialism," in: Jon Elster/Rune Slagstad (eds.), *Constitutionalism and Democracy*, Cambridge: Cambridge UP, 303-326.

—— 1988b: "Consequences of Constitutional Choice: Reflections on Tocqueville," in: Jon Elster/Rune Slagstad (eds.), *Constitutionalism and Democracy*, Cambridge: Cambridge UP, 81-99.

—— 1993: "Constitution-Making in Eastern Europe: Rebuilding the Boat in the Open Sea," in: *Public Administration* 71, 169-217.

Fiorina, Morris P. 1996: *Divided Government*, New York: Macmillan.

Grimm, Dieter [2]1994: *Die Zukunft der Verfassung*, Frankfurt/M.: Suhrkamp.

Holmes, Stephen 1988: "Precommitment and the Paradox of Democracy," in: Jon Elster/Rune Slagstad (eds.), *Constitutionalism and Democracy*, Cambridge: Cambridge UP, 195-240.

Jung, Otmar 1995: "Landesverfassungspolitik im Bundesstaat: ein listiger Umweg der Geschichte?" in: *Zeitschrift für Parlamentsfragen* 26, 41-57.

Lehmbruch, Gerhard 1985: "Constitution-making in Young and Aging Federal Systems," in: Banting/Simeon (eds.), 30-41.

Lijphart, Arend 1994: *Electoral Systems and Party Systems. A Study of Twenty-Seven Democracies, 1945-1990*, Oxford: Oxford UP.

——/Grofman, Bernard (eds.) 1984: *Choosing an Electoral System. Issues and Alternatives*, New York: Praeger.
Loewenstein, Karl 1961: *Über Wesen, Technik und Grenzen der Verfassungsänderung*, Berlin: Gruyter.
Marshall, Thomas H. [1950] 1992: *Bürgerrechte und soziale Klassen. Zur Soziologie des Wohlfahrtsstaates*, Frankfurt/M.: Campus.
McWhinney, Edward 1981: *Constitution-making. Principles, Process, Practice*, Toronto: University of Toronto Press.
Merkel, Wolfgang (ed.) ^{2}1996: *Systemwechsel 1. Theorien, Ansätze und Konzepte der Transitionsforschung*, Opladen: Leske & Budrich.
—— et al. (eds.) 1996: *Systemwechsel 2. Die Institutionalisierung der Demokratie*, Opladen: Leske & Budrich.
Nohlen, Dieter 1984: "Changes and Choices in Electoral Systems," in: Lijphart/Grofman (eds.), 217-224.
—— 1992: "Präsidentialismus versus Parlamentarismus in Lateinamerika," in: *Lateinamerika Jahrbuch*, 86-99.
—— 1994: "Institutional Reform in Latin America from the Perspective of Political Engineering," working paper 14, IPW, Lateinamerikaforschung, University of Heidelberg.
—— ^{3}2000: *Wahlrecht und Parteiensystem*, Opladen: Leske & Budrich.
——/Kasapovic, Mirjana 1996: *Wahlsysteme und Systemwechsel in Osteuropa. Genese, Auswirkungen und Reformen politischer Institutionen*, Opladen: Leske & Budrich.
Pal, Leslie A./Seidle, Leslie F. 1993: "Constitutional Politics: the Paradox of Participation," in: Susan D. Phillips (ed.), *How Ottawa Spends 1993-1994. A More Democratic Canada...?* Ottawa: Carleton UP, 143-202.
Przeworski, Adam 1988: "Democracy as a Contingent Outcome of Conflicts," in: Jon Elster/Rune Slagstad (eds.), *Constitutionalism and Democracy*, Cambridge: Cambridge UP, 59-80.
—— 1991: *Democracy and the Market. Political and Economic Reforms in Eastern Europe and Latin America*, Cambridge: Cambridge UP.
Russell, Peter H. 1993: *Constitutional Odyssey. Can Canadians Become a Sovereign People?* Toronto: University of Toronto Press.
Sartori, Giovanni 1976: *Parties and Party Systems. A Framework for Analysis*, Cambridge: Cambridge UP.
—— 1994: *Comparative Constitutional Engineering. An Inquiry into Structures, Incentives and Outcomes*, London: Macmillan.
Scharpf, Fritz W. 1993: "Versuch über Demokratie im verhandelnden Staat," in: Roland Czada/Manfred G. Schmidt (eds.), *Verhandlungsdemokratie, Interessenvermittlung, Regierbarkeit. Festschrift für Gerhard Lehmbruch*, Opladen: Westdeutscher Verlag, 25-50.
Schultze, Rainer-Olaf 1985: *Das politische System Kanadas im Strukturvergleich*, Bochum: Brockmeyer.
—— 1993: "Statt Subsidiarität und Entscheidungsautonomie – Politkverflechtung und kein Ende: Der deutsche Föderalismus nach der Vereinigung," in: *Staatswissenschaften und Staatspraxis* 4, 225-255.
—— 1996: "Interessenrepräsentation und Westminster-Modell: Kanada – ein abweichender Fall?" in: *Staatswissenschaften und Staatspraxis* 7, 163-193.

——/Schneider, Steffen (eds.) 1997: *Kanada in der Krise. Analysen zum Verfassungs-, Wirtschafts- und Parteiensystemwandel seit den 80er Jahren*, Bochum: Brockmeyer.

Thunert, Martin 1991: *Grundrechtspatriotismus in Kanada? Zur politischen Integrationsfunktion der Canadian Charter of Rights and Freedoms*, Bochum: Brockmeyer.

Tocqueville, Alexis de 1945: *Democracy in America*, 2 vol., ed. by Phillips Bradley, New York: Vintage Books.

Constitutionalism and the Transformation of the State

Petra Dobner

In contrast to many other certainties that are fading away with the second millennium, the constitution is still considered a rock of certainty. While the turmoil of economic and technological globalization, the diffusion of power formerly concentrated in the state, and differentiation and individualization as the societal features of a worldwide process labeled the "postmodern" era or the "second" or "late" modernity are calling into question many of the institutions associated with the Westphalian system of sovereign states – including the state itself –, the basic trust in constitutions has not yet been shaken.

Indeed, the success of the constitution in framing the political, in guiding legislation, and in uniting societies in tacit consensus is impressive, and this success has sustained the worldwide conviction that the political has to be organized constitutionally, or else will fail to meet the demands of democracy, if not modernity.

By now, most nations follow the United States in pursuing their happiness by means of pressing its preconditions into the sparse words of a constitutional order – notwithstanding the fact that some of the constitutional latecomers are still awaiting the apogee of their happiness while retaining hope that the gap between constitutional imagination and constitutional reality will finally be closed in favor of the former.

Neither contradicting the constitution's glorious past nor questioning its theoretical justification as the key to the legitimation and limitation of power in secular societies, I will nevertheless argue here that we have little reason to be confident about the future of constitutionalism – or about the constitutionalization of the future. This conclusion follows analytically and logically from the constitution being an institution deeply rooted in, and highly adjusted to, a form of statehood that is vanishing. We have good reasons to worry about the constitutional future – this conclusion should be evident once we have progressed through the following steps:

- First, I want to clear the path for my argument by questioning the political attitude of constitutional trust (*Verfassungsgewissheit*) as a useful guide for research in constitutional theory.

- Second, an understanding of the constitution as an institution of and for the state will be defined.
- Third, the general features of the transformation of the state will be outlined as these are affecting its classical elements – its territoriality, its sovereignty, and its people.
- Fourth, I will discuss how these transformations may undermine constitutional efficiency.
- The fifth and final part will be dedicated to some concluding thoughts on the prospects of politics beyond constitutionalism.

1. Constitutional Trust

More than – and sometimes even rather than – in God, modern societies place their trust in constitutions. Trust in constitutionalism has many sources:

- Constitutional history shows that the variety of constitutional options is sufficiently large to be adapted to very different political and societal circumstances. In the global set of past and present constitutions we find a world heritage of solutions to the problem of organizing the political, which encourages a basic trust that constitutions can also cope with the political future, regardless of what it may bring.
- Constitutions are the closest approximation of reality to the ideal of a social contract, maintaining that a subjugation of otherwise freewheeling powers must be advanced in the sociopolitical act of consenting to establish and limit these powers in time and space, and thereby to subordinate them to the free will of the subjected.
- The climate of constitutional trust is probably especially strong in (West) Germany. Despite the fact that it was intended to be preliminary, the *Grundgesetz* (Basic Law) fulfilled the postwar hope and need for political stability and justice, and proved to be a worthy vessel for the patriotic feelings vagabonding after the ultimate loss of national innocence in the Third Reich. Dolf Sternberger's (1991) term *Verfassungspatriotismus* now extends beyond a mere general faith in the constitution, including the idea of the *Grundgesetz* as the "last taboo" (Isensee 1986: 14) which may not be impugned. The strength of this taboo was impressively demonstrated when the *Grundgesetz* was not revoked in the course of German unification even though according to its former article 146, this should have been done in order to make way for a new constitutional process for all citizens of both Germanys.

Constitutional trust is a necessary resource for the validity of a constitution because a constitution cannot be defended by material forces alone. Constitutional respect is a mandatory political attitude to fulfill the demands of a democracy. But constitutional trust misleads the academic approach to constitutionalism if it is taken for granted that our normative need for constitutions as such guarantees their lasting efficiency. This certainty is expressed by Ottfried Höffe, for example:

"Institutions will provide for a coherent form of elementary justice in the next century, above all the democratic constitutional state. I know that this argument is a truism in social theory." (Höffe 1996: 20)

Ottfried Höffe indeed refers to a commonplace – but it is exactly the underlying equation of a normative need for institutions and the assumption of their lasting efficiency which has to be put into question if we take the transformation of the political seriously. Trusting blindly in the ongoing continuity of institutional solutions despite obvious changes in the causes and features of the problems these institutions were invented to solve is neither historically nor analytically convincing. We have no a priori evidence that the constitution, invented for the specific political structure of the sovereign state, can easily – or at all – cope with the altered set of political, social, and legal organizations that is arising in the transformation of state structures. Hence despite or rather because of our normative need for constitutions, despite or rather because of the fact that we have no ready alternative to constitutionalism, the viability of the constitution as an institution has to be reconsidered, for the classical terrain on which constitutionalism has grown is transforming into a new political landscape.

Rather than insisting firmly on constitutional stability one should consider as an open question if the constitution can be adapted to the political and social needs of a world that is escaping territorial borders, the concentration of power in the state, and the social bonds that have characterized political modernity thus far – or, put differently, one should ask how the functions of a constitution are altered if the state which the constitution is addressed to undergoes structural changes.

2. Constitution as an Institution

Constitutions are places for competing ideas about the norms and forms of political organization in the state. This competition leads to a diversity of constitutions and contradictory concepts of constitutionalism, and it precludes a notion of "constitution" beyond theoretical or political differences. Therefore, whenever a set of laws and rules is identified as a constitution, the abstract understanding of constitution and constitutionalism which is inevitably applied is a part of, and cannot escape, particular political values or preferences (cf. Frankenberg 1996: 19). Still, the different notions of constitutions can incorporate more or less political values. For the following approach in examining the relation between constitution and state, a definition of constitution was sought which is sufficiently concrete to enable clear identification and sufficiently abstract to leave out judgment on "good" or "bad" constitutions as far as possible.

Embedding constitutions in the broader framework of institutional theory meets these criteria. Institutions are defined as "sets of rules to produce and perform valid, socially relevant decisions and authorities for the symbolic presentation of a society's means of orientation" (Göhler 1994: 39). Within this general framework constitutions can be understood as impersonal formal institutions which symbolically and instrumentally enable political and social control and orientation.

Some additional characteristics of constitutions as specific institutions have to be added to this rather abstract definition:

- The (modern) constitution is an *historical* institution, in the sense that it was invented as a reaction to the only hierarchically developed and historically specific needs of societies organizing as states. As opposed to previous instruments of power, the constitution does not only limit power, but also founds it; it includes everybody, not only some people, and it covers the basic issues of a society comprehensively, not only punctually (cf. Grimm 1988: 12).
- The constitution is a *democratic* institution, in the sense that it leaves the traditional or religious legitimation of government behind and fills the "empty place of power" (Claude Lefort) by means of consent, however fictional, of the people. The constitution is tied to the idea of rationality and social unity.
- The constitution *bundles different functions*, in the sense that it is the general order of the state and therefore has to constitute and unite the state in its elemental components – territory, sovereignty, and people. The constitution mirrors these elements by providing a territorial, power, and societal order within a single entity, and thus makes a significant contribution to the unity of the state's components.
- The constitution is a *legal order which binds the political and guides the law*, and therefore is situated beyond politics and law as much as within them.
- The constitution has to have a certain *stability* and *endurance* to regulate issues otherwise exposed to changing and contradictory opinions. It bridges experience of the past with anticipation of the future and balances the political desires for conservation and progress.

Constitution, as I refer to it, is defined as an historical and democratic institution which symbolically and instrumentally provides the means for orientation and control in the state. The constitution is a territorial order, an instrument of power, and a means of social integration in one. The constitution claims legitimation by expressing the basic consent of the people and can therefore keep the dissent on political and social issues within generally civilized limits.

3. State Transformation: Territoriality, Sovereignty, People

Talking about "the" state raises epistemological obstacles which have been the subject of debate for some time without yielding a satisfactory solution. How can we talk about "the" state without falling victim to the manifold traps of reductionism and essentialism? We get "too much complexity and heterogeneity on our screen," as Luhmann (1984: 626) puts it, if we talk about "the" state. We should stay away from any combination of the definite article and state, John Dewey (1996: 9) argues.

Nevertheless, the systematic approach to state structures – even if they are broken down into autopoetic parts for which autonomy, diversity, and peculiar forms of logic have to be taken into account – is still based as much on an understanding of what characterizes the state as talking about constitutions is based on an understanding of constitution.

A pragmatic way to deal with the problem of complexity inevitably associated with the state is to use the classical characterization of the state as the unity of territory, sovereignty, and people, proposed by Georg Jellinek (1960: 178ff.), as a basic guideline for the analysis of state structures. This definition does not only represent a broad consensus on statehood, it also excludes any criteria as to how these general elements are to be put together or how they are organized, thus leaving enough room for the multitude of existing states.

Territoriality

The modern state relies on the acceptance of territorial borders as the material limit to the exercise of power. Prepared by the 1555 peace treaty of Augsburg and resolved in the 1648 peace treaty of Osnabrück and Münster, overlapping power claims based on personal loyalties have been substituted by a system of defined territorial borders: "The distinguishing characteristic of the modern state is that it is territorial, it is a geographical construct" (Kobrin 1997). Modern states

"explicitly claim, and are based on, particular geographic territories, as distinct from merely occupying geographic space which is true of all social organizations. [...]. Territory is typically continuous and totally enclosed by a clearly demarcated and defended boundary." (Anderson 1986: 117)

Altogether, the system of modern territorial states organizes geographical space through a system of "territorially disjoint, mutually exclusive, functionally similar, sovereign states" (Ruggie 1993: 151).

The territorial foundation of the state is an issue that was taken for granted as soon as it was established. The political philosophers of the period in which the shift from personal to territorial systems took place easily incorporated the geographic border into their theories. Despite its revolutionary effects on the structures of legitimation, the extension of power, the general self-understanding of states, the organization of the international system, the concept of security, and the formation of a people, territoriality has only become a major issue of political and scientific concern in the last few years.

This concern follows from the fact that the territorial basis is fading due to changes both *in* and *of* space:

- The EU is leading the way in dissolving the territorial unity of the state: The territory of the state is no longer a border for money, law, politics, police, people, or even the military.
- Worldwide politics and legal structures are being reorganized into a complex set of overlapping trans- and subnational regions, relativizing the geographical unity of the state.
- The worldwide mobility of capital is weakening the most important backbone of the national state, an economy serving the nation, and leaving the economically dependent and territorially fixed state hostage to the threat or fact of labor and/or money being transferred out of the state's territory.
- Environmental developments do not respect the state territory as the significant border at which the state can be defended against danger. Modern military technology may also undermine the geographical border as division between safety inside and potential threat outside by means of microbiological and microtechnological weapons which enable a kind of warfare that the state under attack does not even have to realize as being one. A noteworthy indication of the change in perspective is the shift in focus from external to internal security.
- Transnational migration challenges the political fiction of a "closed society" (Benhabib 1998: 237), a fiction which is at the foundation of democratic theory and the democratic practices in most countries.
- The sense of territoriality in general is being questioned by the growing importance of non-geographic spaces such as virtual space. Without taking the position that geography does not matter any more, the geographically organized state is still losing control of the growing virtual space, which also undermines its authority in geographical territories.

With a restructuring of geopolitical structures on the one hand and a redefinition of space in general on the other, the state enters into a new competition over the control of space and territory. Being territorially fixed, and having a concept of agency and power adjusted to geographic space understood in terms of an unquestionable property, the state is "territorially left behind" (Narr/Schubert 1994: 28) vis-à-vis other actors enjoying the opportunities of territorial fluidity. Once an unquestioned and reliable structure of the political, territory is today marked by an increasing number of contingencies.

Sovereignty

When the idea of sovereignty was first transferred from its original theological background to a political context in the 16th century, the main concern was to pacifiy a multitude of competing powers by means of centralization and hierarchy, and to put an end to religious and civil war. Following the philosophical reasoning about sovereignty up to the Federalists and the constitution of the United States, the concept of sovereignty has been successively enriched: Whereas Bodin basically argued for the centralization of power, Thomas Hobbes claimed the rationality of absolute power, and although his intentions were different, opened rather than closed the door to a democratic sharing of this power. This door was swung wide open by John Locke, who argued that there is no remedy to the uncertainties of the state of nature as long as power is held by an absolute monarch who, "commanding a multitude, has the Liberty to Judge in his own Case, and may do to all his Subjects whatever he pleases, without the least liberty to any one to question or controle those who Execute his Pleasure" (Locke 1963: 316). Locke therefore claims that government has to be resigned to the public, for "there and only there is a Political, or Civil Society" (Locke 1963: 368). Following this line on to the Federalists as the ones to finally constitutionalize sovereignty, one should not neglect the contribution made by Thomas Paine with "Common Sense," demanding and promoting a mass democratic acceptance of the right to self-government.

Ever since the first constitution of modern times, sovereignty has shown a double-sided face: It claims the centralization of power in the state *and* binds it to democratic consent. The concept of democratically exercised sovereignty (*Volkssouveränität*) now links two questions about power: the question as to the objects and extension of power, located within the state; and the question of formal responsibility for the exercise of this power, which is ultimately situated with the people.

The concept of sovereignty has had its critics for a long time. During the First World War, Harold Laski asked whether sovereignty was but a hiding place for the issue of power, and if there was any more legitimation to locating it in the state than in the individual wills of the people. Hans Kelsen argued early on that sovereignty is incompatible with international law (*Völkerrecht*), and his preferences were clearly in favor of the latter. This early theoretical reasoning for a critical view on the concept of state sovereignty has gained new support over the last years in the factual development of the state gaining the status of primus inter pares – as a national actor within the "corporate state," as an international actor within the structures of global politics.

Taking up the differentiation of the objects and extension of power as one side of sovereignty and the democratic responsibility as the other, the changes in sovereignty can now be analyzed in two steps. First, we see an exodus of objects of power out of the state, in the sense that an increasing number of basic issues such as environmental matters, trade relations, legal affairs, and also legal sanctions and tax matters are no longer either adequately or completely covered by any one state. And secondly, this also leads to a decrease in the number of democratic options for controlling the ways in which this power is exercised, for these options have been located in the state and nowhere else thus far.

I would argue that these two processes, which are linked but can be differentiated analytically, should be valued differently. Assessing the loss of the state's supremacy is purely a matter of measuring the output efficiency of decision-making processes, and this assessment should be based on empirical studies rather than political passions. But political passions quite rightly have their place in evaluating the loss of democratic control accompanying this process.

Democracy depends on the state; it is addressed to the state and organized by the state. If the significance of the state is compromised, democracy is endangered. This is a development challenging the rational legitimation of government for which we have no solution thus far.

People

Political theory insists that the legitimation of the constitutional order has to be based directly or indirectly on the consent of the people. Ever since Rousseau's formulation of the social contract, the problem has been how consent can be formed if the people have free and different wills. One answer has prevailed, namely the assumption of homogeneity on the basis of traditional, cultural or ethnic bonds, which either legitimates the exclusion of dissenters as irrelevant "others," or ideally includes the dissenting minority into the community by assuming that sooner or later they will be part of a majority again.

The construction of homogeneity can come about aggressively such as in the version of Carl Schmitt, be seen as a constitutional goal such as by Otto Kirchheimer, or simply be presented as a normatively necessary precondition for success in the general deliberation as maintained by Jürgen Habermas.

Homogeneity and consent have been theoretical constructions as opposed to realistic descriptions ever since they were introduced into constitutional theory. Nevertheless we seem to have reached a period in which these fictions have become less convincing, if we take the sociological observation of a growing self-reflexitivity (Anthony Giddens), individualization and differentiation seriously. Growing individualization and differentiation generally increase the potential for individual justifications and therefore competing standpoints. If values depend on individual preferences more than on social or cultural traditions, the consensus of the people will probably diminish, and/or competition will increase to claim group desires as collective desires. If this is a realistic prospect for constitutional matters, two processes are possible: either the constitution incorporates group rights and dissolves the universality of its order, or the constitution ignores these claims and loses the consent it needs for its validity.

4. Effects of State Transformation on the Constitution as an Institution of the State

These developments affect the constitution's efficiency in organizing and uniting the different elements of statehood: As a territorial order, the constitution is no longer the universal, comprehensive and supreme law of political organization. The constitution as the expression of the state's "right to its own right" (Häberle 1994: 26) can be universal and comprehensive only if it extends throughout the state's territory, by which it is also limited. But the state's borders, the state's authority, and the constitution have to be co-extensive if the constitution is to be the supreme guideline for politics and law. The borders that politics and law encountered in space are weakened by territorial restructuring and territorial competition, and this vacuum is not filled by any different but equally effective categories for the embedding of power structures. As an instrument of power (*Machtordnung*), the constitution founds, limits, and organizes the power concentrated in the state. But a shift of power towards trans- and subnational actors undercuts the state as a central and hierarchical actor and therefore weakens the constitution as the central instrument for the rationalization of power as well. Moreover, political decisions made outside the democratic structures of the state undermine the constitution as the expression of the free will of the subjected.

Social integration and political legitimation are achieved via the consent of the people as authors and recipients of constitutional law. The consent is being called into question by an increase in divergent and competing claims. If these are made part of constitutional law, they will destroy the universality of the constitution. If they are rejected, they will lead to important issues of society being addressed incompletely, and hence affect constitutional universality as well. In both cases the claim for universal and complete coverage, which distinguished the constitution from other instruments of power, is given up. The character of the constitution as a social contract is further questioned by transnational migration, which separates the subjects and objects of constitutional law. For some of these problems, constitutional theory does indeed offer suggestions. Especially the last issue, namely how constitutional law might respond to a society undergoing differentiation and individualization, has been addressed comparatively well. However, a systematic evaluation of the different approaches in constitutional innovation leads one to conclude that the prospects for keeping the constitution as the universal and comprehensive order experienced over the last two centuries are poor. The main reason for this concern is that the various developments which have been sketched out here are taking place simultaneously, whereas the cures are punctual. The constitution has reacted to the territorial, political and societal needs of modern societies, and has expressed this by balancing the different functions of organization and control, social integration and legal guidance in a given territory. Any constitutional reform that concentrates on only one of these problems will significantly alter the character of the constitution.

5. Conclusion: Politics beyond Constitutionalism

I conclude that the constitution's efficiency in universally, comprehensively and generally regulating the relevant political and social issues for a given territory is undergoing a structural decrease. The specific achievement of constitutions (and the state) as historical formations of modern times was bound to the co-extension of political power, societal organization, and legal structures in clearly defined territories, a co-extension which is dissolved by a transformation of political organization in which the state is relativized first, necessarily followed by the constitution as its legal order.

If this is true, it leaves us with the prospect of a period of "turbulence" (James Rosenau), namely a simultaneous and interactive change in the parameters of the political world of sovereign states. This turbulence will not be "so powerful as to sweep away existing institutional arrangements and cultural patterns without resistance" (Rosenau 1990: 11), but it will nevertheless lead to a shift in political structures and institutional arrangements, including the constitution.

One obvious change is taking place already – the replacement of a homogeneous law under a constitution by legal heterogeneity. Legal heterogeneity already includes forms of self-regulation (as intended by the "netiquette" of the internet), state, sub-state or trans-state legal regulation, law-free spaces, and different forms of paralegal agreements. All in all, the legal unity of the state is threatened, and the constitution as the supreme guideline for legislation and politics is questioned. The political impact of this development may well be an increase of extra- or paraconstitutional politics, including not only the political outputs but also the actors striving for a share in the political processes. If constitutional guidance is becoming precarious, we have to anticipate entering a period of struggle over the hegemony in these different spaces.

Constitutionalism pacified politics by limiting possible claims in time and space and withdrew some issues from the bargaining processes of daily dispute. If constitutions fail to fulfill these expectations, the political process will successively move beyond its constitutional restraints. I agree with Kobrin (1997) that

> "the modern system of political and economic organization may well have been an exception to the norm. [...]. The postmodern era may well resemble the medieval in terms of ambiguity, multiple loyalties, multiple levels of authority and the coexistence of political and economic actors."

One significant distinction has to be made, however. If ambiguity and multiplicity take over, and if we do not find ways to protect the previously achieved constitutional and democratic advances under these changed conditions, we will be very far removed from medieval times in the sense that back then at least the future of constitutionalism and democracy was yet to come.

References

Anderson, James 1986: "Nationalism and Geography," in: James Anderson (ed.), *The Rise of the Modern State*, Brighton: Harvester Press, 115-142.

Benhabib, Seyla 1998: "Democracy and Identity. Dilemmas of Citizenship in Contemporary Europe," in: Michael Greven (ed.), *Demokratie – eine Kultur des Westens? 20. Wissenschaftlicher Kongress der Deutschen Vereinigung für Politische Wissenschaft*, Opladen: Leske & Budrich, 225-248.

Dewey, John 1996: *Die Öffentlichkeit und ihre Probleme*, Bodenheim: Philo.

Frankenberg, Günter 1996: *Die Verfassung der Republik. Autorität und Solidarität in der Zivilgesellschaft*, Baden-Baden: Nomos.

Göhler, Gerhard 1994: "Politische Institutionen und ihr Kontext. Begriffliche und konzeptionelle Überlegungen zur Theorie politischer Institutionen," in: Gerhard Göhler (ed.), *Die Eigenart der Institutionen. Zum Profil politischer Institutionentheorie*, Baden-Baden: Nomos, 19-46.

Grimm, Dieter 1988: *Deutsche Verfassungsgeschichte 1776-1866*, Frankfurt/M.: Suhrkamp.

Häberle, Peter 1994: *Europäische Rechtskultur. Versuch einer Annäherung in zwölf Schritten*, Baden-Baden: Nomos.

Höffe, Otfried 1996: "Individuum und Gemeinsinn – Thesen zu einer Sozialethik des 21. Jahrhunderts," in: Erwin Teufel (ed.), *Was hält die moderne Gesellschaft zusammen?* Frankfurt/M.: Suhrkamp, 15-37.

Isensee, Josef 1986: "Die Verfassung als Vaterland," in: Armin Mohler (ed.), *Wirklichkeit als Tabu. Anmerkungen zur Lage der Nation*, Munich: Oldenbourg, 11-35.

Jellinek, Georg [3]1960: *Allgemeine Staatslehre*, Bad Homburg vor der Höhe: Gentner.

Kobrin, Stephen 1997: *Beyond Symmetry. State Sovereignty in a Networked Global Economy*, www.gsia.cmu.edu/afs/-andrews/gsia/bosch/work/kobrin/kobrin.html.

Locke, John 1963: *Two Treatises of Government* (critical edition, introduction and apparatus criticus by Peter Laslett), New York: Mentor.

Luhmann, Niklas 1984: *Soziale Systeme*, Frankfurt/M.: Suhrkamp.

Narr, Wolf-Dieter/Schubert, Alexander 1994: *Weltökonomie. Die Misere der Politik*, Frankfurt/M.: Suhrkamp.

Rosenau, James N. 1990: *Turbulence in World Politics. A Theory of Change and Continuity*, Princeton: Princeton UP.

Ruggie, John Gerard 1993: "Territoriality and Beyond: Problematizing Modernity in International Relations," in: *International Organization* 47, 1, 139-174.

Sternberger, Dolf 1991: *Verfassungspatriotismus*, Frankfurt/M.: Suhrkamp.

II. Constitutional Governance – Institutional Structures, Actors and Policy Fields

1. Changes in the Legislative and Executive Branches

The Politics of Constitutional Reform in Canada and the United States

R. Kent Weaver

Understanding the politics of institutional reform is a task that has been approached from many different angles. Rational choice theorists, based primarily in the United States, have attempted to understand why governing institutions in the U.S. and elsewhere show such stability.[1] Why don't ascendant political majorities more regularly use their political power to alter institutional arrangements in ways that will advantage their own political and policy interests? Canadian scholars have in recent years focused on a seemingly very different set of questions surrounding Québec sovereignty and the repeated failure of multiple rounds of constitutional negotiations. Why does Canada repeatedly engage in these masochistic exercises, and is there any solution short of the institutional suicide of the Canadian nation-state?

This paper immodestly attempts to provide an analytical framework that can be used to address a variety of questions about institutional reform, with a focus on the politics of reforms of executive and legislative institutions in Canada and the United States. Why do some reform proposals emerge from the broad "discussion agenda" on which debate is occurring onto what Cobb and Elder (1972: 85) have called government's "institutional agenda" – "that set of items explicitly up for the active and serious consideration of authoritative decisionmakers?" Why are some proposals accepted when others are rejected? Is the politics of institutional reform in the two countries similar or different? My objective here is to provide a common vocabulary and set of categories that can be used to illuminate parallels and differences within and across the two countries rather than a close examination of specific Canadian and U.S. cases.

Several caveats should be noted at the outset. First, I confine my attention here to changes in *governmental* institutions that have a non-trivial impact on the way that societies are governed.[2] Changes in the rules and procedures governing political parties, laws governing campaign finance, and

1 For an excellent introduction to the choice perspective, see Shepsle/Bonchek 1997. For a critique, see in particular Green/Shapiro 1994.

2 This same analysis could also be applied to other aspects of governance in these and other countries, such as the structure of the judiciary and federalism. But the focus of this paper is limited to executive and legislative changes in the national government.

developments in civil society and interest group institutions will not be discussed here, although they, too, may of course have impacts on governance and on policy outcomes. Similarly, I will discuss sector-specific changes (e.g., changes in congressional budget rules in the United States) only insofar as they are part of a broader cross-sectoral pattern of institutional change.

Second, my focus here is on changes in *formal* rules and structures under which individual institutions select their members, govern their own operations and their relationships with other institutions, and set the rules under which future rules changes themselves are decided. Thus it excludes consideration of informal changes in practice that become embedded in regular patterns of behavior and perhaps in normative patterns about what are the limits of acceptable behavior. A trend toward shorter careers for members of the U.S. Congress, either as a result of members' self-limitation or voters' declining taste for incumbents would thus not be included here, but formal rules establishing legislative term limits would be included. A change in the informal norm that seniority be observed in selecting congressional committee chairs would similarly be excluded unless an explicit new procedure were put in place, but a change in congressional caucus rules that increases incentives for voting with the party leadership (i.e., for party discipline) would be included. And while the creation or abolition of organizations such as the Congressional Budget Office to increase the expertise available to legislators is included here, the expansion or contraction of resources to existing bodies is not. Similarly, if Canadian Prime Ministers decided informally to make their cabinets larger and more religiously and ethnically inclusive, that informal change could have important changes for governance but it would not be included here. Conversely, formal institutional changes that may turn out to be less portentous in practice if all of the political actors continue to behave as if change had never occurred are nonetheless included.[3]

Third, as noted above, our concern here is with how proposals make it to government's "institutional agenda" rather than a broader discussion agenda. Issues that are raised by powerful opinion leaders such as the editorial page of the *New York Times* or the Toronto *Globe and Mail* may be on the discussion agenda without receiving serious attention from policymakers who have the leverage to move it forward. Proposals backed by the U.S. President or given serious consideration by congressional committees are on the institutional agenda in the United States, however, while proposals pressed by Canada's Prime Minister or seriously considered for adoption in First Ministers' Conferences are on government's institutional agenda in Canada.

3 A good example is the U.S. Supreme Court's overturning in 1983 of the legislative veto. Some observers have suggested that the practical impact of this decision has been minimal, as Congress either found ways around the court decision or simply ignored it. For a discussion, see Korn 1996.

The first section of the paper develops a framework for analyzing the politics of institutional reform that integrates what Sarah Binder (1997: chapter 1) refers to as "macro" and "micro" factors. I begin at the macro level by outlining what can be labelled a structural approach to institutional reform, drawing upon and modifying the theory of two-level games developed by Robert Putnam and others. This approach is supplemented with what I call a "sophisticated actor" approach that attempts to fill in important gaps in structural theories by making more complex assumptions about the objectives and strategies of participants in the institutional reform process. In particular, it is important to look at the participants as having multiple objectives, with preferences that are interdependent and evolve over time. The middle section of the paper provides a brief overview of recent experiences with several types of institutional reform in the two countries. The concluding section of the paper draws conclusions about patterns of agenda-setting for institutional reform and adoption or rejection of specific institutional reforms in light of the theoretical perspectives outlined in the first section.

A Structural Perspective on Institutional Reform

Analysis of institutional reform can take several forms. *Society-centered* explanations view governmental institutions as a reflection of the push-and-pull of societal interests (the pluralist approach) or the interests of the dominant groups in society (the power elite or neo-Marxist approach). *Rational choice* explanations focus on the interest that politicians have in maintaining their hold on political power and state resources – and in some versions, in achieving their policy preferences and/or those of their constituents. *Institutional* or *structural* approaches emphasize the role that existing institutional rules play in determining whether reform proposals make it onto the agenda and the hurdles that they face in winning adoption.

In practice, these approaches are far from watertight, mutually exclusive alternatives. Few rational choice theorists would argue that politicians pay no attention to constituents – which may include economic interests. And while institutional structures can be helpful in understanding the likelihood that some institutional change occurs, they are less helpful in understanding which changes get adopted, when and why.

Institutional reform, like virtually all aspects of political life, is a complicated process that cannot easily be captured in a simple model. But complexity for its own sake is no virtue, and an effective analytical framework must begin somewhere, giving primary attention to some variables and somewhat less focus to others. In trying to develop a framework that can be used to analyze the politics of institutional reform, I will begin with a model that focuses on the preferences of participants (who are usually, but not always, politicians) and the decision rules under which reforms are made. Constituents and other societal interests may both shape these preferences and constrain politicians more directly in how they exercise their preferences. Often they do not, however, especially on matters of institutional reform.

In developing this framework, I will draw on the branch of game theory that Robert Putnam (1998; see also Moravsik 1993) has labeled two-level games. In its original application to international relations, negotiators are simultaneously playing an "international" bargaining game and a "domestic politics" game, and neither of these two levels is seen as causally dominant – each interacts with the other. For example a negotiator's ability to convince others that his hands are tied by domestic opposition can be a powerful bargaining tool in winning concessions from negotiating partners, but simultaneous participation in domestic and international games also poses important constraints on negotiators. The tactics, arguments and alliances necessary to win agreement at Level I may conflict with the moves necessary to win ratification at Level II. At the extreme, followers may feel betrayed by concessions their leaders make at the bargaining table. The realization that any agreement made there must at some point be approved elsewhere must always be prominent in the mind of successful negotiators. The more closely Level I negotiators are constrained by Level II, whether by formal decision rules or democratic norms, the narrower the range of negotiating outcomes they can accept. Of course, the nature of Level II ratification mechanisms may vary widely, from virtually none at all (in autocratic regimes) to complex, multi-stage processes including minority vetoes.

The two-level games paradigm can also be applied to labour negotiations and a variety of other bargaining situations where negotiators face "domestic" constraints in their choice of positions and/or face the need for formal ratification. Consociational bargaining among elites of segmented societies with varying degrees of authority over their followers can be seen as another example of a two-level game (see for example Lijphart 1977, 1984). And analysts of intergovernmental negotiations in Canada have long utilized the concept of bargaining between governments – and even two-level games – as a theoretical paradigm, most notably in Richard Simeon's *Federal-Provincial Diplomacy* (1972).

In applying this approach to analyze institutional reform, however, thinking of the reform process as composed of two levels, negotiation and ratification, misleads and reifies where there should be flexibility. Institutional reform processes vary greatly from single-stage processes to multi-level processes in which a single level or venue may have no precise temporal order or order of importance. A structural "n-level games" approach to institutional reform, then, must include an analysis both of the parameters which characterize individual levels or venues of the game and an analysis of how the interaction of the various levels or venues affects the prospects for the successful adoption of institutional reforms. And while it is inappropriate in many institutional reform processes to characterize a specific decision-making level or venue as a primary or "Level I" stage the way that Putnam does, it is appropriate to recognize that in any given process, those who act first or at early stages are likely to face a different calculus than those who act later. I will here differentiate roughly between "instigators" who make temporally earlier decisions necessary to enact institutional reforms and "ratifiers" who act later.

The major parameters that are likely to affect prospects for ratification parameters are outlined in the left-hand columns of Table 1, along with some of the determinants and implications of those parameters. These parameters fall roughly into three categories: (1) characteristics of decisionmakers in a particular decisionmaking arena or venue and their distribution of preferences (a-d); (2) number of venues required for approval (e); and (3) inter-venue effects (f-g).

(a) *Distribution of decisionmakers' preferences:* The distribution of policy-makers' preferences, and the degree of overlap among those preferences, is clearly the most critical feature in any process of negotiating institutional reform. Most structural analyses begin with the assumption that participants have an "ideal point" – a position that they prefer over all others on each dimension in an n-dimensional space. But they may vary greatly in what can be called their "zone of acceptable outcomes" – the range of outcomes around their ideal point that they are willing to accept. If participants in a decisionmaking venue are willing to accept reform proposals that are relatively distant from their ideal point, the range of reform proposals that can win approval in a specific venue (the "win set") is likely to be higher, as are the prospects for approving a reform proposal in that venue.

Decisionmakers' preferences, in turn, reflect their perception of their own substantive interests, and in some cases, those of the collectivity they represent. Even if we assume that they are "rational" – i.e., they seek to maximize their self-interest as they perceive it – their strategic calculus is often quite complicated. The simplest form of a choice approach views policy conflict as purely a struggle among groups of self-interested politicians to maximize their own prospects for re-election and power (Mayhew 1974; Arnold 1990). This is far too simplistic, however. Most politicians and other policymakers also have multiple objectives that go beyond electoral concerns. In particular, policymakers are likely to have value preferences for what they perceive to be "good policy" that are informed by ideology, experience and other factors besides the balance of constituency preferences. In addition, they are likely to value preservation of *coalitional unity* within their party (or in some cases, a faction within the party). The incentives for members of the same political party to operate in unison tend to be especially strong where the costs of non-unity are especially strong; virtually all votes in the Canadian House of Commons and beginning-of-Congress votes on organizational issues are in this category.

Even within these three broad categories of electoral, coalitional and policy objectives, politicians often pursue multiple goals that may require difficult trade-offs. In the case of electoral objectives, policymakers may be simultaneously attempting to claim credit with some constituents or sources of campaign funds, minimize blame for actions that offend other important interests, and generate blame against political opponents. Pursuing these multiple electoral objectives frequently requires trade-offs: A choice that maximizes credit-claiming, for example, may cut down on opportunities for blame-generating against opponents. While policymakers do not have a single hierarchy of objectives (for example, always placing credit-claiming or other electoral objectives above their policy preferences or coalitional unity), they are likely to be especially attentive to avoiding blame from constituents. Concern with avoiding blame is paramount because voters tend to be much more sensitive to losses that have been imposed on them than to things that have been done to benefit them (Weaver 1986).[4]

(b) *Decisionmakers' perceptions of the acceptability of the default position:* Along with a most preferred alternative, or ideal point, one of the most important determinants of the size of decisionmakers' zone of acceptable outcomes is the consequence of not reaching an agreement at any given point in time. In general, we might expect that policymakers will accept reform proposals that are (i) relatively close to their ideal points, and (ii) closer to their ideal points than the default position.

In fact, however, there are two elements of the default position that are likely to enter into a decisionmaker's calculus: the policy default and the negotiating default. Usually the policy default position is the status

---

4 Of course, when blame-avoiding is not a concern – if a politician's stance on a proposed institutional reform is of low salience to constituents, for example – politicians and other policymakers can pay more attention to their other objectives. But politicians can rarely ignore the potential for blame entirely: interest groups and political opponents may mobilize a previously inattentive public even around issues that had previously seemed obscure and inconsequential (Kingdon 1981: 60-68; Arnold 1990). Another factor influencing decisionmakers' preferences is the information relating to the impact of reforms. Policymakers often operate with far-from-perfect information about the advantages and disadvantages of various reform alternatives, and therefore must make decisions with a great deal of uncertainty – and perhaps with results that are less than optimal even from their own perspective. Because the future costs and benefits of institutional reform options are uncertain, and information about those costs and benefits is often impossible to obtain, politicians are especially likely to "discount" potential costs and benefits that are fairly distant in time.

quo. If all decisionmakers find that acceptable, incentives for participants to make sacrifices to secure agreement on reform are relatively low. On the other hand, if failure to agree on a reform is perceived to lead to a change in the status quo that involves losses for many or all of them – for example, if current institutional arrangements lead to decisionmaking gridlock when the status quo is unacceptable to all – then they are much more likely to make sacrifices or take more risks to ratify an institutional change (Putnam 1988: 452-453). The choices facing ratifiers are frequently different from those of instigators, however. Those at later stages of an institutional reform process rarely confront the full range of options considered at earlier stages. Often they cannot even make marginal changes in proposals to bring them closer to their own ideal points. Their choice is likely to be limited to accepting or rejecting a specific alternative proposal.

Decisionmakers' default calculus also depends on their perceptions of the "negotiating default:" whether negotiations will continue in the absence of an agreement or break down. If they believe that a later round of negotiations may result in an agreement closer to their ideal point than the reform proposal currently under consideration, they again have low incentives to ratify – a point that will be discussed further below as part of the discussion of the "strategic disagreement strategy."

(c) *The number of elements in a reform package:* Institutional reforms are frequently considered one-at-a-time, especially when they involve the decision-making rules of individual organizations (e.g., Senate filibuster rules in the United States). But they are also sometimes considered as packages – the several rounds of Canadian constitutional reform negotiations, for example. Although having a larger number of issues creates opportunities for trade-offs and log rolls among conflicting interests, it is also likely to complicate and prolong negotiations, and to increase the probability that coalitions of intense minorities of opposition will mobilize on specific issues to kill a proposed reform at some level of a multi-venue reform process. In addition, if decisionmakers perceive that only one package of institutional reforms has a chance of winning approval in the near future, they have increased incentives to hold the entire package hostage to make sure that their preferred elements are included in the package.

(d) *Decision rules:* In any decision-making process or institutional reform, it is much easier for negotiators in a specific venue to reach an agreement if approval only by a bare majority of involved parties rather than when super-majority requirements (or majority vetoes, like filibusters in the U.S. Senate) are in place.

(e) *Number of decisionmaking venues:* Institutional reform proposals may be subject to multiple ratification requirements in several different venues.

Constitutional reform packages negotiated between Ottawa and the provincial first ministers, for example, must be ratified by the federal and provincial legislatures. All other things being equal, institutional reform initiatives are more likely to be rejected if approval in multiple decisionmaking venues is required, especially if decisionmakers in each venue are electorally accountable to different political constituencies with different interests and preferences. And as the previous point suggested, these odds are further increased if there are super-majority approvals required within any of those individual venues.

(f) *Level of trust and deference in actors in other venues*: As noted earlier, actors at later stages of the reform process often must choose between ratifying or rejecting an agreement rather than modifying it. Available information is often biased, and information costs for ratifiers are often high – especially when ratifiers consist not just of a few hundred legislators but the general public acting through a referendum. In this situation, the willingness of ratifiers to accept reform proposals may depend in large part on their general level of trust in those who have already accepted the reform proposals in earlier-acting venues.[5] The greater ratifiers' level of trust in those actors, the more likely they are to accept an agreement about which they have some misgivings. On the other hand, if they strongly distrust those actors, they may be disinclined to ratify any agreement that is presented to them, even if it is close to their own policy ideal point.[6] Canadian voters' rejection of the Charlottetown Accord is an obvious case in point.

(g) *Ratifiers' perceptions of probability of reform acceptance in other venues:* In considering whether to accept or reject a reform proposal, ratifiers must consider the relationship between *their* failure to ratify and that of other ratifiers. If ratifiers believe that their own approval is necessary for overall approval of a proposal, their incentives to approve go up (assuming that they support the agreement themselves). If a ratifier believes that an agreement is unpopular with their constituents, but will come into effect anyway without their approval, it may be rational for them to do nothing, or to vote against ratification. Similarly, if (i) they believe that a reform proposal is likely to fail no matter what they do because of the

---

5 LeDuc and Pammett (1995: 6) have noted that "the past performance and personal credibility of politicians does appear to play a significant role in the referendum voting calculus."

6 As Putnam (1988: 451) notes in the context of a two-level game, this has two seemingly perverse consequences. First, high popularity for Negotiator A may actually weaken that negotiator's bargaining position, because other negotiators know that there is a lot of flexibility in the positions he or she adopts. Second, Negotiator A has a high stake in their opposite numbers' popularity, both because the overall win set increases in size and because a very popular Negotiator B has more flexibility to move to Negotiator A's ideal point.

actions of other ratifiers, and (ii) their constituents are divided on the issue and they face potential blame regardless of whether they ratify or reject, they may choose to take no action even if they believe that the policy default is worse than what would result from ratification.

Sophisticated Actors, Political Agendas and Repositioning

In a simple political world where politicians only have to worry about policy concerns and not electoral or coalitional ones, politicians could operate according to a fairly simple decision rule: Endorse any institutional reform that is likely to produce outcomes closer to their ideal point than the default position, and reject those that are further away. In a simple credit-claiming political world, politicians will generally endorse a reform proposal closer to the ideal point of median constituents than the status quo. In the real political world, of course, decisionmaking on institutional reform is far more complex, involving coalitional objectives as well as electoral and policy ones and (intertwined with the other considerations) a calculation about whether an option has a significant chance of being adopted.

In understanding whether bargaining over policy will result in some change from the status quo, understanding politicians' ideal points is less important than their zone of acceptable outcomes – those outcomes that they will accept in a choice between the default position and that alternative. Because politicians set this zone based in part on electoral (especially blame-avoiding) and coalitional considerations as well as policy preferences, this range may include points quite far from their ideal points. Policymakers' zones of acceptable outcomes are likely to be especially broad when they realize that the status quo is very unpopular with their constituents, and they wish to avoid being labeled as defenders of the status quo. Moreover, policymakers may change their zones of acceptable outcomes over the course of a bargaining process in order to hold a coalition together, facilitate or block an agreement, or avoid blame for the failure of an agreement. The "sophisticated actor" approach suggests several arguments about how institutional reform agendas are likely to be made and limited and which sorts of reforms are likely to be adopted.

Getting on the Agenda: While politicians recognize the necessity of making trade-offs, they do not like to do so. *Thus they are drawn to policy options that make them better off on several objectives and worse off in none.* An institutional reform proposal that allows politicians to avoid blame but gives them few credit-claiming opportunities and makes them worse off with respect to several of their policy priorities is unlikely to be greeted by politicians with great enthusiasm. If, however, policymakers develop or encounter an institutional reform option that makes it more likely that they will be able to attain their policy preferences while offering credit-claiming opportunities and incurring little risk of blame or of splitting the party coalition, they are likely to embrace it, try to move it up on the agenda of issues being debated, and try to move it forward to adoption.[7]

If politicians were omniscient, we might expect that the list of institutional reforms reaching the institutional agenda and the list of reforms actually adopted would be very similar. Pushing for institutional reforms is, after all, an investment of scarce resources and time that could perhaps be more efficiently invested elsewhere. A sophisticated actor perspective, however, suggests several reasons in addition to lack of omniscience on the part of politicians to expect that the fit between institutional agendas and actual policy adoption will not be particularly close. First, the reform agenda is likely to be broader if a political system is relatively open, allowing a broad range of politicians other than the central executive to put items on the agenda. Second, the reform agenda is likely to be broader if politicians have electoral incentives to fight and lose – that is, to press for a change that is popular with their constituents even if it has little chance of winning. Third, reform agendas are likely to be broader than the changes actually adopted if the rules for considering change create greater uncertainty about outcomes – for example, if party lines in the legislature are weak, so that endorsement by leaders of the majority party in the legislature is less likely to lead to legislative passage, or if the two chambers in a legislature have different party majorities. In this situation, politicians may instigate a losing institutional reform initiative because they overestimate its prospects for success. In general, the United States is farther away from a close "agenda-adoption" linkage on each of these criteria, so we should expect to see a longer list of failed reform initiatives that actually made it to the agenda in the United States than in Canada.

Agenda Limitation: Policymakers will try to keep options that are costly to themselves from being considered, so that only alternatives that they consider "good choices" remain. Or if they view all plausible options as less desirable than the status quo, they may try to prevent any alternative to the status quo from being considered.[8] Because Canada's Westminster-style par-

7 This process need not necessarily involve a truly new proposal – a reframing of old proposals that makes new claims about old policy ideas may do. The key is that it presents politicians with a win on political, policy and coalitional terms.

8 If policymakers cannot keep undesirable options off the agenda, they may try to mitigate their negative consequences. Legislators, for example, may prevent open votes on legislative proposals that they favor on policy or personal grounds but that they know are unpopular with the public, so that the political risks of supporting those proposals is lowered. On the other hand, politicians may also try to put on the agenda choices that they know pose political problems (hard choices or bad choices) for their opponents – for example, requiring opponents to openly accept or reject a welfare reform proposal that is

liamentary system offers such centralized control over the institutional agenda of the federal government, we would expect that agenda to be more limited than that in the United States, and the falloff of proposals that have been approved in one institutional venue but been rejected in another to be lower than in the U.S.

Repositioning: Policymakers who cannot control the agenda must use other strategies to achieve their policy and political interests. In particular, they may change their positions on issues. Usually this repositioning does not involve changing ideal points, but rather their zone of acceptable outcomes. Policymakers' reassessments of their zones of acceptable outcomes are not based solely on relatively fixed calculations of those options' political and policy merits; instead, *choices about what positions to take are also relational – that is, they are determined in large part in relation to the positions taken by other participants.*[9]

Politicians may engage in several different forms of relational positioning, some of them largely reactive, and some more "pro-active" – that is, trying to stake out distinctive positions of their own. And while most repositioning involves an expansion of politicians' zones of acceptable outcomes, it sometimes involves a shrinking, and rejection of positions that had previously been deemed acceptable.

There are several clearly identifiable strategies for altering a policymaker's zone of acceptable outcomes. For example, politicians who have an ideal point far from that of their constituents may engage in a "matching" strategy – expanding the outward boundary of their zone of acceptable outcomes to match the position taken by a respected "moderate" who is as close to their position as possible, thus providing themselves with political cover. Thus Prairie politicians in Canada may believe it to be politically necessary to be no softer on the issue of a "Triple E" Senate than the premier of their province. If the premier's position becomes more intransigent, they are likely to shift their zone of acceptable outcomes in the same direction. Both before and after the premier's shift, they may view all options on the table as undesirable and prefer no change from the status quo – or abolition of the Senate. But if they are forced into an open choice between the unpopular status quo and a policy change that they dislike but leading spokesmen of their region have endorsed, they may feel that they have to go along.

Politicians may also attempt to tie their own hands by announcing in advance a set of demands that define the outer boundaries of their zone of acceptable outcomes, but are short of concessions deemed necessary by political competitors to reach an agreement. The objective of this "hand-tieing" strategy is to convince political adversaries that they cannot and will not

---

popular with constituents but inconsistent with those opponents' own policy preferences.

9 In the jargon of political science, politicians' preferences are endogenous to the bargaining game. For a contrary argument, see Brady/Volden 1997: chapter 1.

consent to a position any further from their ideal point. If this maneuver succeeds, it narrows the agenda of alternatives "on the table" to those that are relatively close to their own ideal point and within their self-proclaimed zone of acceptable outcomes.[10] The strategy of Québec Premier Robert Bourassa during the Meech Lake Round of constitutional negotiations of outlining five minimum conditions for agreeing to accept the 1982 constitution is an (initially successful, but ultimately unsuccessful) example of such a strategy.

"Triangulation" is a somewhat more pro-active form of repositioning, in which a policymaker or group of policymakers reposition themselves roughly midway between two or more political competitors to appeal as the "moderate" alternative. This has several potential advantages. If the policymaker's previous position was distant from that of most constituents, triangulation can help to avoid blame as being outside the political mainstream on an issue. It may also allow them to obtain credit for achieving policy change through compromise. Triangulation is probably most likely to occur when the distribution of public preferences clusters toward the center. If constituency preferences are highly polarized, a move toward the center is likely to alienate one group of constituents while being insufficiently attractive to those at the other pole.

Even if a political competitor moves substantially closer to a policymaker's ideal point, there may be reasons to engage in a strategy that John Gilmour (1995) has labeled "strategic disagreement:" moving their zone of acceptable outcomes away from the competitor in order to maintain the original policy distance between the two. In this case, the group or individual moving may actually shrink its zone of acceptable outcomes, rejecting as unacceptable some of the policy space that it had previously signaled that it found acceptable.

Strategic disagreement may occur for several reasons. If an election is approaching, for example, and one side expects to make gains in those elections, it may be in their long term policy and political interest to eschew an agreement now and hold out for a better deal (that is, one even closer to their ideal point) later. In this situation, reaching an agreement on institutional

---

10 See Schelling 1963: 22 and Putnam 1988. Of course, hand-tieing strategies pose important risks as well as advantages. The most obvious risk is that political competitors will view these conditions, intended as a maximum concession, as a minimum. They may refuse to accept anything less than the outer limit of what the "tied" politician has announced as their zone of acceptable outcomes, while probing to see if they can get more. There are other risks as well. If the politician or group whose hands are tied is not necessary to build a winning coalition for policy change, they may find themselves excluded from that coalition, failing to obtain concessions that could have been won if they had used a less rigid negotiating stance. A hand-tieing strategy may also result both in the failure to obtain policy change (because it increases the probability that no agreement will be reached) and in the "tied" politician or group being blamed for that failure due to their intransigence.

reform now has four key disadvantages: (1) it may lower the probability that the issue will be revisited after the election, when the resolution would be closer to their ideal point; (2) it may alienate core supporters and key interest groups, who view compromise as selling out (Gilmour 1995: 26-32); (3) it may neutralize an issue that will benefit their party in the next election, when highlighting partisan differences would be more advantageous; and (4) it likely forces them to share credit for the policy change with their political adversaries. Of course, strategic disagreement also carries risks: if the hoped-for electoral gains do not appear, an opportunity to move closer to their ideal point may disappear as well. Moreover, political opponents may try to generate blame against those pursuing the strategy as politically obstructionist. And if the group making the initial move is persistent in its pursuit, a bidding war can break out that results in irresponsible legislation (Gilmour 1995: 56). Overall, however, pursuit of strategic disagreement lowers the prospects for policy change.

The strategy of "strategic pursuit" involves moving closer to the position of a political opponent, even if it falls outside the politician's pre-existing zone of acceptable policy outcomes. Strategic pursuit is frequently motivated by changing public preferences, and politicians' desire to avoid blame for failure to adjust to those preferences. When this situation occurs, politicians may also engage in strategic pursuit for coalitional reasons: they may see moving part, but not all, of the way toward an opponent's position as a way to provide a defensible collective position that is closer to the opponent's position than the position they held earlier, and thus prevent some of their normal political partners from defecting entirely to the opponent's camp.

Policy agreement may arise not only because one actor or set of political actors unilaterally decides to move their zone of acceptable outcomes much closer to the position of others (as in matching and strategic pursuit), but because two or more actors move to joint intermediate positions, pursuing "splitting the difference" strategies. Several conditions may contribute to this outcome: (1) if all those moving, and large shares of the public, view the status quo as unsatisfactory, (2) if the ideal points of all those involved are fairly close, and (3) if splitting the difference provides significant opportunities to claim credit for favoring or achieving policy change. It may also be helpful if policymakers and publics differ in the salience they ascribe to at least some of the issues being debated, facilitating trade-offs in which policymakers can make gains on issues about which they and their constituents care a great deal while making concessions on dimensions that they view as less salient. Splitting the difference is likely to be less feasible if (1) constituencies are highly engaged in, and highly polarized on, all dimensions of policy under discussion, and (2) a substantial portion of policymakers and their constituents view the status quo as preferable to any plausible compromise position.

This analysis of the factors that constrain policymakers' strategic choices suggests several conclusions about when the prospects for movement away from the institutional status quo are likely to be greatest. In particular, it suggests that prospects for institutional change are maximized when:

- Most participants have a broad and flexible zone of acceptable outcomes, making it more likely that "splitting the difference" strategies will result in some policy space that is broadly acceptable. Policymakers are most likely to have broad zones of agreement, in turn, when the status quo or default position is extremely unpopular with their constituents or the policymaker and his or her constituents view the issue as one of low salience. When the issue is of high salience to constituents (e.g., Senate reform in Canada), policymakers' zones of acceptable outcomes are likely to be highly constrained rather than flexible, and the prospects that they will expand those zones to facilitate agreement on institutional reform are low.
- Key participants (e.g., the President in the U.S. system) decide to make institutional reform one of their top priorities, placing it above the many other issues that vie for their attention.
- Participants with similar ideal points and political interests control the agenda (which alternatives are considered and in which order) at all venues in the policymaking process, making it less likely that one group of policymakers will succeed in using agenda limitation to block a policy change that is favored by most others.
- There are few (or only one) decision venues needed for the reform to be adopted.
- Simple majorities rule in each decision-making venue, making it less likely that relatively small groups that are "preference outliers" will use minority vetoes or agenda limitation strategies to block change.

Institutional Reform in Canada and the United States

The analytical framework outlined above suggested a number of hypotheses about when institutional reform proposals (and what type) are likely to reach government agendas for Canada and the United States and which ones are likely to be adopted and in what sorts of packages. This section of the paper briefly reviews the reform agendas in the two countries over the past quarter century as well as touching on some items that have not made it to the agenda and why they have failed to do so.

Selection Rules for the Lower House of the Legislature

In both Canada and the United States, changes in the selection procedures for the lower house of the national legislature have very rarely made it to government's agenda. Absence from the agenda is particularly striking for Canada, because the country's single-member plurality (SMP) electoral rules have been linked by critics to a variety of ills, ranging from disproportionality in weighting of votes for different parties to virtual exclusion of some regions from the governing party caucus in the House and dramatic overrepresentation of other regions, inability to produce consistent single-party majority governments, and underrepresentation of women, visible minorities and aboriginals (Weaver 1997; Milner 1999).

Part of the reason for the failure of House of Commons reform to make it onto the agenda is that many of the problems produced by Canada's electoral system have been rotating rather than persistent: for example, minority governments in the 1960s and early 1970s, extreme regional exclusion in the late 1970s and early 1980s, and tremendous overrepresentation of a single region (Ontario) in the early 1990s (Weaver forthcoming). The more important constraint on any electoral reform proposal for the House of Commons, however, is that political parties which benefit from current plurality rules control the electoral rule-setting process. The Liberal Party has been the dominant party federally in the twentieth century, showing a remarkable ability to reinvent itself when its existing regional bases of support have been threatened. Understandably, Liberal governments have considered electoral reform only occasionally and half-heartedly. Liberal enthusiasm for electoral reform has been especially muted in the 1990s, when the collapse of the Progressive Conservative Party left the Liberals as the only political party with a realistic prospect of forming a government. The Progressive Conservative Party, which was normally disadvantaged by plurality electoral rules, presumably could have used one of its intermittent periods in power to introduce greater proportionality. It never did so because at least until their crushing defeat in 1993, the Conservatives hoped to replace the Liberals as Canada's dominant party. And this hope was not entirely unreasonable: the two most overwhelming general election victories in recent Canadian political history, in 1958 and 1984, were both by the Progressive Conservatives. Then-PC leader Jean Charest did make some comments favorable to electoral reform after the 1997 election (Studlar 1998: 75) but the Conservatives now have no bargaining leverage to get it on the agenda, let alone implement it. Smaller parties, notably the New Democratic Party, have never had sufficient bargaining leverage to force a change in electoral rules, even when they were propping up minority Liberal governments.[11] Regionally concentrated parties have not

---

11 The NDP's position on getting rid of plurality electoral rules was somewhat ambivalent,

pressed for electoral reform as they have lacked incentives to do so. The Bloc Québécois was able to form the official opposition after the 1993 election without contesting a single constituency outside Québec, and Reform became the official opposition after the 1997 election without winning a single seat (although it contested many) outside Western Canada.[12] As a result, the closest a change in selection rules came to being adopted was inclusion of a permanent 25 percent floor for Québec in House of Commons seats that was included in the Charlottetown Accord. This was not a provision that Québec had sought; it was instead included as a compensation for the provision that gave each province equal representation in the Senate.

Selection rules for the House of Representatives in the United States have also been off the agenda more than they have been on. Certainly there has been no significant pressure for movement away from the single-member plurality district system that the United States shares with Canada (Richie/Hill 1999). But two issues have made it to the agenda in recent years: term limitation for members and drawing of congressional districts to facilitate districts in which African-Americans and Hispanics constitute a majority or near-majority of the districts. The former has significant headway in state legislatures (notably California). But efforts to enact term limitations for members of the federal legislature through state-level legislation or citizen initiatives, while they have been enacted in several states, have all been overturned by the courts. A parallel effort to enact congressional term limits through an amendment to the U.S. constitution was considered by Congress as part of the House Republican's Contract with America in the 104th Congress. However, four separate versions of a term limits constitutional amendment failed to secure the two-thirds majority required to win approval in the House of Representatives in March 1995 (Cooper 1995).

---

moreover. NDP leader Ed Broadbent proposed the introduction of proportional representation for the House of Commons in 1979, but this proposal was rejected by the NDP convention in 1981. By the early 1980s, with the Liberal Party appearing to be in strong decline in the waning years of Pierre Trudeau's leadership, NDP leaders hoped that they could supplant the Liberals in a two-party duopoly in Canadian federal politics. But the era of Liberal minority governments had already ended in 1974, ending any hope that the NDP could force a change in the electoral "rules of the game." The NDP may also have been influenced in its reluctance to move away from plurality electoral rules by the fact that the party has frequently benefitted from just those rules, and a split in the "anti-NDP vote," at the provincial level. Of the three NDP provincial governments in power in early 2000, only one (in Manitoba) won more than forty percent of the popular vote, and the other two (in British Columbia and Saskatchewan) actually won fewer votes than the largest opposition party.

12 The relatively young Bloc Québécois has consistently benefitted from plurality electoral rules since its inception, and has little incentive or interest in devoting scarce resources to the reform of electoral institutions for a country it is trying to leave. Moreover, because its pro-sovereignty stance makes it "uncoalitionable," there is no plausible reform that would allow the Bloc to share in governmental power.

The story of "majority minority" congressional districts is more complicated. Congress directed that such districts be created where feasible as part of its reauthorization of the Voting Rights Act in 1982. This enjoyed substantial support among congressional Democrats, both for ideological reasons and because it was popular among the black and Hispanic caucuses among House Democrats. When redistricting took place after the 1990 census, a number of bizarrely shaped districts were created to maximize majority minority districts, especially in the South. As with term limits, however, the courts intervened, placing limits on the degree to which these non-compact districts could be created through "racial gerrymandering." To date, however, this has not resulted in loss of seats by the affected legislators (Lublin 1999).

Selection Rules for the Upper House of the Legislature

While selection rules for Canada's House of Commons have essentially been off the institutional agenda except for a few brief moments, Senate reform has been on the agenda during both the Meech Lake and Charlottetown constitutional rounds. Indeed, these two facts are closely related: the concentration of analytical and political effort on Senate reform has helped to "crowd out" discussion of electoral reform for Canada's House of Commons. While the House certainly has shortcomings as a governing institution, its defects are dwarfed by those of the Senate. Even more important is the fact that western spokespersons (including the Reform Party) have focused primarily on creation of a more powerful Senate that could serve as a check on the House of Commons rather than a change in electoral rules for the House. Exactly what form this Senate should take has been the subject of much dispute, however. In the late 1970s, Alberta's powerful premier Peter Lougheed was a strong advocate for turning the Senate into a body representing provincial governments, on the model of Germany's *Bundesrat*. However, when Lougheed left the political scene, the *Bundesrat* model withered away.[13] More recently, the strongest advocate for Senate reform has been the Reform Party, which has argued for a "Triple E" (popularly Elected, Effective in the sense of having powers similar to those of the House, and providing Equal representation to all provinces) Canadian Senate, modeled more on the U.S. Senate. A Senate elected by proportional representation has gained support among some non-Reformers as well as a means of checking the power on the "manufactured majority" in the House of Commons.

13 The *Bundesrat* model was also supported in the Pepin-Robarts Commission report and resurfaced as a "House of the Federation" in the Mulroney government's 1991 constitutional proposals (Canada 1991). For a history of *Bundesrat*-style proposals for Senate reform, see Janda 1992.

In fact, however, there was no overlap in the zones of acceptable outcomes of western Canadian provincial leaders and those in Québec, either on provincial equality or on the mechanisms through which Senators should be selected, let alone on the powers of the Senate. A reformed Senate was included in the Charlottetown Accord package of constitutional reforms that Canadian voters rejected in a referendum in 1993, but it was not explicit on a particular method of election. In fact, the Accord provided that provinces could choose between having Senators elected by provincial or territorial assemblies or electing them by popular vote (with the method to be specified later by federal legislation). This was intended to give Québec's provincial government the authority to appoint its members to the Senate.[14] The recent dominance of variations on the "Triple E" theme for Senate reform, however, reflects the nature of backing for any type of Senate reform. Among Canadian voters, the most favored Senate reform is simply its abolition, and among the current Canadian government, Senate reform is not of interest. Thus Senate reform remains off Canada's institutional agenda until another round of constitutional negotiations, or perhaps a minority government, gives the backers of Senate reform the institutional leverage needed to force it back on.

Senate reform is even more on the backburner in the United States. Of course, Senate selection was dramatically changed in the early part of the twentieth century, when the 17th Amendment to the U.S. Constitution moved from selection of U.S. Senators to direct election (a practice that had already become widespread in any case). But despite widespread recognition of the inequities of equal representation for states of wildly varying populations in the U.S. Senate, a move to change apportionment has not made it to government's agenda in recent years. The reason is simple: it would be a waste of time and resources for its proponents, because the Constitution contains a special amending formula relating specifically to Senate apportionment: "no state, without its consent, shall be deprived of its equal suffrage in the Senate" (Article V). And because the status quo both gives small states more power in Congress and allows them to win more funding in federal grant programs, it is implausible to imagine that they would ever agree.[15] Only term limits has made it to the institutional agenda in the U.S., where it has en-

---

14 Russell 1993: 214-215. The Accord directed that "federal legislation [...] be sufficiently flexible to allow provinces and territories to provide for gender equality in the composition of the Senate" (Russell 1993: 243). The Mulroney government's September 1991 constitutional proposals had called for direct election of the Senate simultaneously with House elections based on the principle that "the size of Senate constituencies should be large enough to allow for proportional representation and, in the larger provinces, numerous enough to represent different regions within the province" (Canada 1991: 18). See also Seidle 1992.

15 On the consequences of equal representation of states in the U.S. Senate, see Lee/Oppenheimer 1999.

countered the same obstacles of court and congressional rejection as term limits for the House. Abolition of the Senate has been suggested only by a few crackpot academics like myself (Weaver/Rockman 1993).

Operating Rules in the Legislature and Inter-Branch Relations

A variety of changes in the organization and operating rules of the Canadian and United States legislatures have been made in recent years. In the United States, the power of House subcommittees was dramatically expanded in the 1970s, and trimmed back in the 1980s, as party leaders tried to reassert control (Smith 1989). And while term limits for members of Congress were rejected in 1995, both the House and Senate Republican caucuses that year approved six-year term limits for committee chairs and ranking minority members of their party, with the former taking effect in 2001 (Dewar 1995). Significantly, this move required only a majority vote in their own caucuses rather than the multi-stage super-majority requirement needed for a congressional term limit. But even these groups were unable to agree on changes to caucus rules that would increase incentives for party discipline by stripping committee chairs of their posts if they failed to back the party leadership in floor votes on key items in the party's agenda (the House Speaker has informal authority to do so already, however) (Dewar 1995). The failure of these measures lies in the electoral interest that all U.S. legislators have in being responsive to constituency interests and opinion rather than the party leadership when these two considerations come into conflict, because their constituents expect it and because the decentralized, candidate and constituency-oriented nature of congressional politics makes them highly vulnerable to criticism on such grounds by opponents if they deviate from constituency views.

Other distinctive elements of the fragmented character of congressional decisionmaking remain largely intact, however, surviving even the dramatic change in party control of Congress in 1994. Most obviously, the Senate has made only modest changes in its rules for imposing cloture on debates, changing from a requirement of two thirds of all members to sixty percent of those present and voting in 1975 (Binder/Smith 1997).

Some sector-specific procedural changes have been made, however, to make Congress and inter-branch relations operate more effectively (Sinclair 1997). Congress has made a series of revisions to its budget process that had the effect of restricting unlimited debate on major budget bills and hence restricting the rights of minorities to block legislation that they did not like. In the budget case, for example, there was a perception that if Congress did not get its act together, it would lose control of taxing and spending policy to the President (Sundquist 1981: chapter 8). Similarly the War Powers Resolution of 1973 was enacted (over President Nixon's veto) in response to perceived presidential unilateralism in foreign affairs, most notably in Southeast Asia (Sundquist 1981: chapter 9). Successive Presidents have branded the resolution unconstitutional. They have, however, generally abided by its reporting requirements (although generally avoiding reporting under provisions of the Resolution that would require congressional ratification of continued troop deployment after sixty days), but not its requirements for consultation "in every possible instance" before introduction of troops or regular consultation after they are introduced (Sundquist 1981: chapter 9; Katzmann 1990). The common features that gave rise to these sector-specific institutional changes are (1) a bipartisan perception that the status quo (or default position) was unacceptable, frequently because it was seen as weakening congressional power and prerogatives vis-à-vis the President, and (2) the ability of Congress to enact changes solely through legislation or changes in its own rules, minimizing procedural obstacles to change. Similarly, Congress granted (but under President Clinton, failed to renew) so-called "fast track" negotiating authority to the President for trade agreements – although the perceived problem in this case was that the United States would not be able to lead in the negotiation of multilateral trade agreements if Congress was able to pick and choose which provisions it liked rather than having to abide by the entire package (Destler 1992). In any case, these sector-specific adjustments did not change the fundamental character of the American legislature and executive as separate (and in the former case fragmented) institutions sharing power. They merely adjusted processes and the balance of powers between the two at the margins.

In Canada, there have been numerous changes over time in the way that Cabinet has operated. The number of Cabinet committees has expanded and shrunk, and an Inner Cabinet was created by Joe Clark and abolished by his successor (Savoie 1999). This was easily doable because the governing party (and in fact the Prime Minister) could implement these changes without need for further ratification.

Serious (rather than cosmetic) reforms to lower party discipline and/or increase minority party rights in the Canadian House of Commons rarely even made it onto the agenda in Canada, however. The reason is clear: it is never in the interests of governing parties to do so. No matter how attractive such a reform may be to a party when it is in opposition, the bloom quickly falls off the rose once such a party gains power.

Constitutional Amending Procedures

Canada-U.S. differences are starkest in the area of constitutional amending procedures. In the United States, the hurdles to a constitutional amendment that would itself revise the rules for amendments to the U.S. Constitution are so formidable that it has remained entirely off the agenda. Proponents of major change in the U.S. Constitution have instead focused on the provision in the U.S. Constitution (Article V) that says that Congress "may" call a new constitutional convention to consider amendments if two thirds of state legislatures request that it do so.

In Canada, on the other hand, the perceived need to put in place a workable amending formula for Canada's constitution was (along with ending the requirement that any changes be ratified by the British Parliament) a leading cause of Canada's early rounds of "mega-constitutional politics" prior to the 1982 Constitution Act. Recognizing the potential high costs of failure, the issue was addressed only when there were strong indicators that a consensus between Ottawa and the provincial premiers might be possible. In each case, however, that consensus broke down – usually because Québec's premier feared electoral retribution for not getting enough for Québec. The 1980-82 round had a more specific cause: Prime Minister Trudeau's need to make good on his pledge during the 1980 referendum campaign to achieve constitutional renewal. But it became clear during that process that the "conventional" process of unanimous consent of Ottawa and the provinces would not work. Indeed, the federal government came to believe that there was no overlap achievable between their zone of acceptable outcomes, and that of the Parti Québécois government in Québec City. When the Supreme Court, in a 1981 decision, ruled that a constitutional package including substantial but not complete provincial assent would be legal (if not especially wise), it decisively eased the rules for approval in the only decisionmaking venue that really mattered – negotiations between Ottawa and the provincial premiers. In so doing, it also altered the incentives acting on provincial premiers to expand their zones of acceptable outcomes to ensure that they were not left out of an agreement between Ottawa and the other provinces. The four-part amending formula that Ottawa and the nine anglophone-majority provinces agreed to reflected a compromise between the preferences of Ottawa and those provincial leaders.

Revisions to the 1982 amending formulae was one of the demands made by Premier Bourassa in the process leading up to the Meech Lake and Charlottetown Accords. However, several of Québec's constitutional demands required use of the unanimity amending formula under the 1982 Constitution Act, which sunk the Meech Lake Accord when the Manitoba Legislature failed to ratify the Accord within the three year ratification period. Later efforts to revise the amending formula (and other aspects of Canada's constitution) in the Charlottetown Accord fell victim to the addition of further decisionmaking venues – provincial referenda – to the amending process, each with a veto over changes to the constitution. These additions came about not as a result of changes in the Constitution Act, but rather as a result of provincial legislation in Alberta and British Columbia to require a referendum on all constitutional amendment packages and in Québec requiring a referendum on the Charlottetown Accord.

After the failure of the Charlottetown Accord, changing Canada's constitutional amending formula – and constitutional amendments in general – remained off the agenda until the final days of the 1995 sovereignty referendum in Québec, when Prime Minister Chrétien, seeking to bolster the "No" side in the referendum campaign, pledged to bring about a package of constitutional reforms responding to Québec's concerns, including an enhanced Québec veto over constitutional amendments. It quickly became obvious that the other provinces had no interest in such a package. Prime Minister Chrétien instead used ordinary legislation to pledge that Ottawa would not approve constitutional amendments under the 7/50 amending formula unless a super-majority of provinces including Québec (as well as British Columbia and, implicitly, Alberta) approved it first. Thus Canada moved to an informal "normal" amending formula that was even harder to use than the one in the 1982 Constitution Act – and it did so only by avoiding the multiple decisionmaking venues (executive federalism, public referenda and votes in provincial legislatures) where previous changes in the amending formula had been blocked.

Conclusions

This study suggests a number of patterns of interest, some of which suggest similarities in cross-national patterns of institutional reform, while others suggest distinctive practices in Canada and the United States.

Agenda Formation

Institutional reform agendas in the two countries have had more differences than similarities, reflecting both the different pathologies of the two systems and the differing interests of those who have power to put issues on the agenda.

First, in both countries, high visibility and persistence of a policy problem increase the likelihood that a problem will make it to policymakers' institutional agenda. In Canada, the "on its face" illegitimacy of an unelected Senate and, prior to 1982, the non-patriated character of Canada's constitution, increased the prospects that those issues would be a major part of any institutional reform package that is considered in Canada. In the United States, incumbency advantages and high re-election rates in the House of

Representatives that were widely seen (especially by Republicans) as unfair and undemocratic helped to fuel demands for congressional term limits. On the other hand, problems that in theory could be serious but which have in fact occurred almost never (e.g., a presidential candidate in the U.S. failing to win the support of a majority of the electoral college after winning a plurality or majority of the popular vote) or seldom (a party winning a plurality or majority of Canada's House of Commons seats after failing to win a plurality of the popular vote) seems less likely to make it to the institutional agenda. Changes in the operation of the legislature have been much less frequent, and less visible on the reform agenda in Canada than in the United States both because the stakes are so much smaller and because control over the reform agenda is much more centralized in the government of the day in Canada.

A second conclusion, however, is that developments in what John Kingdon (1995) has called the "problem stream" are generally insufficient to move institutional reform proposals to the institutional agenda. Developments in the "political stream" are also important. In particular, there must be actors who have both an interest or commitment to a particular institutional reform and the leverage to get the issue on government's institutional agenda. Policymakers' incentives in putting issues on the agenda are complex rather than simple, however. The commitment of the new Republican congressional majority to instituting term limits, for example, was based primarily on a prior campaign commitment rather than their self-interest as a new congressional majority.

Third, as one might expect given the differences in the two countries' political institutions, how reform agendas for national political institutions are set differs substantially in the two countries. In the United States, the diffusion of power in the legislature allows multiple sources with different political and policy interests to get issues on the institutional agenda. The ubiquity of divided government over the past thirty years has made this even more salient. Thus consideration of institutional reform has been less concentrated into a few "rounds" than in Canada. In Canada, only the governing party has been able to put institutional reforms on the agenda except during the grand rounds of "mega-constitutional politics," where provincial premiers, and more recently aboriginal leaders, have also had leverage to do so.

Fourth, there appears in both countries to be some diffusion of institutional reform proposals between levels of government. In the United States, the widespread use of line-item vetoes in the states has clearly had an impact on the federal debate and helped to propel it onto the agenda. The case of term limits is more complex, with most of the early interest in term limits being with respect to Congress, but all of the early success occurring with respect to state legislatures. In Canada, the diffusion of referenda on constitutional issues from the provinces (Alberta, British Columbia, Québec) to the federal level can be seen very directly in the case of the Charlottetown referendum, where the perceived illegitimacy of citizens in some provinces having a vote on constitutional reform while others did not helped to lead to the decision to hold a nation-wide referendum (technically, the referendum in Québec was run separately, under distinct rules). There are barriers to diffusion, however. There has not yet been a spread of recall legislation from British Columbia to the federal Parliament, for example, because its primary proponent, the Reform Party, does not have the institutional leverage to get it on the federal institutional agenda. There is also some evidence of cross-border diffusion of ideas in the usual U.S.-to-Canada direction with respect both to ideas for Senate reform (the idea of a Triple E Senate and a Senate role in confirming certain government appointments) as well as the populist ideas of referendum, recall, and weaker party discipline in the legislature.

Fifth, the evidence presented here suggests that having one type of reform proposal on the agenda may help to "crowd out" others. A good example is Canada's serious and persistent problems of overrepresentation of some regions in the House of Commons while other regions are underrepresented. The fact that Western Canadian political elites have consistently seen Senate reform as the preferred mechanism to deal with this problem has meant that Senate reform has been on the agenda in each round of constitutional negotiations, while making it less likely that an alternative mechanism, reform of electoral rules for the House of Commons, could make it onto the reform agenda.

Adoption and Rejection of Reform Proposals

The evidence reviewed here also suggests a number of conclusions about adoption and rejection of institutional reform initiatives that *do* make it onto government's agenda. First, contrary to the hypothesis suggested at the outset of this chapter, there has been a large gap in both countries (not just in the United States) between the list of items that make it to the institutional agenda of government and those that actually get adopted. This can be accounted for by the dismal record of recent rounds of "executive federalism"-driven constitutional reform in Canada.

Second, decisions on adopting or rejecting institutional reforms have been made in very different venues and using very different mechanisms in Canada and the United States. These differences reflect broader differences in existing political institutions in Canada and the United States. In the U.S., the constitutional amendment has rarely been attempted, because the procedural barriers to success for such a route are so high, and are perceived to be high by all parties. The major exceptions, term limits for members of Congress and a balanced budget to the U.S. constitution, were recognized by their proponents as both long-haul propositions and political long-shots; they were pursued as much for their potential to generate blame against (mostly Democratic) opponents as for their prospects for adoption. In addition, the prospect of generating blame against opponents of these measures led supporters of both measures to believe that they could compel opponents to expand their zone of acceptable outcomes if they could force those opponents to vote directly on them. In Canada, on the other hand, attempts at institutional reform through the constitutional route have been frequent, and have been concentrated in the several great rounds of constitutional reform that have bedeviled Canada over the past three decades.

Why has the constitutional amendment route been pursued so much more frequently in Canada, and with so little success? Four reasons stand out for its pursuit. First was the fact that Canada's constitution had not been patriated and lacked a clear amending formula prior to 1982. Until the early 1960s, the absence of a domestic amending formula was, in the words of Peter Russell (1993: 57), "more of an embarrassment than a practical inconvenience." The federal government of Canada amended its constitution through the British Parliament nine times between 1930 and 1964, obtaining the unanimous consent of provincial executives (but not legislatures) on matters that affected the division of federal and provincial powers (e.g., an amendment giving the federal government sole jurisdiction over unemployment insurance), and acting unilaterally on other issues. Increasingly, however, the lack of a clear amending formula was seen as both a national embarrassment and an inconvenience that repeatedly brought the constitution to government's attention whenever there was a glimmer of hope that a consensus between Ottawa and the provinces could be reached. Second, the 1982 constitutional reform set off an expanding cascade of demands for redress (notably from Québec) that could only be met through further constitutional amendments. Third, it took a while for Canadian elites to realize just how much the obstacles to constitutional reform had been increased by the 1982 constitution, since until that time an agreement of Canada's eleven First Ministers (and in the 1980-82 round, something less than consensus) was all that was required for an amendment to be adopted. Since then, the requirement that provincial legislatures also ratify amendments made that route more tricky. The underlying reason here is that each of Canada's provinces is on an independent electoral cycle: thus a provincial premier who commits to a constitutional reform package may not be in power long enough to see it through to ratification.

The growing perception that the default position, no agreement on constitutional revisions, would lead to the breakup of Canada also helped to put the issue on the agenda and keep it there. Belief that the default was unacceptable may also have led political elites to believe that when push came to shove, fellow elites would expand their zones of acceptable outcomes until they overlapped. There was some truth to this belief – provincial premiers did compromise in agreeing to the Meech Lake and Charlottetown Accords.

But fear of the default did not bring new signataries on board, either because they had strong convictions (Elijah Harper and Clyde Wells), their constituents would not accept it (Preston Manning), or they welcomed the default (the Parti Québécois and the Bloc Québécois).

A fourth conclusion is that institutional reform procedures – both the number of venues through which institutional reform proposals must pass and the decision rules within those venues – matter a lot. Procedural barriers – multiple venues in which affirmative decisions were required, and minority vetoes or unanimity requirements in some venues – have made constitutional amendment an impractical route for institutional reform in both countries. These procedural barriers are especially visible in the abortive constitutional Canadian reform rounds since 1982. The addition of more decisionmaking venues, all of which required approval, sometimes with unanimity (notably in the instigating "executive federalism" phase), severely complicated negotiations in the Meech Lake and Charlottetown Rounds. But other elements of the process were also working against reaching a deal. A defining characteristic of Canadian constitutional negotiations is that the major societal interests have different, and incompatible, zones of acceptable outcomes regarding how the Canadian federation should be altered: most notably, Québec governments have consistently sought increased fiscal and policy autonomy, and freedom from federal controls, while negotiators from the Western provinces have most often sought an increased voice in central institutions, but have sometimes (most notably when they are flush with natural resource revenues) endorsed a devolution agenda as well. As Campbell and Pal (Campbell/Pal 1994: 154) said about the Charlottetown Round, English Canada and Québec were "on different tracks, with different agendas." In particular, Québec has sought recognition as a "distinct society," which English Canadians have greeted with reactions ranging from indifference to hostility. In addition, Québec governments have continued to worry about amendments that would threaten their interests; but they also sought a constitution flexible enough to allow Québec to acquire new powers from Ottawa. Québec's amending formula concerns could be addressed most directly by a formula that allowed significant flexibility but gave Québec a veto; such "special status" was, however, unacceptable to most of the other nine provinces. Extending a veto to all the other provinces would remove the flexibility sought by Québec.

Chances for reaching agreement on a constitutional package were also lowered by overloading of the constitutional agenda with contentious new players and new dimensions of conflict that required a more complex reform package. Prior to the 1987-1990 Meech Lake Round of constitutional negotiations, the parties negotiating, as well as those ratifying, were limited almost exclusively to the federal government and the ten provincial governments. In the Charlottetown Round, there were a whole series of new actors who were pushing their concerns into the policy making process, and some old actors lengthened their list of demands. These concerns included (a) aboriginal self-government; (b) Ottawa's concerns with economic union; (c) territories' desire to become provinces; (d) women and linguistic minorities' concerns; and (e) Social Charter concerns from the Ontario government and others. But as the Meech Lake Accord showed, proceeding with smaller constitutional packages, involving fewer issue dimensions, was not an option. The reason is that given the high public resistance to constitutional negotiations and the high barriers to a successful outcome, all sides tended to believe that any constitutional round that won ratification was likely to be the last train leaving the station for a long time. Waiting for the next round of constitutional negotiations would likely mean postponing indefinitely a possible move toward their preferred position (ideal point) on a desired issue dimension.

The defeat of the Charlottetown referendum suggests that popular mistrust of elites may also require referenda if such reform packages are to be seen as legitimate. The practical result, as Patrick Monahan has noted, is that the Canadian constitution has become virtually unamendable. (An exception is amendments that affect only one province, which take place under a separate amending formula requiring only the consent of Ottawa and that province. Amendments under this formula have been made with respect to denominational schools in both Quebec and Newfoundland, for example [see Hurley 1996]). Thus it is not surprising that the Chrétien government has tried to steer clear of the constitutional route to institutional reform since coming into office.

A final notable pattern in acceptance or rejection of institutional reform initiatives in the two countries is that courts have played a much more active role in overturning reforms in the United States than in Canada, notably with the legislative veto, majority-minority House districts, the line-item veto, and legislative term limits for Congress enacted at the state level. Three factors appear to account for this difference. First and most obvious is the greater deference of Canadian courts to the legislature on institutional issues, even in the post-Charter of Rights era of a more activist Canadian Supreme Court. Second is the greater use of non-constitutional reform mechanisms as a vehicle for institutional reform in the United States than in Canada. These types of reforms are inherently more vulnerable to constitutional challenge than reforms that are included in the constitution. Third, the fragmented nature of governmental power in the United States (and especially the potential for divided government) gives access to government's institutional agenda to a broader array of elected politicians, and provides political incentives to force through institutional changes that they know (or at least strongly suspect) will ultimately be overturned by the courts.

Table 1: Attributes of Multi-Venue Games and Their Application to Institutional Reform

Game parameters and their consequences			
Game parameters	Determinants of parameters	Impact on prospect for agreement	Optimal conditions for approving institutional reform
	Negotiating parameters		
(a) Distribution of decisionmakers' preferences and degree of overlap in those preferences at each venue	Perceptions of self-interest (including desire to win re-election) and benefits of cooperation; accountability of decisionmakers to others; predictability of reform impacts	Differing preferences and small zones of acceptable outcomes limit prospects for agreement	Individual participants have broad zones of acceptable outcomes with substantial or complete overlap
(b) Negotiators' perceptions of acceptability of default position	Decisionmakers' policy preferences and their perceptions of other actors' response to failure to reach or ratify agreement	High acceptability of default for critical actors lowers prospects for agreement	Lack of agreement unacceptable to all negotiators
(c) Number of different elements in an institutional reform package	Number of participants and their preferences	Larger number of institutional reform proposals creates opportunities for trade-offs and log rolls but complicates and prolongs negotiations, increasing probability of mobilizing coalitions of intense minorities of opposition on specific issues	A single reform proposal for a single institution
(d) Rules for approval in each decisionmaking venue	Rules of decisionmaking venue	Unanimity rules empower holdouts; deviations from unanimity rule give incentives to compromise to avoid exclusion from agreement	Simple majority decision rule
(e) Number of decisionmaking venues where approval is required	Rules for institutional reform (e.g., constitutional amending formulae)	Multiple venues in which reform can be vetoed increase prospects for stalemate	Single-venue approval requirement for institutional reform

(f) Ratifiers' trust and deference in decisionmakers at prior levels	Past performance of "instigators" and political linkages between instigators and "ratifiers"	High deference lessens ratifiers' willingness to incur search costs to find out more information about agreements and increases their willingness to ratify	Very high trust and deference
(g) Ratifiers' perception of probability of acceptance in other critical venues	Past experience with similar reform initiatives	Perception that agreement may fail in another venue may increase probability of inaction	Combination of perceived high probability of acceptance and preference for adoption

Table 2: Selected Institutional Reforms in the United States, 1975-1999

Reform	Stage reached	Period under consideration	Mechanism
Selection rules for lower chamber of legislature			
Term limits for members of House of Representatives	Rejected in Congressional vote; approval in some states before being overturned by courts	1995 (Congress); early 1990s (states)	State ballot initiatives; constitutional amendment
Encouragement of "majority-minority" districts for House of Representatives	Adopted and partially overturned		Legislation and court decisions
Selection rules for upper chamber of legislature			
Term limits for members of Congress	Rejected in Congressional vote; approval in some states before being overturned by courts	1990s	State ballot initiatives; constitutional amendment
Internal operation of legislative chambers			
Cloture rule in Senate for debate on most matters lowered from 2/3 of present and voting to 3/5 of membership	Adopted	1975 (revised in 1979 and 1986)	Senate rules
Sanctions for House and Senate committee chairs who violate party discipline on key votes	Rejected	1995	House and Senate Republican caucus rules
Term limits for House and Senate committee chairs	Adopted	1995	House and Senate Republican caucus rules
Increased subcommittee independence in House of Representatives	Adopted	1970s	House committee rules
Greater openness of floor voting procedures in House	Adopted	1973	House rules for Committee of the Whole

Development of budget reconciliation procedure, fast track and similar mechanisms provide vehicles for avoiding multiple veto points, unlimited debate and super-majority requirements in Senate legislative process	Adoption for budget; adoption on time-limuted basis for trade negotiations	1974 (budget)	Congressional rules
Relationships between branches			
Formal end to legislative veto	Adopted and later overturned	Gradual adoption; overturned in 1983	Adoption in individual pieces of legislation; overturned by Supreme Court decision
Creation of Congressional Budget Office gives Congress alternative sources of expertise to executive	Adopted	1974	Legislation and chamber rules
Constitutional amending procedure			
None			

Table 3: Selected Institutional Reforms in Canada, 1975-1999

Reform	Stage reached	Period under consideration	Mechanism
	Selection rules for lower chamber of legislature		
Québec guaranteed minimum of 25% of House seats	Included in Charlottetown Accord and rejected	1992	Constitutional amendment, including referendum/plebiscite
	Selection rules for upper chamber of legislature		
Bundestag-style House of the Federation	Proposed by Government of Canada but later dropped	1991	Constitutional amendment
Partially "Triple E" Senate with proportional representation or provincial option election/appointment procedures	Included in Charlottetown Accord and rejected	1992	Constitutional amendment, including referendum/plebiscite
	Executive/cabinet		
Inner cabinet established	Adopted and then abolished	1979-1980	Privy Council Order
Cabinet committees proliferate and are cut back in number	Adopted and revised	1988-1993	Privy Council Order
	Constitutional amending procedure		
Four-part amending formula	Included in 1982 constitutional reforms and adopted	1982	Constitutional amendment
Constitutional changes involving national political institutions would require unanimity of Ottawa and provinces; compensation to provinces opting out of amendments transferring jurisdiction to Ottawa	Included in Meech Lake Accord; provincial ratification failed	1987-1990	Constitutional amendment

Constitutional changes involving national political institutions would require unanimity of Ottawa and provinces	Included in Charlottetown Accord and rejected	1992	Constitutional amendment, including referendum/pelbiscite
Adoption of referendum requirement for constitutional amendments in Alberta and British Columbia	Adopted	Early 1990s	Provincial legislation
Addition of statutory regional vetoes to amendments undertaken under 7/50 amending formula	Enacted by Parliament	1997	Statute

References

Arnold, R. Douglas 1990: *The Logic of Congressional Action*, New Haven: Yale UP.
Binder, Sarah A. 1997: *Minority Rights, Majority Rule. Partisanship and the Development of Congress*, Cambridge/New York: Cambridge UP.
——/Smith, Steven S. 1997: *Politics or Principle? Filibustering in the United States Senate*, Washington: Brookings Institution.
Brady, David W./Volden, Craig 1997: *Revolving Gridlock. Politics and Policy from Carter to Clinton*, Boulder: Westview Press.
Campbell, Robert M./Pal, Leslie A. [3]1994: "The Rise and Fall of the Charlottetown Accord," in: Robert M. Campbell/Leslie A. Pal (eds.), *The Real Worlds of Canadian Politics*, Peterborough: Broadview Press, 142-187.
Canada 1991: *Shaping Canada's Future Together. Proposals*, Ottawa: Supply and Services.
Cobb, Roger W./Elder, Charles D. 1972: *Participation in American Politics. The Dynamics of Agenda-Building*, Boston: Allyn and Bacon.
Cooper, Kenneth J. 1995: "House Rejects Measures to Require Term Limits," in: *Washington Post*, March 30, A1.
Destler, I.M. [2]1992: *American Trade Politics*, Washington/New York: Institute for International Economics/Twentieth Century Fund.
Dewar, Helen 1995: "Senate Republicans Put a Lid on Seniority By Limiting Terms of Chairmen," in: *Washington Post*, July 20.
Gilmour, John 1995: *Strategic Disagreement. Stalemate in American Politics*, Pittsburgh: University of Pittsburgh Press.
Green, Donald P./Shapiro, Ian 1994: *Pathologies of Rational Choice Theory. A Critique of Applications in Political Science*, New Haven: Yale UP.
Hurley, James Ross 1996: *Amending Canada's Constitution. History, Processes, Problems and Prospects*, Ottawa: Canada Communication Group.
Janda, Richard 1992: *Rebalancing the Senate through Senate Reform. Another Look at the Bundesrat*, North York: York University Centre for Public Law and Public Policy, Background Studies of the York University Constitutional Reform Project, Study No. 11, Part III.
Katzmann, Robert A. 1990: "War Powers: Toward a New Accommodation," in: Thomas E. Mann (ed.), *A Question of Balance. The President, the Congress and Foreign Policy*, Washington: Brookings Institution, 35-69.
Kingdon, John 1981: *Congressmen's Voting Decisions*, New York: Harper and Row.
—— [2]1995: *Agendas, Alternatives, and Public Policies*, New York: HarperCollins.
Korn, Jessica 1996: *The Power of Separation. American Constitutionalism and the Myth of the Legislative Veto*, Princeton: Princeton UP.
LeDuc, Lawrence/Pammett, Jon H. 1995: "Referendum Voting: Attitudes and Behaviour in the 1992 Constitutional Referendum," in: *Canadian Journal of Political Science* 28, 1, 3-33.
Lee, Frances E./Oppenheimer, Bruce I. 1999: *Sizing Up the Senate. The Consequences of Equal Representation*, Chicago: University of Chicago Press.
Lijphart, Arend 1977: *Democracy in Plural Societies. A Comparative Exploration*, New Haven: Yale UP.
—— 1984: *Democracies. Patterns of Majoritarian and Consensus Government in Twenty-One Countries*, New Haven: Yale UP.

Lublin, David 1999: *The Paradox of Representation. Racial Gerrymandering and Minority Interests in Congress*, Princeton: Princeton UP.
Mayhew, David 1974: *Congress. The Electoral Connection*, New Haven: Yale UP.
Milner, Henry (ed.) 1999: *Making Every Vote Count. Reassessing Canada's Electoral System*, Peterborough: Broadview Press.
Moravsik, Andrew 1993: "Integrating International and Domestic Theories of International Bargaining," in: Robert D. Putnam (ed.), *Double-Edged Diplomacy. International Bargaining and Domestic Politics*, Berkeley: University of California Press, 3-42.
Putnam, Robert D. 1988: "Diplomacy and Domestic Politics: The Logic of Two-Level Games," in: *International Organization* 42, 3, 427-460.
Richie, Rob/Hill, Steven 1999: "This Time Let the Voters Decide: The Proportional Representation Movement in the United States," in: Henry Milner (ed.), *Making Every Vote Count. Reassessing Canada's Electoral System*, Peterborough: Broadview Press, 179-185.
Russell, Peter H. 1993: *Constitutional Odyssey. Can Canadians Become a Sovereign People?* Toronto: University of Toronto Press.
Savoie, Donald 1999: *Governing from the Centre. The Concentration of Power in Canadian Politics*, Toronto: University of Toronto Press.
Schelling, Thomas 1963: *The Strategy of Conflict*, Cambridge: Harvard UP.
Seidle, F. Leslie 1992: "Senate Reform and the Constitutional Agenda: Conundrum or Solution?" in: Janet Ajzenstat (ed.), *Canadian Constitutionalism: 1791-1991*, Ottawa: Canadian Study Group of Parliament.
Shepsle, Kenneth A./Bonchek, Mark S. 1997: *Analyzing Politics. Rationality, Behavior, and Institutions*, New York: W.W. Norton.
Simeon, Richard 1972: *Federal-Provincial Diplomacy. The Making of Recent Policy in Canada*, Toronto: University of Toronto Press.
Sinclair, Barbara 1997: *Unorthodox Lawmaking. New Legislative Processes in the U.S. Congress*, Washington: Congressional Quarterly Press.
Smith, Steven S. 1989: *Call to Order. Floor Politics in the House and Senate*, Washington: Brookings Institution.
Studlar, Donley T. 1998: "The Last Westminster Electoral System? Canada Not Britain?" in: *Representation* 35, 1, 70-78.
Sundquist, James L. 1981: *The Decline and Resurgence of Congress*, Washington: Brookings Institution.
Weaver, R. Kent 1986: "The Politics of Blame Avoidance," in: *Journal of Public Policy* 6, 4, 371-398.
—— 1997: "Electoral Reform for the Canadian House of Commons," in: *Canadian Journal of Political Science* 33, 3, 473-512.
—— forthcoming: "Electoral Rules and Electoral Reform in Canada," in: Matthew Soberg Shugart/Martin P. Wattenberg (eds.), *Mixed-Member Electoral Systems. The Best of Both Worlds?* New York: Oxford UP.
——/Rockman, Bert A. 1993: "Institutional Reform and Constitutional Design," in: R. Kent Weaver/Bert A. Rockman (eds.), *Do Institutions Matter? Government Capabilities in the U.S. and Abroad*, Washington: Brookings Institution, 462-481.

Parliamentary Government in Canada: Institutional Stability and Constitutional Reform in the Legislative and Executive Branches

Steffen Schneider

Historical ancestry and geographical proximity underpin the dominant role of two major reference points for institution-building and constitutional reform in Canada: The British Westminster model is the obvious benchmark for the Canadian version of parliamentary (responsible) government. Secured during an early phase of "mega-constitutional politics" (Peter Russell) in the 1840s, it has remained a key element of the Canadian political system ever since its inception in 1867, and hence throughout the protracted transition from colonial dependency to national sovereignty that came to an end with the repatriation of the British North America Act in 1981/82. The prominence of majoritarian principles in the organization of the legislative and executive branches of Canadian government during much of the postwar era was demonstrated by Arend Lijphart (1984). However, 1981/82 also was an important episode in a new phase of "mega-constitutional politics" that had begun in the 1960s and strengthened (federalism) or established (entrenched constitutional provisions and rights, judicial review) a number of institutional features that run against the logic of the Westminster model while being shared with the United States. With the partial exception of the Canadian Senate, the procedures and structures of the legislative and executive branches of government played a clearly subordinate, if visible role in the constitutional reform debates and initiatives of the last few decades, and even organizational changes below that level were quite rare and modest.

This relative neglect, both in the field of constitutional politics itself and in the academic literature,[1] did perhaps not come as a surprise: The "decline of legislatures" (Bryce 1990) in Canada seemed to be the combined effect of explanatory factors shared with other advanced democratic nations and homemade ones, and hence to be even more pronounced in Canada than elsewhere. As a consequence, the intergovernmental arena of federal-provincial relations (and later, the judicial arena of the Supreme Court), rather than the core features of parliamentary democracy, tended to absorb the interest of constitutional reformers and political scientists.

1 Titles more often than not illustrate this neglect (cf. Cairns 1992; Russell et al. 1989); the topic remains underexplored (cf. Atkinson/Thomas 1993).

Yet on an international scale, interest in various aspects of constitutional design has re-emerged over the last couple of years with the rise of the new institutionalism (Evans/Rueschemeyer/Skopcol 1985; Steinmo/Thelen/Longstreth 1992). A growing literature now probes into the impact of different forms of executive-legislative relations – notably, presidentialism versus parliamentary government – on system efficiency, stability, and legitimacy (Lijphart 1992; Moe/Caldwell 1994; Weaver/Rockman 1993). Even the internal organization of legislative bodies themselves is once again considered a meaningful area of study; the question "if parliament matters" (Norton 1993) is now increasingly answered positively (Döring 1995). According to some, we live in an "age of parliaments" where legislative bodies are "dynamic institutions capable of both changing and leading change" (Copeland/Patterson 1994: 1, vii). This emerging literature, however, continues to have a strong bias toward the British Parliament and the U.S. Congress which, due to their longevity and substantive importance, clearly represent paradigmatic, but also highly specific cases.[2]

In light of these developments, the neglect of would-be reformers and political scientists in Canada for their own institutions of parliamentary democracy becomes a phenomenon in need of explanation. This chapter is based on the implicit argument that the legislative and executive branches of Canadian government indeed merit closer examination than they have received so far, and that changes to them have a greater potential impact than acknowledged. As parliamentary government is a core element of the Westminster model, it might seem tempting to broaden the analysis in order to include all of Lijphart's eight dimensions of majoritarian democracy, as well as underlying social conditions. Although I will shortly refer to some of these context factors of Canadian parliamentary government, notably in the conclusion (III.), I do not primarily aim at offering such a broad analysis of the fate of majoritarian democracy in Canada here.[3] Rather, the bulk of the paper (II.) will concentrate on the internal organization and relations of the legislative and executive branches, their constitutional foundations, real or perceived shortcomings and the (few) changes that have been made over the last couple of decades in order to address them. A theoretical framework derived from the new institutional economics (NIE) serves as guiding line of the chapter (I.).

2 More precisely, the British Parliament continues to serve as prototype in the more traditional literature (cf. Kluxen 1983; Hofmann/Riescher 1999), while rational-choice oriented work has so far largely focused on the U.S. Congress, "the most untypical example of the legislative institution" (Döring 1995: 17).

3 For a more encompassing perspective, cf. Thunert 2000; for those elements of the Canadian political system that are solely considered as context factors of parliamentary government here, cf. various other chapters in this volume.

I. Comparing Variants of Parliamentary Government – A Theoretical Framework

A theoretical framework for the comparative analysis of parliaments has to be able to cope with considerable empirical variety, both across the divide of presidentialism versus parliamentary government and within the category of parliamentary democracy – "the most common institutionalisation of popular sovereignty" (Strøm 1995: 77) – itself. The fairly recent application of theoretical insights gained from the NIE to rational-choice inspired work on legislative organization is a major breakthrough in this regard. The conceptual shift implied in the change of key metaphores – from "parliament as market" to "parliament as firm" – sustains a more realistic perspective on legislatures and their relations with executives; its genuinely comparative potential is, however, restricted by a strong U.S. bias.[4]

Previously, the rational choice image of legislatures had been one of utility-maximizing, vote-trading political entrepreneurs – the individual MPs – in an environment of full information and costless exchange. This image is conspicuously inadequate, and even more so for the study of parliamentary regimes with strong parties. Yet by incorporating problems of uncertainty and enforcement, as well as forms of hierarchical exchange and delegation of authority similar to those encountered in the sphere of industrial organization, the more sophisticated NIE framework is able to lay theoretical ground for a systematic analysis of the causes and effects of legislative organization. As "equilibrium institutions" (Shepsle 1986, 1989), parliaments contribute to solving problems of collective action like the famous, if largely hypothetical one of preference cycling in the aggregation of individual preferences. As "institutional equilibria," parliaments impose varying transaction costs and behavioural constraints on legislative actors.

The delegation of authority from entire legislatures as principals to agents both within and outside parliaments is a key aspect of legislative organization, and it represents a particularly useful theoretical lens for the study of parliamentary government – that is, "the institutional arrangement by which the executive is accountable, through a confidence relationship, to the parliamentary majority" (Strøm 1995: 52), and parliamentary democracy – that is, "a system in which the popular majority, through its elected representatives in the legislative branch, effectively controls public policy" (52). In fact, the distinguishing characteristic of parliamentary democracy – at least in theory – is the existence of a single chain of delegation from the

4 On the NIE, cf. Alt/Shepsle 1990; Moe 1984; North 1990; for an application to the U.S. Congress, cf. Weingast/Marshall 1988. The contributions to Döring (1995) use the framework for the analysis of legislatures in Western Europe. The following theoretical sketch is largely based on Strøm's (1995) chapter in that volume.

people to its representatives in the legislature to a government that is supported by a parliamentary majority (and from the cabinet to an administration that implements government policy – a link of the chain that will have to remain largely unexplored in this chapter).

Thus the study of parliamentary government has to focus both on the internal organization of legislatures and on external delegation from legislatures to cabinets and prime ministers. One important aspect in this regard is the unicameral versus bicameral structure of parliaments (and different forms of intercameral relations). Secondly, parliaments as otherwise largely collegial and egalitarian bodies provide for a range of vertical and horizontal differentiations among individual members and their roles; the rules and norms of legislatures define "a set of privileged groups, that is, subgroups of parliamentarians with specific powers, and a set of procedures that specifies the powers of these subgroups with respect to the functions that legislatures perform" (Strøm 1995: 62). These privileged groups include: committees; presidents or speakers; parties with their own caucus and leadership organizations.

As agents of the people, legislatures have a central place and important duties within the logic of parliamentary government – notably, law-making and budget approval, executive selection and oversight. The concept of parliamentary supremacy is a core element of the majoritarian tradition, and yet

> "[t]he contrast between formal power and actual impotence seems particularly striking for legislatures built on the Westminster model of parliamentary democracy and supremacy. The people's representatives seem curiously and frustratingly constrained in their critical role as agents of the popular will." (Strøm 1995: 57)

The reason for this gap is the far-reaching external delegation of powers from the legislative to the executive branch on which parliamentary democracy in general and the Westminster model in particular are based, thus leaving parliaments with executive selection as their main responsibility. Control of the legislative agenda is largely concentrated in the executive branch (and the party leadership of the government majority). Strong executive dominance, which is exacerbated by the complexity of modern industrial society, greatly reduces the legislative and even the oversight functions parliaments once had.[5]

This shift from the legislative to the executive branch, especially in the majoritarian tradition of the Westminster model, is inextricably linked with the role of parties. In parliamentary regimes, parties tend to be the most important privileged group within the legislature and to have an influence on

---

5 This does not mean, however, that legislative organization becomes an irrelevant object of study. Within the NIE framework, and given that assent to binding policy measures remains a decisive responsibility of legislatures, "it is of no concern whether parliaments actually initiate policies themselves or not. What counts are the actual costs involved in parliamentary procedure" (Döring 1995: 28f.).

legislative organization and procedure (timetabling, etc.) that reaches far beyond their formal competences. The caucus and leadership organizations of parties dominate individual MPs, and the government majority dominates opposition parties. Within the NIE framework, parties have long been an underexplored phenomenon due to the American bias of the approach, but are now seen as important solutions for collective action and coordination problems (Cox/McCubbins 1993); they are even more crucial in the context of parliamentary democracy than in the context of presidentialism: On the one hand, the logic of parliamentary government makes party cohesion an important resource for cabinets and prime ministers, who depend on a stable majority for their political survival, for the successful implementation of their programs, and hence for their re-election (similarly, the opposition as government-in-waiting hopes to profit from party discipline). On the other hand, individual MPs have a strong incentive to closely follow real or perceived constituency interests, even against their own leadership, while at the same time using their party label as an additional electoral resource. Left to their own devices, MPs would be likely to oversupply particularistic-benefits legislation through log-rolling and pork-barrel projects, while underproducing collective-benefits legislation. By empowering their leadership to monitor and enforce discipline through selective punishments and rewards, parties – if successful – circumvent the potential danger of "free-riding" by individual MPs, ensure that policy is geared towards broadly encompassing rather than special interests, and increase their re-election chances as a whole. Despite cross-national variations, party discipline – often decried as "evils of faction," but more aptly understood as a functional prerequisite of efficient parliamentary government – is indeed high in most parliamentary regimes.

Delegation of agenda control powers to privileged groups inside legislatures and to external agents thus entails various advantages, distributive and informational gains for parliaments and their government majority: it helps to reduce transaction costs, to ensure stability of choice in the face of the (potential) collective action problem of voting cycles, and to prevent "free-riding." On the other hand, delegation brings about its very own problems – such as "shirking," the risk that agents do not properly execute the intentions of their principals –, and hence together with "the ways legislators seek to solve them, [these problems] provide a coherent and intriguing perspective in which to examine the critical issues of parliamentary democracy" (Strøm 1995: 61).

The risks involved in the above-mentioned forms of internal and external delegation are countered with a range of oversight instruments through which principals impose constraints on their agents: ex ante control through contract design and selection mechanisms; ex post control through monitoring devices and institutional checks. Parties tend to dominate the use of all these instruments in parliamentary regimes. As far as external delegation is concerned, contract design refers to investiture rules and the set of terms on which cabinets and prime ministers take office. Often – especially in the Westminster tradition – legislatures have a merely passive role even in this respect, and formal investiture votes are not required; governments stay in office until they lose a vote of confidence. Incentive compatibility between cabinet members and backbenchers is largely based on shared party membership. The selection of aspiring cabinet members, often after service in minor party and legislative offices, is another form of ex ante control where parties tend to play a key role. Ex post control is achieved through monitoring – the no confidence vote as strongest weapon, but also question period, legislative hearings, audits, parliamentary commissioners/ombudsmen, etc. – and institutional checks like bicameralism and federalism.

However, there are substantial variations among actual parliamentary regimes with regard to structures, procedures, and important context factors like societal cleavages, voting behaviour, electoral and party systems. At the one end of the scale, there is the majoritarian principle, which combines parliamentary government with strong executive dominance, one-party cabinets, first-past-the-post elections, and a two-party system. Yet parliamentary government can also be combined with features of the consensus model, which "give protection to the rights of minority parties and individual deputies, both at the government-opposition and at the cross-party level" (Döring 1995: 13) – proportional representation, multi-party systems, coalition governments and aspects of legislative organization that strengthen individual MPs vis-à-vis their party caucus and leadership, opposition parties vis-à-vis the government majority, and parliament as a whole vis-à-vis the executive branch.

These different arrangements vary in terms of transaction costs. A distinction between internal and external costs has to be made, though. The standard argument in favour of majoritarian arrangements has it that they reduce the internal costs of decision-making for the majority (time and resources invested), and hence increase government efficiency: the number of participating actors with veto points is small, and thus undue influence of minority positions is prevented. Yet on the other hand, the external costs of decision-making – that is, disadvantages imposed on the excluded minority – decrease with a higher number of veto points. There is an obvious trade-off between efficiency (lower internal costs) and inclusion (lower external costs), and no readily discernible optimal point – the balance of efficiency and inclusion varies among different examples of parliamentary government, too. Once again, electoral and party systems belong to the most important underlying factors with regard to internal and external costs of decision-making (Saalfeld 1995; Tsebelis 1995a, 1995b).

The details of legislative organization are quite rarely entrenched in constitutions, but rather laid down in ordinary statute law or standing orders adopted by assemblies for themselves. Furthermore, they interact with context factors like societal cleavages and voting behaviour. The role of parties is a case in point. Therefore, an attempt will be made here to distinguish informal constraints, including those that are based on norms and conventions of political culture, and formal constraints, entrenched in constitutions, statute or common law, and standing orders. Both forms of constraints are "restriction[s] on the set of feasible outcomes that [are] beyond the short-term control of the players" (Strøm 1995: 58) and have a measurable impact on the behaviour of legislative actors, on legislative choice and output (Tsebelis 1999).

II. Parliamentary Government, Institutional Development and Constitutional Reform in Canada: An Overview

In marked contrast with the British situation (Saunders 1995), the bulk of Canada's "master institution" (Alan Cairns) is made up of formal, entrenched constitutional law: the British North America (BNA) Act, 1867, and the Constitution Act, 1982. Various important aspects of the constitutional framework in a wider sense are, however, stipulated in pieces of ordinary, non-entrenched law, standing orders and conventions (Heard 1991; Hogg 1992). Entrenched constitutional law regulates in some detail the "dignified parts," as well as the innovative and specifically Canadian elements of the constitutional order – such as federalism and the privileges of religious and linguistic minorities –, while the elements of the Westminster model that it shares with the United Kingdom – notably, the "efficient secret" (Walter Bagehot) of parliamentary government – are largely based on ordinary legislation, standing orders and conventions.

Thus the BNA Act states that Canada is "to be federally united into One Dominion under the Crown of the United Kingdom of Great Britain and Northern Ireland, with a Constitution similar in Principle to that of the United Kingdom" – and further, in section 17, that "[t]here shall be One Parliament for Canada, consisting of the Queen, an Upper House styled the Senate, and the House of Commons" (quoted in Archer et al. 1995: 165). In other words, the role of the Crown as formal executive, the central position and bicameral nature of the legislature, as well as the principles of "King-in-Parliament," are entrenched in constitutional law, but there are, for instance, no detailed references to the electoral system, to the internal organization of the legislature, or to the selection, removal and authority of the political executive (prime minister, cabinet). This amounts to a rather implicit entrenchment of parliamentary democracy as the Canadian form of government.

Both ceremonial and substantive aspects, then, illustrate the continuing importance of the Crown and the Westminster model as shared institution and common reference point of Canadian and British government. However, parliamentary democracy in Canada has evolved against the backdrop of an extremely heterogeneous society and of a constitutional reality that is also characterized by elements such as federalism and judicial review that are lacking in the United Kingdom and alien to the Westminster model. Adjustments to this double reality have been made, and the rules and norms of parliamentary government have been adapted to them from the outset. Yet to what extent the majoritarian and non-majoritarian elements in the Canadian political system are compatible remains a contentious question (Lijphart 1984; Schultze 1996).

Welfare state expansion and the unfolding of the national unity crisis in the postwar era have not only strengthened the Canadian executive vis-à-vis the legislature, but have also privileged intergovernmental relations and the judicial branch vis-à-vis the parliamentary arena. The ensuing phase of "mega-constitutional politics" has seen the emergence of reform debates and initiatives with regard to parliamentary government as secondary, albeit persistent theme. While the constitutional discontent associated with Québec nationalism since the 1960s has largely focused on aspects of federalism, and minority groups since the 1980s have focused on the judicial branch, the challenge against manifestations, consequences – and ultimately, basic tenets – of parliamentary democracy has so far been mostly driven by the engine of western alienation. This challenge became more acute during the Meech Lake and Charlottetown episodes of failed constitutional reform, and was drastically confirmed by the 1993 and 1997 federal election results (Schneider 1997; Schultze/Schneider 1997).

A cabinet-centred view of parliamentary government – that is, a view that embraces the Westminster model – has long dominated among Canadian political elites and academics, and probably continues to be the majority opinion (but cf. Franks 1987 versus 1999b). A growing part of the Canadian public, however, "has been alternatively confused, bemused, and offended by the practices it engenders" (Atkinson 1995: 361), and a quick glance at the parliamentary reform debates and initiatives of the last decades confirms that a legislative-centred view has gained in importance: most failed or successful initiatives have aimed at strengthening parliament as a whole vis-à-vis the executive, opposition parties vis-à-vis the government majority, and individual MPs vis-à-vis their party caucus and leadership. Both chambers of parliament have been the subject of reform proposals during the era of "mega-constitutional politics" since the 1960s, less so the formal and political executive.

The background, scope and fate of these proposals will now be examined. First, however, one should point to the fact that in contrast with many other aspects of the constitutional order – notably, federalism –, the elements of parliamentary democracy were in principle accessible to reform even before the repatriation of the BNA Act. While a reform of federalism would, in the absence of an amending formula and as a matter of convention, have necessitated a joint resolution of both chambers of the legislature, consent of (affected) provinces and referral of the proposed amendment to the British Parliament, section 91 (1) and 92 (1) of the BNA Act (section 44 and 45 in the revised Constitution Act) had already given provincial and (since 1949) federal governments limited authority to change at least some aspects of their own institutional arrangements through ordinary legislation, although perhaps not to implement a large-scale reform of parliamentary government. This limited authority was used, for instance, to introduce a retirement age for senators and parliamentary representation for the two (now three) Canadian territories. In spite of this, most actual changes were implemented below the constitutional level proper – for instance, as changes to standing orders.

1. The Legislative Branch

1.1. The House of Commons

The House of Commons is the confidence chamber of Canada's bicameral parliament and hence, in a formal sense, the "centre of the institutional complex that constitutes the Canadian state" and the "primary arena for debates over the character and direction of public policy" (Archer et al. 1995: 165). Its political role is, however, qualified as weak and even declining by most observers, and its internal organization has long been criticized as "underdeveloped, immature, retarded and defective" (quoted in Franks 1987: 157). An increasingly prominent line of criticism explains this lack of clout and internal strength as a consequence of the excessive party discipline, adversarialism and government dominance under which the Canadian lower chamber operates even if measured against the standard of the Westminster model, let alone the U.S. Congress.[6]

Government control of the legislative agenda and procedures has become all but complete, party discipline all but guaranteed over the decades. Most bills, including all money bills, are now government initiated rather than private or private members' bills. Executive dominance and party discipline are, or have long been, secured through a range of instruments: the appointment of Liberal and Progressive Conservative caucus representatives (House leaders, whips) by the party leadership rather than their election by backbenchers like in the United Kingdom, the de facto selection of committee chairpersons, the speaker and other House officials by the prime minister and

6 On the House of Commons, cf. Atkinson 1995; Courtney 1985; Franks 1987; Frazer 1993.

cabinet, etc. As newcomers quickly find out, individual MPs have almost no genuine legislative or policy role. MPs are servants of their parties rather than independent political entrepreneurs. Backbenchers tend to find refuge in constituency work or else, to quit soon (Docherty 1997). Extended periods of Liberal dominance have led to a firmly anchored obstructionist mentality on the opposition benches, while the government side has increasingly found ways to circumvent parliament altogether. The adversarial mode and ritualistic character of floor debates, question period, committee work and plenary decisions, the excessive influence of party leaders on the government and opposition side, and the ensuing low quality of parliamentary life have been major points of criticism at least since the so-called pipeline debate of 1956.

Various factors – some implied in the logic of parliamentary government, others specifically Canadian – have contributed to this exacerbation of majoritarian elements. One is historical: In the colonial situation of British North America, institutions of both the formal and the political executive had already been firmly established when representative institutions and conventions were secured. Other factors are contextual, such as welfare state expansion, the national unity crisis, and the rise of executive federalism in the postwar era:

> "Executive dominance in parliament is closely related to the dominance of the executive in intergovernmental relations [...]. The one reinforces the other, with often the real opposition being the other level of government, not the nominal opposition within the legislature." (Franks 1999b: 7)

Moreover, the "product" of the legislature, ordinary statute law, has increasingly been devalued by the growing influence of minority groups that expect symbolic constitutional recognition for their demands. Yet still other factors are more directly tied to aspects of legislative structures and internal organization. One of these is the composition of the House, which itself is the combined result of intense societal cleavages, fickle voting behaviour, single-member simple-plurality elections, and the ensuing multi-party system in Canada. The well-documented effects of this combination have, on the one hand, produced several minority governments in the postwar era.[7] On the other hand, and more importantly, they have enabled the Liberals to encroach on power and to become the "natural" government party, rather than guaranteeing the regular alternation of majority governments implied in the Westminster model. As a consequence, a typically weak, regionally and ideologically fragmented opposition is often unable to perform its control functions or to serve as government-in-waiting in a credible way. Furthermore, electoral volatility and high drop-out rates lead to a rapid turnover of MPs; the continuously high percentage of inexperienced parliamentarians in the House

7 Like coalitions, minority governments may be considered part of Lijphart's consensus model.

strengthens the position of the government and party leaderships.[8] Representational biases and problems of short-term amateur membership have been exacerbated in the 1993 and 1997 House elections, which brought two fundamental opposition parties – the Reform Party and the Bloc Québécois –, as well as an unprecedented number of newcomers, to the legislature.

These overly lopsided and dysfunctional election outcomes, which can almost be expected where first-past-the-post elections are combined with a multi-party system, are further compounded by specifically Canadian representative biases. The representativeness of the lower chamber is a major requirement for the legitimacy of any system of parliamentary government, including Westminster regimes: the far-reaching delegation of authority to a government majority in these regimes is unproblematic if and only if minority groups are not systematically or permanently excluded from access to power. More than anywhere else, however, these questions of representativeness are linked with wider questions of constitutional recognition for societal groups and communities in Canada. The introduction of a provincial level of government and of an upper chamber of parliament in 1867 was supposed to facilitate adherence to the principle of representation by population in the House, a principle that is now respected to a considerable extent. Regular demographic adjustments have enlarged the size of the lower chamber to its current 301 seats and have at the same time reduced, although not ended, imbalances in the size of rural and urban ridings. The number of MPs from the ten provinces closely approximates their respective population shares. Exceptions apply to the huge, sparsely populated territories, which have at least one MP each. Prince Edward Island and New Brunswick profit from a so-called senatorial floor granting them at least as many MPs as senators. A grandfather provision guarantees the number of MPs reached in 1974 to Newfoundland, Nova Scotia, Manitoba and Saskatchewan. As a result, small provinces are now slightly over-represented, the larger ones slighty under-represented (but nevertheless dominant in absolute figures). There is no special provision for non-territorial communities such as aboriginal peoples, which remain as much under-represented as other (functional) minority groups. These distortions might be qualified as minor and within the limits of the Westminster model if they were not combined with sectional asymmetries in the electoral bases and caucus membership of the government and opposition parties. For instance, the membership of the Liberal caucus is now extremely skewed towards Ontario, but also – a novelty – towards English Canada, while the Reform Party and the Bloc Québécois draw their membership exclusively from Western Canada and francophone Québec, respectively.

8 The fact that the Canadian House regularly looses more members because of personal choice than the British and American legislatures for all reasons combined is a clear sign of the frustration experienced by many backbenchers (Franks 1999b: 2).

In a society as diverse and fragmented as the Canadian one, it hardly comes as a surprise that the ensuing problems of inclusion (external costs of decision-making) tend to be more of a concern than efficiency considerations (internal costs). House reform initiatives since the 1950s – and notably, during the 1960s and 1980s – have therefore concentrated on the insertion of consensual elements into the largely majoritarian and adversarial organization and procedures of the Canadian lower chamber. Recent changes in the United Kingdom or even the American congressional system have been the implicit or avowed reform models; the bulk of implemented changes have remained at the level of standing orders, informal rules and norms (D'Aquino/Doern/Blair 1983; Gunther/Winn 1991).

The committee system – an element of parliamentary life where the American example looms particularly large – has been at the centre of most reform initiatives in Canada. The NIE has amply demonstrated the collective benefits, distributive and informational gains that can be reaped from an intra-parliamentary distribution of labour through committees (Shepsle/Weingast 1987). However, there is a great variety in the selection and permanence of members, the jurisdictions and functions of committees – and once again, a clear divide between presidentialism and parliamentary government, while differences between continental European legislatures and those adhering to the Westminster tradition are also substantial. Committees in Westminster legislatures tend to be microcosms of parliament as a whole: the government party has the majority in them and often provides all chairpersons; like procedures and budgets, the selection of members from the government side and of chairpersons, who represent a more or less random sample of MPs with more or less expertise or interest in the policy areas under deliberation, is under executive control.

Unlike the United Kingdom, Canada has nominally had a system of specialized standing committees since Confederation, but apart from a few exceptions, they have remained moribund and strongly government dominated in practice. Prime Minister John Diefenbaker was the first to appoint an opposition member as chairperson of the Public Accounts Committee, Lester B. Pearson continued his attempt to revive committee activity, and Pierre Elliott Trudeau at last ushered in the era of modern parliamentary government through a drastic overhaul in 1968. A comprehensive system of specialized committees overlooking government departments and programs, with regular meetings and serious functions (review of bills and scrutiny of spending estimates, independent investigations), was established. Another intense phase of reform activity was initiated by the 1982 Special Committee on Standing Orders and Procedure, which was created in the wake of the so-called bell-ringing episode, and the 1985/86 Special Committee on Reform of the House (McGrath Committee). The creation of ad hoc legislative committees, which had been suggested by the McGrath Committee, led to a surge in the number of committees and made immediate adjustments necessary, with the result that every eligible member could subsequently count on one position on a standing committee and one on a legislative committee. Later, committees were given the authority to review (not reject) order-in-council appointments.

As a result of these efforts, most of which aimed at enhancing the role of private members and at fostering a less partisan, more in-depth and consensual study of topics, there are now four types of committees: legislative committees, which give clause-by-clause consideration to bills that have passed second reading; standing committees, which debate broad policy areas and review departmental estimates; special committees, which tend to have a specific task ending with the parliamentary session; finally, (standing or special) joint committees, which include senators. The legislative committees are still not firmly established; after 1989, the standing committees have gained back some ground. Most of the approximately 20 standing committees focus on departmental policy areas and responsibilities, but others like Public Accounts have more specific jobs. Their size is now relatively small (seven to 14 members), but they increasingly delegate work to subcommittees and hire research staff. As the scrutiny of spending estimates is often considered futile – estimates can only be reduced –, committees have discovered independent investigations of more encompassing questions as a meaningful activity. In the 34th parliament (1988 to 1993), standing committees started investigations and produced reports, to which government must respond, on a range of issues.

Despite a certain success in terms of resources, influence and public attention, the positive impact of these changes to the committee system should not be overestimated and certainly fell short of British developments, where a system along Canadian lines was introduced later (1979), but quickly became more independent and effective.[9] By contrast, reforms in Canada have ultimately done little to strengthen the role of individual MPs, the opposition, or the House as a whole. The committee system is still embedded in an overall adversarial and executive dominated context. Chairpersons, membership and working procedures have emerged as the major, and largely unresolved, problem areas. Chairpersons continue to be selected from the government side with one exception, the Public Accounts Committee, and the inequality between government and opposition members remains pronounced: in the United Kingdom, chairpersons are chosen by backbenchers and act like quasi-speakers; half of them are drawn from the opposition side. Short tenures of chairpersons, membership substitution, low attendance, and the ensuing lack of corporate spirit further undermine the role of committees. The

---

9 As a footnote, it is worth mentioning that these reforms allowed the British Foreign Affairs Committee to play an important role in the repatriation process of the Canadian constitution.

ratio of MPs and committee positions contributes to these problems: while only half of the eligible members of the British House of Commons sit on committees, the situation is almost inverse in the Canadian House. And the inclination of the executive and government majority to allow independent investigations, or to follow up on them, remains low. Even as these changes to the committee system were made, other forms of deliberation – for instance, in task forces and Royal Commissions – were tried; the McGrath Committee itself had the form of a task force.

Presidents or speakers represent the second important privileged group in legislatures – and here again, forms of selection and responsibilities vary greatly. Tasks performed by speakers typically include the everyday control of the parliamentary agenda and of the rules and norms of floor debates and plenary decisions, but may also include coordinating functions such as assigning members and bills to committees, discharging bills from committees, administering parliamentary staff, and communicating with the executive branch. Speakers may exercise these tasks in a partisan or non-partisan fashion. In this respect, the U.S. Congress represents the extreme of partisanship, the British House of Commons the pole of non-partisanship.

In Canada, the secret election of the speaker – traditionally quasi-accomplice of party leaders in the maintenance of party discipline rather than neutral arbiter –, as well as new disciplinary powers and responsibilities, were only introduced in 1986. Prior to that date, the speaker had been chosen by the prime minister in consultation with the leaders of the opposition parties. The growing dissatisfaction after the bell-ringing incident had served as catalyst for this reform, too, and it represented one of the major breakthroughs of the two afore-mentioned parliamentary reform committees. Yet in comparison with the British speaker, who enjoys far more powers and independence, the office continues to be tainted by adversarialism, short tenures and inexperienced office-holders, as well as the ongoing practice of having other House positions filled through orders-in-council.

While excluded from many privileges, the backbenchers of parties – and notably, the government backbench – can be an important source of criticism and, as principals, dispose of more or less effective instruments to control their agents, party leaders. Many of these instruments are of course informal and/or at the discretion of the parties themselves. Canada is no exception in this respect. The Liberal caucus has been relatively active over the last few decades. Starting in 1969, it has insisted on being informed on the government's legislative and policy initiatives beforehand; a system of ad hoc caucus committees was created. Since 1970, the Liberal caucus has elected its own officers, including the caucus chairperson, without direct interference of the party leadership. Regional caucuses and task forces were also established. Strong caucus opposition can prevent or at least modify policy initiatives of the government.

Privileged groups and actors typically control various important aspects of legislative procedure in parliamentary regimes, such as the agenda and character of floor debates and question period, the number and scope of legislative amendments considered, and the form of plenary decisions. Time is the crucial – and scarce – resource of parliamentary life. Control over the legislative calendar and schedule, over the allocation of time between floor debates and committee deliberations, and over the time spent on particular bills therefore is a powerful weapon in the hands of the executive and the leadership of the government majority, both against opposition parties and individual MPs. The centralization of timetabling and procedure in general varies among parliamentary regimes, but tends to be high in Westminster systems even though there is some informal cooperation with the opposition side in the United Kingdom.

In Canada, attempts have been made since the 1960s to limit obstruction and improve timetabling. Procedural tools like closure were reformed, but the result was still unsatisfactory. In 1983, the Special Committee on Procedure (Lefebvre Committee) reached the adoption of a set of measures that had some positive effects on the circumstances of debates and included a new system for private members' bills. The Committee stressed the theme of reduced government control and enhanced private members' rights, but did not deal with the crucial issue of timetabling. Further reform proposals along these lines were developed, and partly implemented, by the McGrath Committee. A set of changes made in 1991 shortened the parliamentary session to a maximum of 134 days, and also shortened the amount of time for opposition days and other general debates. Another attempt to strengthen backbenchers and committees was made in 1994.

These changes to the standing orders of the House have certainly had some beneficial effects on parliamentary life in Canada. Their impact should, however, not be overestimated. Despite the described efforts, the confrontational approach of the government and opposition side has largely gone unabated in the 1980s and 1990s. For instance, the Mulroney cabinet made unprecedented use of closure and other timetabling instruments – that is, more often than in the entire previous history of the Canadian legislature (Franks 1999b: 16) – in order to push through controversial legislation such as the Free-Trade Agreement and the GST against a Liberal opposition that used obstruction even more systematically than the PC opposition in the decades before. An indicator for this is the fact that the success rate of government bills has remained surprisingly low in comparison with the United Kingdom (around 70% versus 90%), despite the more frequent use of countervailing instruments like omnibus bills and orders-in-council. Thus adversarialism has hardly been reduced, and private members' business hardly made easier. Party discipline remains high; in marked contrast with the recent British practice of government backbenchers as "Her Majesty's Unofficial

Opposition," a firmly anchored confidence convention, although no formal constitutional requirement, continues to make virtually every vote in the Canadian House a matter of confidence. Free votes or successful initiatives of private members, by contrast, remain the exception – and ironically, this holds true even for the Reform Party caucus with its supposedly anti-parliamentarian stances.

As a topic of genuine constitutional reform, the House has been sidetracked by debates and proposals regarding federalism and bicameralism. In line with the preoccupations of the francophone province, the Québec Round of constitutional negotiations and the Meech Lake Accord had focused on intergovernmental relations. A reform of the House was postponed.[10] In the Canada Round, it was initially removed from the agenda despite clear signs of public discontent with overly adversarial elements such as question period. Later, it reappeared in the context of proposed changes to the Senate. If accepted, the Charlottetown Accord would have enlarged the lower chamber of the Canadian parliament from 295 to 337 MPs; the proportionality of the regional seat distribution would have marginally improved through seat shifts from Atlantic and Western Canada to the central provinces. On the other hand, as a concession to the two-nations perspective of the Québec government and in an attempt to gain its support for Senate reform, the province would have received a guaranteed 25% floor of MPs – a percentage that already is, and will probably remain, above its population share. This provision of course became one of the most controversial and unpopular elements of the entire agreement, especially in Western Canada, and died a quiet death with it. Conspicuously absent from the constitutional negotiations of the 1980s and 1990s, and from political debates in general, was an aspect of institutional reform with potentially far-reaching consequences for the operation of parliamentary democracy in Canada: electoral reform, which has only recently become a more serious topic of academic debates (cf. Weaver: this volume).

1.2. The Senate

That the precise type, rules and norms of (incongruent versus congruent, symmetrical versus asymmetrical, strong versus weak) bicameralism influence its effects on the operation of parliamentary government is now a well-documented result both of traditional comparative and NIE oriented work (Lijphart 1984; Tsebelis/Money 1997). Among the crucial variables are the modes of appointment or election of upper-chamber members and the institutional mechanisms for resolving inter-chamber differences.

10 In light of the executive dominance in the House, it is rather ironic that newly assertive provincial legislatures and MPPs like Elijah Harper played an important role in the eventual demise of the agreement.

The Senate as upper chamber of the Canadian bicameral system was an important part of the compromise that led to Confederation. Its name and the ambiguous role it was given by the fathers of Confederation reveal two main reference points: the British House of Lords and the American Senate. The Canadian upper chamber was to serve, on the one hand, as a forum of "sober second thought," a counterbalance against the feared radical tendencies of an elected House of Commons. Appointment of members by the federal government, age and property qualifications, as well as life-long tenure (a retirement age of 75 years was introduced in 1965), are linked to this purpose. On the other hand, the Canadian Senate was to provide regional representation as a counterweight to representation by population in the lower chamber. Its initially 72, now 105 members are drawn from the originally three Canadian regions (24 each for the Maritimes, Québec and Ontario), the four western provinces (six each), Newfoundland (six), and the two (now three) territories (one each) – a distribution that owes more to historical compromise and circumstances than to the demographic reality then and now.

Although unelected, senators have virtually the same legislative powers as members of the House. Legislation moves through the same stages in both chambers, although the hurdles are sometimes lower in the Senate. The Senate can amend legislation passed by the House, and ultimately has an absolute veto (a suspensive veto over constitutional amendments). Money bills, however, can only be introduced in the House, and the federal government is solely accountable to the lower chamber. Despite almost complete formal equality, the actual legislative tasks of the Senate have long been quite restricted and are not highly visible in practice. Their focus is on private bills and the review of statutory instruments, while legislation originating in the House, which carries democratic legitimacy, often receives only perfunctory treatment. Like in the United Kingdom, uncontroversial bills are often initiated in the upper chamber in order to reduce the workload of the Commons. Investigations of social and policy questions in the committees of the Senate have gained in importance relative to the revision of legislation since the 1950s, and have often been more thorough than similar endeavours in the House.[11]

The combination of functions derived from British traditions and from the American innovation of federalism is as unique as it is contested. The Senate is now, and has been for many decades, "the most criticized institution of government in Canada" (Franks 1987: 186). Both aspects of its role have increasingly come under scrutiny. As a chamber of "sober second thought," it suffers from serious representational biases and from the abuse of appointments for patronage purposes. The composition of the chamber is, for instance, male-dominated and skewed towards property interests. It over-repre-

11 On the Senate, cf. Zinterer 2000.

sents members of the federal government party – usually the Liberals – and virtually excludes third-party members (CCF/NDP and Social Credit, now Reform Party and Bloc Québécois), as well as non-territorial minority groups (the first Indian was appointed by Diefenbaker). Even more importantly, its role as forum of intrastate federalism is jeopardized by the fact that senators are appointed by the federal government on the basis of an antiquated and questionable regional allocation formula.

Far-reaching changes to the role, structures and internal organization of the Senate have therefore been discussed over the last couple of decades; would-be reformers have looked at the upper chamber as the most promising location for a reconciliation of parliamentary government and federal principles. Yet surprisingly, the upper chamber has remained essentially unchanged since its creation even if measured against the minor changes implemented in the House. The conspicuous lack of agreement on the direction of reforms is part of the explanation; with hindsight, it is remarkable that reform proposals have become so prominent "despite the fact that virtually all of the existing institutional actors would lose" (Archer et al. 1995: 197). Leaving aside the most radical of changes, abolition, these proposals fall into two groups: those which attempt to improve the existing Senate and those which suggest to transform it into a more genuine forum of intrastate federalism.[12]

A first series of sweeping proposals was published in the 1960s and 1970s, against the backdrop of an increasingly powerful Québec nationalism and of western alienation – for instance, in the 1969 and 1978 white papers of the Trudeau government, as part of the 1978 Bill C-60, by the 1972 Joint Committee of the Senate and the House of Commons on Constitutional Reform, and by the 1979 Pepin-Robarts Task Force on Canadian Unity. The common denominator of most of these proposals was the idea of a House of Provinces along the lines of the German *Bundesrat* model, which would have given provincial governments more direct representation – and sometimes also new powers – in and through the Senate. By contrast, Bill C-60 suggested to replace the Senate with a House of the Federation, whose members would have been partly appointed by the federal government, partly by provincial legislatures in proportion with seat shares in those legislatures.

By the mid-1980s, the House of Provinces concept had lost ground, but calls for reform subsisted. The years between 1984 and 1996 brought two periods of divergent majorities in the chambers of parliament, and with them came a return of Senate assertiveness in the revision of legislation – for instance, with regard to the FTA, the GST, and abortion legislation. The attempt of the Liberal Senate majority led by Allan MacEachen to serve as unofficial opposition was a reaction to the weak official opposition in the

12 Cf. Franks 1999a; Lijphart 1987; Sturm 1998; White 1990.

House after 1984, and obstruction of business from the Commons was even extended to questions of supply. In the fight over the GST, the government finally resorted to a previously unused clause of the BNA Act in order to create a Progressive Conservative Senate majority. Despite the unpopularity of the particular federal government bills involved in this development, the intrusion of partisan battles into the Senate and the new disrespect by its unelected members for the supremacy of the House remained highly controversial, though. Reform proposals now shifted to the idea of an elected Senate and most prominently, to the concept of a Triple-E (elected, equal, effective) upper chamber. In the Québec Round of constitutional negotiations and the Meech Lake Accord, Senate reform was still postponed, but the Mulroney government subsequently made concessions to western proponents of the Triple-E concept by appointing senators from lists provided by the provinces (Alberta even forced the issue of Senate election onto the constitutional agenda).

After the failure of the Meech Lake Accord, the continuing momentum for an elected and equal, although not necessarily effective Senate became visible in the public discontent with parliamentary government and executive federalism aired through the Spicer Citizens' Forum and other arenas of constitutional debate. In 1991, the House of the Federation model briefly resurfaced in Mulroney's constitutional proposals. The Charlottetown Accord, final product of the Canada Round of negotiations, tried to reconcile Québec and western demands by taking up the concept of a Triple-E Senate. If it had been implemented, membership in a smaller upper chamber would have been based on equal representation of the provinces (six seats for each of them, plus two senators from the territories). However, in order to make the reform concept more palatable to Québec, the Accord left open the possibility to have senators elected indirectly by provincial legislatures (or de facto appointed by provincial governments). In a further step away from the Triple-E model, disagreements between the Senate and the House, where Québec was to have a 25% seat share, would have been resolved by simple majority vote in a joint sitting, thus giving the House an edge over the Senate. While Triple-E provisions, despite these modifications, paid tribute to an equal-provinces vision of Canada, provisions for a double majority requirement on cultural and linguistic subject matters would have meant a renewal of the quasi-consociational post-Act of Union (1840) practice, as well as a concession to a two-nations (or even three-nations) vision: francophone and aboriginal senators would have enjoyed absolute veto rights on legislation affecting their cultures and languages, while western provinces were to be lured into acceptance of the package by an absolute Senate veto on new taxes and natural-resources legislation. Furthermore, the logic of intrastate federalism contained in these proposals would have been balanced by the constitutional entrenchment of first ministers' conferences, an interstate element.

There is no doubt that this reform concept, if accepted, would have meant an important shift away from majoritarian principles; an elected and arguably more legitimate Senate might indeed have become a genuine institutional check against the executive dominance implied in the Westminster model – and at worst, an obstacle for the operation of parliamentary government. However, like the Accord writ large, its Senate reform proposals were a badly conceived attempt to balance competing interests and ultimately incompatible constitutional perspectives. Therefore, even western support for these proposals remained surprisingly lukewarm with hindsight.

2. *The executive branch*

2.1. The Crown and Governor General

Like many other parliamentary regimes, Canada has a double-headed executive. This division of the executive branch into a formal part – the monarch and institutions associated with the Crown – and a political executive is another obvious element of British constitutional inheritance. The legislative and executive role of the Crown as symbolic and legal entity is detailed in entrenched constitutional law and remains a consequential fact of political life (Smith 1995b). The Crown is one of the three parts of which parliament consists. But section 9 of the BNA Act also states that "the executive government and authority of and over Canada is hereby declared to continue and be vested in the Queen," and section 12 points out that it is "vested in and exercisable by the Governor General, with the advice, or with the advice and consent of or in conjunction with the Queen's Privy Council for Canada, or any member therefore, or by the Governor General individually [...]" (quoted in Archer et al. 1995: 214).

Yet the vast powers of the Crown in constitutional theory gave way to a largely ceremonial role a long time ago; probably even more than in the United Kingdom, it has become one of the "dignified" rather than the "efficient parts" of the constitution. In parliament, its formal role includes the speeches from the throne, Royal assent to and proclamation of legislation; its role in the appointment or dismissal of prime ministers has been severely curtailed, however, and its independent prerogative has been restricted to very difficult and contentious circumstances at least since the so-called King-Byng affair. Executive authority remains vested in the Crown and its institutions – notably, the Privy Council – in a formal sense, but has shifted to the political executive (prime minister, cabinet) in constitutional practice.

The Crown is an ongoing expression of the constitutional and historical ties between the United Kingdom and Canada; the right to choose the Governor General has, however, passed from the British to the Canadian government. Candidates are appointed on the advice of the prime minister for normally five to seven years, and since 1951, only Canadians have been selected. As representative of the monarch, the Governor General symbolizes the separation of the government of the day from the Canadian state – a role performed by presidents in many other parliamentary regimes. Leaving aside purely ceremonial functions, the Governor General exercises his/her powers upon the "advice and consent" of the political executive; the room for discretionary action is narrowly circumscribed by conventions. The abuse of the office for patronage purposes has further contributed to its declining importance. On the other hand, however, the recent appointment of Hongkong-born Adrienne Clarkson confirms the by now well-established practice of instrumentalizing the post for the symbolic accommodation between the cultural and linguistic communities of the country. John Diefenbaker was the first to choose a French Canadian as Governor General. Today, alternation between English and French Canadians, proficiency in both official languages, as well as the occasional selection of other minority candidates or women, have become standard requirements in the appointment process – and hence, a slight concession to a more consensual form of parliamentary democracy.

Perhaps this relatively new and valued integrative role of the Governor General, together with the largely "invisible" position of the Crown in the institutional framework, contributes to explaining why the monarchy as such has so far not become an item on the constitutional reform agenda despite the fact that it is clearly flawed as symbol of national integration.[12] Not even the method of selecting the Governor General itself has been part of recent constitutional negotiations.

2.2. Prime minister and cabinet

Despite the formal notion of parliamentary supremacy and the constitutional responsibilities of the Crown, the majoritarian logic of the Westminster model, together with the specifically Canadian elements touched upon at various points in this chapter, privileges the institutions of the political executive – the prime minister and his/her cabinet – in Canada. In constitutional theory, the cabinet and its head are a subcommittee of the Privy Council, but in practice they can be more aptly described as an executive committee, or agent, of the legislative branch: The prime minister and the other members of cabinet must have seats in the House or Senate, and a defeat of the government in major legislation or a successful nonconfidence vote in the lower chamber force the resignation of the prime minister. While being ultimately responsible to its principal, the Commons, the Canadian executive dominates

---

13 Australia provides a contrasting experience in this respect.

legislative business even more strongly than the governments of most other parliamentary regimes.[14]

In line with the Westminster model (Weller 1995), Canadian government has clearly moved towards the pole of prime-ministerial rather than cabinet government over the last few decades – and this despite the fact that the office of the prime minister is not even mentioned in the BNA Act. The prime minister decides on the internal organization of government, appoints the cabinet and other members of the political executive, calls the House of Commons and asks the Governor General to dissolve it for new elections. The exceptional powers of the Canadian prime minister are, however, largely based on conventions and strengthened by non-institutional factors: his/her role as leader of the government party, support by its extra-parliamentary branch, increasingly privileged access to the media and the general public, the longevity in office of many Canadian prime ministers, etc. An indicator for growing executive and prime-ministerial dominance in Canada is the fact that prime-ministerial participation in floor debates has been declining for decades.

Like the role of the prime minister, the internal organization of the executive is to a large extent the product of conventions and informal constraints rather than entrenched constitutional law in Canada. The powers described above notwithstanding, Canadian prime ministers are faced with several constraints when selecting the members of their cabinet: The high turnover of MPs often greatly reduces the number of experienced candidates for executive offices. Secondly, the major ideological camps and key members of the government party and caucus have to be represented. Yet the imperative of sectional representation within the federal cabinet is arguably the most important of these constraints. The emergence of cabinet as preeminent national institution for the representation of Canada's religious, linguistic and territorial communities is a consequence of the biases and deficits that both the House and the Senate, as well as the institutions of the Crown, have in this respect.

The office of prime minister itself has been dominated by politicians from Québec (Trudeau, Mulroney, Chrétien) for the last thirty years. As far as ministerial appointments are concerned, representational considerations have a long tradition, as "from early on cabinet proved especially useful as a mechanism for accommodating the social diversities of the colony" (Smith 1995a: 389). In the postwar era, John Diefenbaker expanded the practice of "recognizing" societal groups by selecting the first Ukrainian-Canadian and female cabinet members. Since Pearson and Trudeau, the bicultural and federal nature of the country has been closely reflected in cabinet structure. An

14 On the prime minister and cabinet, cf. Bakvis/MacDonald 1993; Pal/Taras 1988. Despite its prominent role, studies of the federal cabinet are conspicuously rare (Smith 1995a: 382).

attempt has been made to represent linguistic and cultural groups, as well as (almost) each province, in numbers roughly equal to their share of the population. As a result, Québécois and other francophones have been slightly over-represented, and the importance of their portfolios has risen, since the 1960s. The longstanding institution of regional ministers – and notably, a Québec "lieutenant" – illustrates the dominance of the federal and bicultural dimension, and has survived cabinet transformations under Trudeau and Mulroney (Bakvis 1991). Under Mulroney and Chrétien, cabinet representation was further extended to non-territorial and visible minorities. Throughout Canadian history, ministers *from* individual provinces have been considered as ministers *for* them (or conversely, certain portfolios have been identified with specific regions).

The described regional asymmetries in the membership of the government party caucus make it difficult to honour these representational principles. Prime ministers are often confronted with the problem that there are no, or few, caucus members and ministerial candidates from certain parts of the country (for the Liberals, from the western provinces). In the past, the appointment of senators from these under-represented regions was a quite frequently used solution. While the developing conventions of parliamentary democracy and the legitimacy deficits of the Senate have reduced the viability of giving cabinet posts to senators (with the exception of the government leader in the upper chamber), this practice nevertheless illustrates the strength of these representational conventions.

These largely informal principles of accommodation strongly influence the structures and working procedures of the federal cabinet in Canada, which can be easily modified through orders-in-council. The challenge of representing various societal groups and regions has typically been met through large, and growing, cabinet sizes; only Kim Campbell's far-reaching changes, which Jean Chrétien continued as part of his austerity measures, drastically reduced the number of ministers. The constraints of intra-cabinet accommodation have also greatly inhibited attempts to rationalize cabinet structures and procedures; for instance, they made it difficult to emulate the British practice of distinguishing between an inner and outer cabinet whose strength in dealing with the challenges of party discipline and responsible government should otherwise have made it an interesting model for Canadians. The number and scope of cabinet committees is subject to frequent changes. In the early 1970s, Trudeau introduced a Priorities and Planning Committee as de facto inner cabinet, and the short-lived Clark government in 1979/80 also experimented with the distinction, but Chrétien in 1993 was the first to create an outer circle of junior ministers (eight secretaries of state) around a small cabinet of 23 ministers (parliamentary secretaries, not to be confounded with these secretaries of state, have existed since the 1940s).

Combined with the principles of brokerage politics, the logic of responsible government has strengthened cabinet solidarity and decision-making by ministerial consensus in Canada: many important decisions are made through orders-in-council – for instance, decisions on appointments, regulations, and property transactions. This practice, however, reduces the visibility of regional ministers and their efforts to defend regional interests, and the behind-the-door negotiations that come with brokerage politics have become a popular target of criticism at least since the constitutional and national unity crisis of the early 1990s.

The clout and responsibilities of individual ministers have, on the other hand, shrunk over time. General problems of cabinet selection mechanisms in parliamentary regimes apply even more strongly to Canada with its representational conventions:

> "These common forms of ex ante agency controls impose notable constraints on executive decision making. The promotion of the party faithful, and the concomitant hierarchical ordering of political offices, bring to the top generalists rather than specialists. They also reward risk-averse individuals. [...]. The drawbacks can be measured in information costs, and the consequence is that cabinet ministers are ill-equipped for the task of supervising their respective agents, the civil servants." (Strøm 1995: 76)

Secondly, prime ministers since Trudeau have increasingly bypassed cabinet, and have governed with small groups of individual key ministers, deputy ministers and other senior public servants, and with central agencies like the Privy Council Office or the Prime Minister's Office whose director occupies the triple role of prime minister's deputy, cabinet secretary and formal head of the public service (Campbell 1983; Savoie 1999a, 1999b). The formal identification of a deputy prime minister by Mulroney, Campbell and Chrétien, and the growing influence of his/her office within the federal cabinet, seem to have expanded rather than weakened the prime minister's reach. Yet the growing influence of bureaucratic agencies, which at the same time have become more politicized, collides with the notion of a single chain of delegation from the legislature to cabinet and the administration, and hence raises questions about ministerial and parliamentary accountability. The blurring of responsibilities in this emerging structure prevents the simple distinction between policy (ministers) and administrative (public servants) accountability that is sometimes offered as solution. Despite these various problems, however, the internal organization of the political executive has so far been a marginal field of institutional changes, and has been largely absent from constitutional reform debates and initiatives. Some proposals – for instance, the suggestion to include elected senators from a reformed upper chamber in the cabinet (Bakvis 1991) – were explicitly rejected in the Charlottetown Accord.

III. Conclusion

There is no doubt that the societal and institutional environment of parliamentary democracy in Canada has greatly changed over the last few decades. Measured against Lijphart's eight dimensions of majoritarian versus consensual democracy, these developments have more often than not meant a shift away from the Westminster model: Societal and party-system fragmentation, as well as electoral volatility, have further increased, thus reducing the future likelihood of regularly alternating, sectionally balanced majority governments. Tensions between the logic of parliamentary government and federalism, which have persisted throughout Canadian history, are now complemented by (manifest or latent) conflicts with an entrenched constitution, the Charter of Rights and Freedoms and judicial review through an activist Supreme Court, as well as emerging elements of direct democracy – in short, the move from a "'governments'" to a "citizens' constitution" (Alan Cairns). The very careful use of the so-called notwithstanding clause – in principle a powerful way to *defend* parliamentary supremacy –, as well as the fate of the amending formula adopted in 1981/82, illustrate the extent to which these new constitutional elements, which reduce the clout of the legislature, have been accepted in political life: Provincial governments outside Québec have so far hesitated to invoke the notwithstanding clause. And while referenda have been rare in Canadian history (three at the national, some 50 at the provincial level), the constitutional referendum of 1992 has set a precedent at least in the field of constitutional reform, so that the amending formula has de facto become obsolete before it has ever been successfully employed.

Many of the institutional changes that have already been implemented or are still being advocated in Canada have been fostered through diffusion – notably, from the provincial level, the American neighbour, and the United Kingdom (cf. Weaver: this volume). Support for term limits, initiative and recall, which emerged on the prairies between the world wars, has now led to the partial implementation of these features (constitutional referenda in Alberta and British Columbia, recall legislation in B.C.), and demand for their introduction might soon creep from the provincial level into federal politics. They are familiar elements of American (state) politics, too, and the U.S. is also an obvious model for an entrenched constitution and judicial review, a Triple-E Senate, and weaker party discipline in the legislature. The example of the U.S. Congress and the successful, if partial comeback of the British House of Commons should keep pressure in favour of changes that strengthen individual MPs, opposition parties, and the legislature as a whole high.

Moreover, the number of influential reform proponents has grown. Outright anti-centralist and anti-parliamentary stances now have a strong and vocal advocate in the Reform Party. And while parliamentary democracy continues to be practiced, it has become unclear if it is still as deeply anchored in the (elite and mass) political culture of Canadians (or in the academe) as it undoubtedly once was. As part of a more general political cynicism that has spread at least since the early 1990s, public discontent with basic tenets of parliamentary democracy such as adversarialism and party discipline is now quite pervasive. Not *if* reform is desirable, but only how it can be *achieved* seems to be controversial:

"[The] normative attack on the party-discipline foundation of cabinet government may not be sufficient to produce significant institutional change without a reinforcing reform impetus from other quarters. It is interesting to note, however, that a principled defence of party discipline, one based on notions of responsible government and electoral accountability, is not being mounted with any zeal or enthusiasm. Parties differ only in the eagerness with which they embrace parliamentary reform; there is a broad consensus that such reform should be pursued." (Archer et al. 1995: 227)

In short, it is true that the heat is on for parliamentary democracy, let alone parliamentary supremacy, in Canada. Against this backdrop, it is surprising how resistent against changes the internal organization and relations of the legislative and executive branches of Canadian government have so far been. The basic framework of responsible government remains intact. In other words, Canada is still largely majoritarian on Lijphart's dimension I even though developments on dimension II and shifting context factors have reduced the clout of the legislature. A core feature of majoritarian democracy, executive dominance, has been exacerbated. The gap between constitutional reality and the thrust of reform proposals has widened in this respect.

The formidable obstacles to constitutional reform in Canada (a high number of veto points and actors with strongly diverging interests, the complicated amending formula, etc.) are but one part of the explanation for this institutional stability (Lazar/McLean; Weaver: this volume), for many aspects of parliamentary government could have been reformed by the government majority through ordinary legislation without constitutional amendment. Yet many substantial reform proposals have not been put on the institutional agenda, and most of the implemented changes have not had the desired impact, precisely because they contradict the logic of parliamentary government and the interests of powerful actors within Canada's institutional framework.

Which changes and transfers from other political systems might be realistic and effective in the Canadian environment, then, can only be evaluated on the basis of a theoretical framework that takes the institutional mechanisms and constraints of parliamentary democracy, but also its collective action benefits, seriously. For instance, proposals that implicitly or avowedly draw on the American congressional system for inspiration often fail to recognize that the independence and powers of U.S. House of Representatives and Senate members, as well as the strength of congressional committees and the legislature as a whole, are inextricably linked with the institutional logic of presidential government, and with the weak party cohesion in the American system. Most institutional or procedural transfers from the U.S. cannot be successful unless presidential government is adopted – hardly a likely outcome of Canadian reform efforts. Proposals along the lines of the rather flexible, innovative and effective changes undertaken in the United Kingdom might be less difficult to achieve, but even their success depends on context factors that are often not given, and not easy to replicate, in Canada. Thus in order to make future reform debates less simplistic, their protagonists would gain from focusing on measures that are compatible with those elements of the Canadian institutional framework whose reform is not wished or unlikely.

Secondly, reform debates would profit from a less biased approach to the logic and merits of parliamentary democracy itself. So far, the desirability of changes away from the underlying logic of the Westminster model or parliamentary government writ large has often simply been assumed. However, the empirical and normative literature on majoritarian versus consensual democracy, parliamentary government versus presidentialism has not yielded conclusive results yet, and a legitimate case for the virtues of the Westminster model, including its more unpopular features like party discipline, adversarialism and executive dominance, can obviously be made. The relatively few observers who express some doubt about the desirability of massive changes to the Canadian version of parliamentary government (Franks 1987; Thunert 2000) rightly point to the fact that there is precious little evidence to suggest that some of the more radical proposed reforms are likely to be implemented, to achieve their stated goals, or to improve system efficiency, stability, and legitimacy in Canada. The current system deserves to be evaluated, to some extent, on its own terms.

With regard to government efficiency, it is important to note that highly controversial – and consequential – decisions have nevertheless been made by simple parliamentary majority vote in recent years and decades – for instance, the NEP, the ratification of the FTA, or the introduction of the GST. These examples illustrate that the internal costs of decision-making often remain surprisingly low and, at the very least, do no prevent policy change. And as far as the success of government policy is concerned, it would be difficult right now to present Canada as an example for the "English" or "Anglo-Saxon disease," whose alleged causes have preoccupied authors from Mancur Olson to Francis Castles.

With regard to government stability and accountability, the Canadian record has so far, and despite a number of short-lived minority governments, been relatively successful, too. The Mulroney government arguably imposed huge external costs on the Canadian electorate by overusing the majoritarian instruments at its hands – but much to their dismay, the Progressive Conservatives were taught an impressive lesson in accountability by the Canadian voters in their crushing 1993 defeat. Yet the usual lopsidedness and representational biases of the Canadian parliament, and what they mean for government stability and legitimacy, should not be underestimated either. They constitute serious shortcomings. Against the backdrop of increased regional and ideological fragmentation expressed in the party system, minority governments might not only become more frequent, but also more precarious in the future. Or else, if the Liberals continue to profit from the distortion effects of the first-past-the-post electoral system and cling on to power for too long, accountability might suffer. In both cases, the opposition side is likely to remain unduly weak in numbers, divided, severely hampered in the exercise of its parliamentary duties, and no credible alternative to the government. And both scenarios are also likely to perpetuate the representational biases of the House. The inadequate personal continuity and professionalization of the Commons and the ensuing shortage of experienced and capable MPs who can fill committee seats and chairpersonships, cabinet and party offices have emerged as the other important problem areas of the Canadian lower chamber. Together, these shortcomings jeopardize the functioning of majoritarian democracy in the Canadian environment, exacerbate its adversarialism, and prevent the House from playing a stronger investigative, legislative and policy role.

Thus if the discontent with executive federalism and brokerage politics symbolized by the failure of the Meech Lake and Charlottetown Accords is to usher in an era of revitalized parliamentary democracy, adjustments to the House are indeed necessary – particularly in the absence of Senate reform. Structural and procedural changes that give the chamber as a whole, the opposition side and individual MPs a more efficient voice, and the incorporation of consensual elements like the proportional allocation of chairpersonships, might indeed be in order. Reforms along the lines of the consensual model could appeal to the Canadian electorate, "including those who admire the American system, and those (a growing number) who do not like the confrontational, adversarial nature of present parliamentary politics" (Franks 1999b: 30). Relatively modest changes could also strengthen the House vis-à-vis the intergovernmental and judicial arenas (Franks 1999b). Other parliamentary regimes prove that the combination of responsible government with such consensual elements is possible and can indeed have positive effects; in the context of parliamentary democracy, consensual elements can and should only complement, not replace adversarial ones, though. Hence one should not overestimate how far these changes to the lower chamber can or ought to go in Canada: Those aspects of Canadian politics that make substantial adjustments, rather than merely efficiency oriented tinkering, desirable often also make them highly unlikely; the simple imitation of foreign models must fail if they are based on preconditions that are absent in Canada.

For instance, the relatively successful adaptation of the British House of Commons since the late 1970s has had to do with a much higher number of MPs (over 600 as opposed to 301), the greater proportion of safe seats, candidate nominations in the hands of strong constituency associations, a more restricted range of patronage plums and party rewards, as well as the existence of activities and career paths for backbenchers beyond party control. As long as this context is missing, Canadian governments will hardly feel compelled to loosen their stances on matters of confidence as much as British governments have done over the years, and a relaxation of party discipline would only be at the discretion of cabinets and prime ministers. Yet most of the changes that might be adopted in order to emulate the British situation are either not achievable through legislative fiat or conspicuous non-starters in the current climate of Canadian politics: Electoral-system reform was discussed already, and similar points could be made for seemingly unspectacular measures such as attempts to increase the size of the House or to improve remuneration of MPs in general and committee chairpersons in particular.

Senate reform is the one area of institutional change where constitutional amendment is absolutely needed (unless reform is restricted to merely procedural matters), and therefore has not succeeded to date. It is now on the backburner even though the Reform Party continues to propagate it. The experience with failed reform proposals along the lines of the House of Provinces and Triple-E models illustrates several important problems of these more ambitious concepts: Power would almost inevitably shift from the centre to the eastern and western peripheries without the guarantee of an ensuing relaxation of regional tensions and intergovernmental conflict. Serious complications for the representation of Québec and French Canadians, as well as other minority groups, would also be difficult to avoid. Furthermore, the implementation of a reform based on the *Bundesrat* model would have to contend with public discontent with executive federalism. A reform on the basis of the Triple-E concept, on the other hand, implies enhanced Senate powers and legitimacy, and hence would reduce the ability of cabinets supported by a House majority to control the legislative agenda. At the same time, it might reduce the clout of provincial governments, which enjoy a privileged position as voices of regional interests in the current system of interstate federalism, and strengthen a more centralized, intrastate version of federalism. Senate reform proposals to date have often not sufficiently considered the consequences which institutional change might have on the functioning of parliamentary government:

"Comparisons with Australia, where the upper chamber is elected, do not often take into consideration the comparative weakness of the Australian lower House. Nor do comparisons with the United States recognize the weakness of state governments." (Franks 1987: 201)

They have further assumed without strong arguments that partisan competition would not be a central feature in an elected Senate or a House of Provinces – an assumption that is hardly confirmed by the American or German experience. Thus reform proposals have, as Franks (1987) argues, often served as displacement activity that suggested the possibility of easy technical fixes for underlying tensions within the Canadian federal order.

The institutions of the formal and political executive have so far not been at the centre of reform debates and initiatives – perhaps because their elements of accommodation have been relatively more successful in reducing the external costs and enhancing the legitimacy of parliamentary government than the institutions of the legislative branch. Yet representational biases and problems continue; supporters of these consociational features rarely provide evidence for the claim that "balanced Cabinet representation leads to balanced policies" (Smith 1995a: 387). Problems of efficiency and accountability remain unresolved: The Canadian executive branch is able to make authorative decisions on strategic issues that often impose high external costs, but also produces large amounts of distributive pork-barrel legislation.

Thus one should neither overestimate the possible scope of changes to the internal organization and relations of the legislative and executive branches of Canadian government if they are not tied to reforms of the institutional framework writ large nor should one underestimate the room for and the potential benefits of system-compatible adjustments. Despite undeniable flaws of the current situation, many reform proposals tend to downplay the benefits of the Westminster model for Canada. One frequently cited advantage is the concentration of authority which protects a political system against the overly strong influence of single-issue groups and parochial, localist interests that plague the American congressional system: "The Westminster model, it appears, is better suited to development of integrative, national programs than the cultivation of narrow, special interests" (Atkinson 1995: 363). In the already fragmented Canadian environment, then, "a parliament-centred approach might make matters worse, inviting all MPs to concentrate on nothing but locally tailored programs" (Atkinson 1995: 365). One has to ask if the institutions, rules and norms of Canadian parliamentary government have not been a relatively constructive ingredient of the political system so far – one that balances efficiency (the output dimension) and inclusion (the input dimension) rather well:

"Canada is not an easy country to govern. The huge land mass, two languages, many regional economies, strong provincial governments, the prevailing shadow of the United States, all create centrifugal tensions. The central government, parliament, the executive, and especially prime minister and cabinet, are the main institutions and forces holding the country together and asserting a national purpose, national standards, and national concerns over and above those of provinces, regions, and particular groups. The federal government has a critical role as the central expression of the nation as opposed to the numerous bodies expressing the concerns of its parts." (Franks 1987: 268)

Whatever the merits or deficiencies of parliamentary democracy, then, its proponents should not too quickly cede the arena of constitutional reform to the representatives of a fashionable anti-parliamentary populism. That the logic of responsible government is so badly understood, even less appreciated, is alarming – a fact that is true not only for Canada, but also for Germany.

References

Alt, James E./Shepsle, Kenneth A. (eds.) 1990: *Perspectives on Positive Political Economy*, Cambridge: Cambridge UP.

Archer, Keith et al. 1995: *Parameters of Power. Canada's Political Institutions*, Toronto: Nelson Canada.

Atkinson, Michael M. 1995: "Parliamentary Government in Canada," in: Michael S. Whittington/Glen Williams (eds.), *Canadian Politics in the 1990s*, Toronto: Nelson Canada, 360-381.

——/Thomas, Paul G. 1993: "Studying the Canadian Parliament," in: *Legislative Studies Quarterly* 18, 423-451.

Bagehot, Walter [1867] 1990: "The House of Commons," in: Norton (ed.), 36-46.

Bakvis, Herman 1991: *Regional Ministers. Power and Influence in the Canadian Cabinet*, Toronto: University of Toronto Press.

——/MacDonald, David 1993: "The Canadian Cabinet: Organization, Decision-Rules, and Policy Impact," in: Michael M. Atkinson (ed.), *Governing Canada. Institutions and Public Policy*, Toronto: Harcourt Brace Jovanovich, 47-80.

Bryce, James 1990: "The Decline of Legislatures," in: Norton (ed.), 47-56.

Cairns, Alan C. 1992: *Charter versus Federalism. The Dilemmas of Constitutional Reform*, Montreal/Kingston: McGill-Queen's UP.

Campbell, Colin 1983: *Governments Under Stress. Political Executives and Key Bureaucrats in Washington, London, and Ottawa*, Toronto: University of Toronto Press.

Copeland, Gary W./Patterson, Samuel C. (Hg.) 1994: *Parliaments in the Modern World. Changing Institutions*, Ann Arbor: University of Michigan Press.

Courtney, John C. (ed.) 1985: *The Canadian House of Commons*, Calgary: University of Calgary Press.

Cox, Gary W./McCubbins, Matthew D. 1993: *Legislative Leviathan. Party Government in the House*, Berkeley: University of California Press.

D'Aquino, Thomas/Doern, G. Bruce/Blair, Cassandra 1983: *Parliamentary Democracy in Canada. Issues for Reform*, Toronto: Methuen.

Docherty, David C. 1997: *Mr Smith Goes to Ottawa. Life in the House of Commons*, Vancouver: UBC Press.

Döring, Herbert (ed.) 1995: *Parliaments and Majority Rule in Western Europe*, Frankfurt, M./New York: Campus/St. Martin's Press.

Evans, Peter B./Rueschemeyer, Dietrich/Skocpol, Theda (eds.) 1985: *Bringing the State Back In*, Cambridge: Cambridge UP.

Franks, C.E.S. 1987: *The Parliament of Canada*, Toronto: University of Toronto Press.

—— 1999a: "Not Dead Yet, But Should It Be Resurrected? The Canadian Senate," in: Samuel C. Patterson/Anthony Mughan (eds.), *Senates. Bicameralism in the Contemporary World*, Columbus: Ohio State UP, 120-161.

—— 1999b: *Parliament, Intergovernmental Relations and National Unity*, qsilver.queensu.ca/iigr/Working_Papers_Series/Franks.html.

Frazer, John A. 1993: *The House of Commons at Work*, Montreal: Éditions de la Chenelière.

Gunther, Magnus/Winn, Conrad (eds.) 1991: *House of Commons Reform*, Ottawa: Parliamentary Intern Program.

Heard, Andrew 1991: *Canadian Constitutional Conventions. The Marriage of Law and Politics*, Toronto: Oxford UP.

Hofmann, Wilhelm/Riescher, Gisela 1999: *Einführung in die Parlamentarismustheorie*, Darmstadt: Wissenschaftliche Buchgesellschaft.

Hogg, Peter [3]1992: *Constitutional Law of Canada*, Toronto: Carswell.

Kluxen, Kurt 1983: *Geschichte und Problematik des Parlamentarismus*, Frankfurt/M.: Suhrkamp.

Lijphart, Arend 1984: *Democracies. Patterns of Majoritarian and Consensus Government in Twenty-One Countries*, New Haven/London: Yale UP.

—— 1987: "Bicameralism: Canadian Senate Reform," in: Herman Bakvis/William M. Chandler (eds.), *Federalism and the State*, Toronto: University of Toronto Press, 101-112.

—— (ed.) 1992: *Parliamentary Versus Presidential Government*, Oxford: Oxford UP.

Mezey, Michael L. 1993: "Legislatures: Individual Purpose and Institutional Performance," in: Ada W. Finifter (ed.), *Political Science. The State of the Discipline II*, Washington: APSA, 335-364.

Moe, Terry M. 1984: "The New Economics of Organization," in: *American Journal of Political Science* 28, 739-777.

——/Caldwell, Michael 1994: "The Institutional Foundations of Democratic Government: A Comparison of Presidential and Parliamentary Systems," in: *Journal of Institutional and Theoretical Economics* 150, 1, 171-195.

North, Douglass C. 1990: *Institutions, Institutional Change and Economic Performance*, Cambridge: Cambridge UP.

Norton, Philip (ed.) 1990: *Legislatures*, Oxford: Oxford UP.

—— 1993: *Does Parliament Matter?* London/New York: Harvester Wheatsheaf.

Pal, Leslie A./Taras, David (eds.) 1988: *Prime Ministers and Premiers. Political Leadership and Public Policy in Canada*, Scarborough: Prentice-Hall.

Russell, Peter H. et al. 1989: *Federalism and the Charter. Leading Constitutional Decisions*, Ottawa: Carleton UP.

Saalfeld, Thomas 1995: "Rational-Choice Theory in Legislative Studies: Models of Politics without Romanticism," in: *Journal of Legislative Studies* 1, 1, 32-64.

Saunders, Cheryl 1995: "Evolution and Adaptation of the British Constitutional System," in: Joachim Jens Hesse/Nevil Johnson (eds.), *Constitutional Policy and Change in Europe*, Oxford: Oxford UP, 67-94.

Savoie, Donald J. 1999a: *Governing from the Centre. The Concentration of Power in Canadian Politics*, Toronto: University of Toronto Press.

—— 1999b: "The Rise of Court Government in Canada," in: *Canadian Journal of Political Science* 32, 4, 635-664.

Schneider, Steffen 1997: "Regionale Fragmentierung statt nationaler Integration: Das kanadische Parteiensystem nach den Unterhauswahlen vom 2. Juni 1997," in: *Zeitschrift für Parlamentsfragen* 28, 4, 664-682.

Schultze, Rainer-Olaf 1996: "Interessenrepräsentation und Westminster-Modell: Kanada – ein abweichender Fall?" in: *Staatswissenschaften und Staatspraxis* 7, 2, 163-193.

——/Schneider, Steffen (eds.) 1997: *Kanada in der Krise. Analysen zum Verfassungs-, Wirtschafts- und Parteiensystemwandel seit den 80er Jahren*, Bochum: Brockmeyer.

Shepsle, Kenneth A. 1986: "Institutional Equilibrium and Equilibrium Institutions," in: Herbert F. Weisberg (ed.), *Political Science. The Science of Politics*, New York: Agathon, 51-81.

—— 1989: "Studying Institutions: Some Lessons from the Rational Choice Approach," in: *Journal of Theoretical Politics* 1, 2, 131-147.

——/Weingast, Barry R. 1987: "The Institutional Foundations of Committee Power," in: *American Political Science Review* 81, 1, 85-104.

Smith, David E. 1995a: "The Federal Cabinet in Canadian Politics," in: Michael S. Whittington/Glen Williams (eds.), *Canadian Politics in the 1990s*, Toronto: Nelson Canada, 382-401.

—— 1995b: *The Invisible Crown. The First Principle of Canadian Government*, Toronto: University of Toronto Press.

Steinmo, Sven/Thelen, Kathleen/Longstreth, Frank (eds.) 1992: *Structuring Politics. Historical Institutionalism in Comparative Politics*, Cambridge: Cambridge UP.

Strøm, Kaare 1995: "Parliamentary Government and Legislative Organisation," in: Döring (ed.), 51-82.

Sturm, Roland 1998: "Der kanadische Senat und die Lehren aus den Bemühungen um seine Reform," in: *Zeitschrift für Kanada-Studien* 34, 1, 53-65.

Thunert, Martin 2000: "Das Westminstermodell in Kanada: Besonderheiten, Leistungen und Zukunftschancen," in: André Kaiser (ed.), *Regieren in Westminster-Demokratien*, Baden-Baden: Nomos, 95-119.

Tsebelis, George 1995a: "Decision Making in Political Systems: Veto Players in Presidentialism, Parliamentarism, Multicameralism, and Multipartism," in: *British Journal of Political Science* 25, 2, 289-325.

—— 1995b: "Veto Players and Law Production in Parliamentary Democracies," in: Döring (ed.), 83-111.

—— 1999: "Veto Players and Law Production in Parliamentary Democracies: An Empirical Analysis," in: *American Political Science Review* 93, 3, 591-608.

——/Money, Jeannette 1997: *Bicameralism*, New York: Cambridge UP.

Weaver, R. Kent/Rockman, Bert A. (eds.) 1993: *Do Institutions Matter? Government Capabilities in the United States and Abroad*, Washington, DC: Brookings Institution.

Weingast, Barry R./Marshall, William J. 1988: "The Industrial Organization of Congress," in: *Journal of Political Economy* 96, 1, 132-163.

Weller, Patrick 1985: *First Among Equals. Prime Ministers in Westminster Systems*, Sydney: Allen & Unwin.

White, Randall 1990: *Voice of Region. The Long Journey to Senate Reform in Canada*, Toronto: Dundurn Press.

Zinterer, Tanja 2000: "Der kanadische Senat: ungeliebt, undemokratisch, unreformierbar?" in: Gisela Riescher/Sabine Russ/Christoph Haas (eds.), *Zweite Kammern*, Munich: Oldenbourg, 185-199.

2. *Trends in Federalism and Intergovernmental Relations*

Federalism and Constitutional Politics: A Theoretical Perspective

Roland Sturm

I. Introduction

Federalism seems to be a prime candidate for constitutional politics. On the one hand it can be regarded as a constitutional principle; on the other hand it is also a social instrument, a tool to resolve conflict in society and to create consensus for the constitutional framework. In other words, federalism both expresses and sustains the constitutional consensus of a given society. One is tempted to assume that it should not be difficult to list the federal states and then to go on and evaluate the role of constitution-making for federalism.

A legalistic approach to the explanation of the substance of federalism would no doubt search for answers in constitutional documents and would classify countries as federal or non-federal accordingly. What – one could ask – could be a reliable yardstick for such a classification? The fact that the term "federalism" is used in the relevant constitutional document, a certain division of tasks or powers between the national and the regional level of government, the existence of a Second Chamber of Parliament which represents regional interests on the national level, or all three of these elements together?

If we follow the arguments made today with regard to the Spanish constitutional realities (see for example Agranoff 1996; Moreno 1997; Pfeifer 1998), Spain seems to be the classical example for a federal or at least federalising country, although her constitution in its article 2 maintains that the unity of the Spanish state can never be broken up. So quasi-federalism seems to be possible without the blessings of the constitution. And the same goes for the emergence of a quasi-unitary state despite constitutional provisions to the contrary. In the German constitution, for example, special attention is paid to the protection of the federal order. Article 79 (2) excludes the possibility that Germany could ever be anything else but a federal state. But already in the sixties influential commentators began to describe Germany as a unitary state (Hesse 1962, for the current debate see Schultze 1999; Sturm 2000a). So, constitutional documents do not seem to be a very reliable guide for those who are interested in a comparison of federal realities.

And if the two other criteria mentioned, the division of powers and the Second Chamber, are added, we still cannot be sure whether we really deal with federalism. With regard to the first element we may just as well observe an effort to improve administrative efficiency in a unitary state, but it could also hint at a process which leads to the establishment of a regional counter-force. An example for such a case which provoked a great number of interpretations is devolution in Britain. It has so far found its expression in a Welsh Assembly and a Scottish Parliament, and there may be more to come. The devolution acts do not allow any doubt: devolution is not supposed to be a first step to change the unitary nature of the British state. The scientific debate was, however, quick to compare the future British constitutional realities with asymmetrical federal arrangements in Canada and Spain (Brown 1998; Keating 1998). The division of powers argument is therefore no promising tool for verifying the federal qualities of a polity either. And it suffices to mention the Canadian Senate to demonstrate how little the existence of Second Chambers as such can tell us about the quality of federalism in a given country.

If we want to discuss the relationship between constitutional change and federalism we should therefore set aside at least for a moment the thorny problem of a definition of federalism (for a recent effort see Lane/Ersson 1997: 87ff.) and instead concentrate on political realities assuming that at least all the states which have federalism in their constitution plus some quasi-federal ones, such as Spain, qualify as material for our argument. Federalism is a weak substitute for ideological securities. As ideology it is, as has been convincingly argued (Smith 1995: 4), "best considered as an amalgam of doctrines, beliefs and programmatic considerations reflecting the very paradoxes and tensions inherent in thinking about the politics of modernity." Deductions from a stringent ideological framework for the analysis of the relationship between constitutional change and federalism are therefore difficult to make.

The relationship between constitutional change and federalism can best be explored with regard to conditions which to a certain extent control constitutional change in every society:

- context,
- political culture,
- division of powers and implementation, and
- performance.

II. The Context of Constitutional Politics

The context of constitutional politics in federal states is more than the need to adapt constitutional arrangements to functional necessities derived from efforts to secure good government. And it is also more than the division of responsibilities between the national government and regional governments. The context of constitutional change in federal states is structured by two forces, one external and the other internal. The external force is social change which leads to a constant re-interpretation of federalism and its role for society, the other is internal. In addition to external pressures which shape federalism we can observe an internal logic of federalism, a development of federalism driven by the federal arrangements themselves, which also creates permanently new federal realities.

Social change results in new interpretations of the federal order. As a first step social change can make federalism more plausible as constitutional arrangement than other more unitary forms of government. This is typically the case when nationalist and ethnic tensions emerge or resurge. But longtime federal systems are also not immune to external pressures, be they of this kind or different. Constitutional change in Switzerland, the creation of a new canton Jura in 1978, was an instrument to accomodate ethnic tensions which emerged although Swiss federalism had been constituted in the 19th century to avoid their resurgence.

New popular and elite expectations as a result of social change with regard to the goods a constitution in federal systems should deliver can also provoke constitutional change. Alan Tarr has, for example, distinguished three stages in state constitution-making in the United States which illustrate this point: Nineteenth century constitution-makers took it for granted that what was needed was an extension of popular rule. Minimally this required "that all politically relevant people should have the opportunity to participate in governing. So over time state constitutions extended the franchise and removed eligibility requirements for office" (Tarr 1998: 736). In addition the popular election of most state office-holders was enshrined in state constitutions. In the early twentieth century the key concern of state constitution-makers shifted from an emphasis on participation to an interest in effective government:

"In order to promote effective action by state executives, reformers proposed concentrating political authority in the hands of the governor by eliminating the independent election of other executive-branch officers, collecting the myriad independent boards and agencies into a manageable number of executive departments, and enhancing the governor's power over budgetary matters through the executive budget, the item veto, and other devices." (Tarr 1998: 740)

A new set of expectations in society has contributed to the currently last stage in the development of state constitutions. Today skepticism about activist governments and their abilities and programmes has resulted in a reform movement led by "constitutional populists," as Tarr calls them. They agree on the need "to lodge policy-making authority directly in the people, to reverse policies enacted by the established institutions of government, and to limit the powers and tenure of government officials" (Tarr 1998: 742).

The close relationship between the history of a nation and the interpretations of federalism makes it very difficult to come to more general theoretical conclusions with regard to the relationship between external pressures and their constitutional consequences for federalism. One could, of course, try to find factors which influence all societies, such as globalisation or sub-state nationalism. A closer look at existing federal societies will, however, show very quickly that the analytical value of such an approach is limited. A more important question is, however, up to which point can external pressures still be accomodated by federalism, or, in other words, when does federalism break up because external pressures such as ethnic conflict, one example is the former Yugoslavia, or the need for greater institutional flexibility, Canada may be a case here, cannot be defused by the traditional strategies of conflict management in a federal state.

Internal pressures which lead to constitutional change are either a result of inadequate constitutional design or unexpected consequences of constitutional practice. Garth Stevenson (1985: 73) has, for example, argued that in Canada

> "new subjects requiring state interventions have been dealt with through a combination of informal intergovernmental collaboration, judicial interpretation, or unilateral extensions of authority by whichever level of government is the one to take the initiative. The result has been a de facto division of powers that bears an increasingly small resemblance to the division provided in the Constitution, and that singularly lacks the virtue of logic, precision and predictability."

Stevenson sees in the inadequacies of the constitutional design which find an expression in this way a strong incentive for constitutional change not only in Canada, but also in Australia and Switzerland.

Pressures for constitutional change, because of unexpected results of federal arrangements, have been mentioned with regard to German federalism. According to Lehmbruch (^{2}1998) an institutional crisis of German federalism was caused by the fact that party political conflict – especially in the *Bundesrat*, where the *Länder* representatives vote on federal legislation – supersedes the representation of regional interests. In a functioning federal system, so the argument goes, federal institutions define strict boundaries for party political conflict. When party competition ignores these boundaries a federal system is in danger of pathological reactions. Goal conflict may lead – in a worst case scenario – to goal displacement, i.e. federalism as a principle of territorial representation may develop into a Trojan horse for party-political interests (Sturm 1999: 197). Lehmbruch also added to the list of unexpected results of federal arrangements the consequences of the special brand of interlocking federalism in Germany. "It soon became apparent," he wrote (1985: 34), "that this constitutional shift had important and unanticipated dysfunctional consequences."

Lehmbruch's suggestion that the forms of federalism we find, and above all the degree of institutionalised cooperation between the federal and the regional level of government, provide us with a clue for further theoretical deliberations is, however, not convincing. There is no law, as Lehmbruch seems to assume, that dictates that constitution-making which has led to greater cooperation in federalism produces "aging federal systems" (Lehmbruch's term) and vice versa ("young federal systems"). It is simply wrong to assume that constitution-making is unidimensional and irreversible. The German case shows that very clearly. The new debate on German federalism is all about less cooperation and more competition (Sturm 2000b). Does that mean Germany's federalism is on its way to become rejuvenated? And if so, what is this supposed to mean?

III. Political Culture

As with regard to political culture in general it is difficult to identify the elements of the political culture of federalism. It is, however, now well-accepted by students of comparative federalism that constitutional realities of federalism are shaped by national political cultures. Elazar (1993: 193) aptly summarised the possible relationship between political culture and the stability of federal systems in the following way:

> "If the political culture is not supportive, at the very least it must be sufficiently congenial to accept federal constitutional-institutional arrangements and relationships, and to make them work. If the political culture is sufficiently neutral, or if the variety of political cultures within a potential federal entity eventually balance one another, it may be possible to achieve some kind of federal arrangement. But if the political culture is hostile, the possibilities for federalism in any form are greatly diminished."

For political elites the major impact of federalism is "environmental." Federalism shapes the area in which bargaining processes take place and defines, not in the same way in all nations though, the quality of the influence regional elites have on political bargaining. The involvement of regional elites in federal decision-making may be rather indirect, as in the United States, where the governors can only lobby Congress or the President, or fairly central, as in Germany, where the *Bundesrat* today has a veto for almost two thirds of federal legislation. A change in the strategic positioning of regional elites in federalism may, as Smith (1995: 10) has pointed out for the example of Canada, lead to a paradigm change in the constitutional discourse:

"With Québec's so called 'quiet revolution' of the 1960s, the province's political elites became less concerned with defending Francophone interests within a federal Canada and more concerned with pushing for radical solutions to protecting Francophone interests through adopting a secessionist position."

More important for the constitutional realities is, however, the general attitude of the citizens towards a federal-type political system. It has even been argued (Saunders 1996: 47) that given the appropriate attitude of the citizens "the effects of federalism may be obtained in absence of fully federal constitutional arrangements." Attitudes of citizens encapsulate the essence of federalism, namely the balance between unity and diversity in constitutional arrangements, which to a certain extent also imply diversity in policy outputs for different regions in a federal state. It is true that no constitutional "golden rule" exists which defines the degree of disparity between regions that is acceptable in a federation. It is also true, however, that if this disparity goes too far or is underdeveloped regions tend to revolt and the stability of federalism is in danger. There is no evidence – and, for example, the history of federalism in Canada with its ups and downs with regard to centralisation and decentralisation proves this convincingly – that as Saunders (1996: 64) believes, "all federal-type systems exhibit a tendency to centralization, which constitutional mechanisms are likely to be only partially successful in overcoming."

Federalism affects the citizen both as the sovereign and as "consumer" of politics. Citizens may see the decisive advantage of federalism either in the increased possibilities for their political participation compared to participation in unitary states, or in the diversity of policy outputs and the choices available for them at the receiving end of politics. It may be true that citizens today see themselves more as consumers than as "producers" of politics, but one cannot divorce democracy from federalism, otherwise the introduction of federalism and the decentralisation of public administration would be more or less the same thing. I therefore disagree in this respect with – to mention just two examples – Smith (1995: 7) who defines federalism as "above all an organising principle," or Saunders (1996: 62) who has argued that "while federalism is historically or characteristically associated with democracy, it is theoretically possible to create a working federal system in a polity which is not otherwise democratic."

In federal states such as Canada, Belgium or Spain, where there is still an argument about the constitutional formula which clarifies participatory rights of regions in the federal context and the necessary degree of regional autonomy, citizens will take a greater interest in the input side of the political process and the institutional design of federalism. (That is, if mega-constitutional politics does not put them off after a while). In those federal states which have a fairly stable constitutional framework citizens' attitudes towards federalism are much more oriented towards policy outputs. Even in this group of countries important differences in the political culture of federalism exist. Whereas opinion polls in Germany show that a majority of citizens in Germany expect an improved efficiency of policy outputs through a higher degree of centralisation of the decision-making process (Sturm 2000b), the trend in the United States has for a while now been going exactly in the opposite direction (Sturm 1997). The end of big government, pressure for devolution, even a devolution revolution, and a grown interest in community reinvestment seem to be the pillars on which the latest interpretation of federalism in the United States rests, and not to forget "the legal wrangling over the distribution of powers by means of philosophies of constitutional interpretation is expected to continue" (Weissert/ Schram 1998: 20).

IV. Division of Powers and Implementation

A federal constitution provides the framework for the implementation of policies. When powers are handed down to the regional level the freedom of choice with regard to the implementation of policies is greatest. Stevenson (1985:85) stresses that "a federal constitution should minimize the overlap between the powers and responsibilities of different levels of government." This is the ideal the economic theories of federalism would like to see being put into practice. Only a clear separation of powers allows the full application of the principle of "fiscal equivalence," which aims at "a match between those who receive the benefits of a collective good and those who pay for it" (Olson 1969: 483). But even where only a limited degree of freedom for decision-making on the regional level of federal states exists, there is leeway for important variation in the implementation of policies.

There is again no "golden rule" as to which level of government should be responsible for which policy, though Stevenson (1985: 82) has observed that

> "in nearly all federations, the national legislative body is responsible for defence, trade and commerce, customs and excise taxes, the currency and the financial system, postal service, copyrights, weights and measures, social insurance programs, and transportation by rail, air and water. In nearly all federations, the provinces or states are responsible for education, social institutions, health, highways, municipal affairs, renewable resources, regional planning and the environment."

The alternative for the division of powers between the federal and regional level of government is a sharing out of tasks by subject matter or vertically, i.e. the rule-making is to a great extent the task of the federal government and the implementation is mostly the task of the regions. Occasionally it has been argued that the vertical division of powers is a feature of German federalism, but it can be doubted that this was really intended by the original constitutional design. And it is sometimes asserted that the division by subject matter is typical for Canada, where, it is said, the Constitution places most of the economic powers in the hands of the federal government while conferring on the provincial legislatures the powers over sociocultural matters.

Implementation is most interesting with regard to its constitutional implications in federal states which allow their constituent units to differ fundamentally. Here the interpretations of policies on the federal and the regional level may vary widely, even with regard to the nature of policies necessary for peace and stability in a society. Nathan and Gais (1998: 97) describe the effects this may have on constitutional realities focusing on different eras of welfare reform in the United States:

"Most observers of United States domestic affairs would agree that the dynamics of welfare since the passage of the Social Security Act in 1935 have been for the federal government to set a framework for action by the states, a framework which, on the whole has been liberal. This framework and the rules promulgated under it placed pressure on conservative states to provide benefits to the most controversial needy population [...]. But now the ideological tables are turned. The framework of federal law and the pressures it applies from Washington are conservative. The pressure is on the liberal states to terminate welfare benefits and put teeth into work and related family and school behavioral requirements."

What is even more important for the development of the constitutional realities of federalism is that competition between the constituent units of a federal state may lead to policy innovation and in some cases even to constitutional innovation. Examples for the former are the reactions of the American states to the new federalism for Welfare (Nathan/Gais 1998; Rom/Peterson/Scheve 1998). An example for the latter is the extension of direct democracy in the American states which with California's medical marijuana and Oregon's assisted suicide propositions even moved into the dimension of constitutional conflict with the federation.

V. Performance

Lane and Ersson have asked "is federalism superior?" To answer this question they have concentrated on the policy output of federal systems. Though much could be criticised with regard to the variables they test in their article, it is perhaps worth mentioning their results here. They found (Lane/Ersson 1997: 110):

"What federalism means is first and foremost what it should mean according to constitutional theory, namely less central government spending. Federalism has one institutional effect that comes out, however one identifies the set of federal states, and that is fiscal decentralization."

This finding comes close to saying the typical feature of federalism is that it is federal – not a very helpful conclusion. It is also not particularly helpful to identify the performance of federalism only with such broad issues as peace and the removal of trade restrictions, as Riker (1996) did. Unitary states can fulfil these tasks, too, as many examples show. And the idea that peace is a central category for the constitution of a nation and not only identical with the absence of military conflict with a foreign power has been shown before to be of universal relevance (cf., e.g., Sternberger 1986).

More interesting for the analysis of the relationship between constitutional realities and the performance of federalism is the school of research which deals with the price of federalism (e.g., Peterson 1995; Schneider/Schultze 1999). Here the costs of performance are identified as an incentive for constitutional change. Context is, as Schneider and Schultze have pointed out, however, crucial here. The questions of an adequate regional representation must be settled and a willingness to accept diversity must exist if a preference for a new federal system which is designed primarily for a better performance can find a political majority. Otherwise the two most important yardsticks for the performance of a federal system, participation and efficiency, might come into conflict. Whenever there is a great degree of controversy on the constitutional consensus one can expect that efficiency is less important for constitutional settlements which at the end are found than participation. The mutual distrust of opponents in the constitutional struggle tends to result in relatively long constitutional documents which, when measured by the yardstick of efficiency, have the additional disadvantage of a lack of flexibility when it comes to their adaptation to political, social and economic change.

Federalism in by territory ethnically divided societies has a problem of democratic performance which for constitution writers is difficult to resolve. How can one balance individual and collective rights, especially if the latter deny some citizens individual rights in order to protect an ethnic group? At present no easy solution for this problem seems to be in sight. Smith (1995:19) mentions the crucial constitutional issues in this respect, namely: is cultural difference a social good, and if so, which cultures should be supported through territorial recognition, and who should have the right to make this decision?

VI. Conclusion

If there is anything we can be sure about regarding the relationship between federalism and constitutional change it is the path dependency of constitutional realities. The changing context for constitution-making as well as the realities of political culture limit the room for manoeuvre when it comes to constitutional reform. And even before it comes to such a reform context and political culture shape the constitutional realities, no matter what constitutional documents may say.

Participation and efficiency are important criteria for the division of powers in federalism, the implementation of policies and the evaluation of federal systems. It is often difficult to reconcile both of them when writing a constitution, and for the stability of a federal system it may be important that constitutional change with regard to both participation *and* efficiency remains always possible. But the most important precondition for constitutional change, and a resource often in short supply, is consent:

"Federal systems are normally established around the consent of the people in a number of polities to establish common framing institutions, usually through a comprehensive 'package' known as the constitution." (Elazar 1993: 193)

Consent is the glue which holds federal systems together and which finds its expression in a federal constitution.

References

Agranoff, Robert 1996: "Federal Evolution in Spain," in: *International Political Science Review* 17, 4, 385-401.

Brown, Archie 1998: "Asymmetrical Devolution," in: *Political Quarterly* 69, 3, 215-223.

Elazar, Daniel J. 1993: "International and Comparative Federalism," in: *PS: Political Science and Politics*, June, 190-195.

Hesse, Konrad 1962: *Der unitarische Bundesstaat*, Karlsruhe: C.F. Müller.

Keating, Michael 1998: "What's Wrong with Asymmetrical Government?" in: *Regional and Federal Studies* 8, 1, 195-218.

Lane, Jan-Erik/Ersson, Svante 1997: "Is Federalism Superior?" in: Bernard Steunenberg/Frans van Vught (eds.), *Political Institutions and Public Policy*, Dordrecht etc.: Kluwer, 85-113.

Lehmbruch, Gerhard 1985: "Constitution-making in Young and Aging Federal Systems," in: Keith G. Banting/Richard Simeon (eds.), *The Politics of Constitutional Change in Industrial Nations*, London: Macmillan, 30-41.

—— [2]1998: *Parteienwettbewerb im Bundesstaat*, Opladen: Westdeutscher Verlag.

Moreno, Luis 1997: *La federalización de España*, Madrid: Siglo Veintiuno de España.

Nathan, Richard P./Gais, Thomas L. 1998: "Early Findings About the Newest New Federalism for Welfare," in: *Publius: The Journal of Federalism* 28, 3, 95-103.

Olson, Mancur 1969: "The Principle of 'Fiscal Equivalence'. The Division of Responsibilities among Different Levels of Government," in: *American Economic Review* 59, 479-487.

Peterson, Paul E. 1995: *The Price of Federalism*, Washington, D.C.: Brookings.

Pfeifer, Bernd 1998: *Probleme des spanischen Föderalismus*, Berlin: Duncker & Humblot.

Riker, William H. 1996: "European Federalism. The Lessons of Past Experience," in: Jens-Joachim Hesse/Vincent Wright (eds.), *Federalizing Europe?* Oxford: Oxford UP, 9-24.

Rom, Mark Carl/Peterson, Paul E./Scheve, Kenneth F., Jr. 1998: "Interstate Competition and Welfare Policy," in: *Publius: The Journal of Federalism* 28, 3, 17-37.

Saunders, Cheryl 1996: "The Constitutional Arrangements of Federal Systems. A Sceptical View from the Outside," in: Jens-Joachim Hesse/Vincent Wright (eds.), *Federalizing Europe?* Oxford: Oxford UP, 46-99.

Schneider, Steffen/Schultze, Rainer-Olaf 1999: *The Price of German Federalism: Paul E. Peterson's Analytical Framework and Intergovernmental Dynamics in the German Federal System, 1949-1998*, paper presented at the CPSA Annual Conference, Université de Sherbrooke, June 6-8.

Schultze, Rainer-Olaf 1999: "Föderalismusreform in Deutschland: Widersprüche – Ansätze – Hoffnungen," in: *Zeitschrift für Politik* 46, 2, 173-194.

Smith, Graham 1995: "Mapping the Federal Condition: Ideology, Political Practice and Social Justice," in: Graham Smith (ed.), *Federalism. The Multiethnic Challenge*, London: Longman, 1-28.
Sternberger, Dolf 1986: *Die Politik und der Friede*, Frankfurt/M.: Fischer.
Stevenson, Garth 1985: "The Division of Powers," in: Richard Simeon (ed.), *Division of Powers and Public Policy*, Toronto: University of Toronto Press, 71-86.
Sturm, Roland 1997: "Föderalismus in Deutschland und in den USA – Tendenzen der Angleichung?" in: *Zeitschrift für Parlamentsfragen* 28, 2, 335-345.
—— 1999: "Party Competition and the Federal System: The Lehmbruch Hypothesis Revisited," in: Charlie Jeffery (ed.), *Recasting German Federalism. The Legacies of Unification*, London/New York: Pinter, 197-216.
—— 2000a: "Breaking Through the Barriers of Interlocking Federalism," in: Ludger Helms (ed.), *Institutions and Institutional Change in the Federal Republic of Germany*, London/Basingstoke: Macmillan.
—— 2000b (in print): *Föderalismus*, Opladen: Leske & Budrich.
Tarr, Alan 1998: "Models and Fashions in State Constitutionalism," in: *Wisconsin Law Review* 3, 729-745.
Weissert, Carol S./Schram, Sanford F. 1998: "The State of American Federalism, 1997-1998," in: *Publius: The Journal of Federalism*, 28, 1, 1-22.

Courting Devolution: The U.S. Supreme Court and Contemporary American Federalism

Timothy J. Conlan

The Republican party took control of the U.S. Congress in 1995, promising to make dramatic changes in American government. Whole federal departments were scheduled for elimination; hundreds of federal grant-in-aid programs were slated for termination or reform; large reductions in federal spending were advocated; and sweeping regulatory reforms were proposed. As Newt Gingrich, the architect of the new Republican majority, put it: "We are going to rethink the entire structure of American society, and the entire structure of American government [...]. This is a real revolution" (Conlan 1998). Academic observers agreed that big changes were underway. Richard Nathan dubbed the Republican program a "devolution revolution," because of its proposed reductions in the size and power of the federal government and the anticipated return of governmental responsibilities to the states. Even President Bill Clinton conceded in early 1996 that "the era of big government is over."

In the end, the Republican revolt stalled and its revolutionary changes were avoided. By 1999, Bill Clinton had been reelected while Newt Gingrich had lost his leadership position and left office. Republicans had lost seats in Congress. Few federal programs and agencies had been abolished, and federal spending had increased.

Away from the spotlight of attention on Congress and the White House, however, the U.S. Supreme Court had opened a second front in the devolution battles of the 1990s. Between 1992 and 1999, the Supreme Court overturned all or portions of five congressional statutes on the grounds that they intruded into protected spheres of state sovereignty or exceeded Congress's delegated powers under the Constitution. These developments were all the more significant because the Court had been an energetic agent of governmental centralization for most of the previous sixty years, ever since the last so-called "revolution" in constitutional interpretation during the New Deal. According to one political scientist, the Court had launched "the most fundamental debate over federalism since the 1930s" (Kettl 1999).

Has the Supreme Court embarked on a new constitutional revolution, rewriting the rules of American federalism as the United States enters its third century? If so, what do recent cases tell us about the core tenets of this new judicial federalism? If not, what significance should be placed on the Court's recent decisions? This chapter examines such questions, beginning with a brief synopsis of the Supreme Court's doctrines shaping federalism during the 20th century, an assessment of the recent cases decided by the Rehnquist Court, and an analysis of their significance for American federalism and the Court's own role in our constitutional framework.

The Supreme Court and the Centralization of American Federalism

The American federal system has evolved dramatically over the past two hundred years. With surprisingly few formal amendments to the Constitution, the national government has grown from a tiny federal establishment "out of sight and out of mind" (Young 1966) into the nerve center of a military superpower and the dominant partner of a domestic welfare state. It transfers over $250 billion annually to state and local governments, which in turn have become the chief agents of implementation for scores of federal programs.

Many of the members of the founding generation did not believe that such changes would be possible without major amendments to the Constitution. Antifederalist opponents of the federal Constitution, early presidents like Jefferson and Madison, and their successors in the early Democratic party, all believed and sometimes insisted that formal constitutional amendments were required to go beyond a literal, minimalist reading of Congress's powers in Article I, section 8. Jefferson, for example, opposed the constitutionality of the Bank of the United States and sought a constitutional amendment to legitimate the purchase of Louisiana from the French. Madison and Monroe vetoed bills for "internal improvements," which they otherwise supported, out of deference to their narrow view of the national government's authority under the Constitution. Both called for passage of amendments to the Constitution to permit such projects in the future.[1]

In contrast, the early Supreme Court, especially under Chief Justice John Marshall, took a more expansive view of the powers of Congress and the new national government. Equally important, the Court proceeded to address such issues through the process of judicial review – seeking to settle such policy differences through its interpretation of the Constitution's expansive and often ambiguous language. Ultimately, all parties came to accept this judicial role as legitimate, and subsequent constitutional battles generally focused –

1 For a richly detailed analysis of this constitutional debate in the early Republic, see Lacey 1999.

not on the adoption of new amendments to the Constitution – but on issues like the scope of the interstate commerce clause, the meaning of the elastic clause, whether the tax and spending powers comprised independent grants of power, and the substance of the 10th Amendment.[2]

Within the latitude afforded by the Constitution's broad language, great swings have occurred in the Court's reigning doctrines. The Supreme Court was an agent of nationalization under John Marshall. It assumed the role of protector of property rights and defender of capitalism in the post-Civil War era. By the early 1930s, the Court was the last bastion of conservative opposition to social change.

The Court's modern era began in the mid-1930s, when it once again became an engine of nationalization. It first did so in a permissive way, interpreting key provisions of the Constitution expansively and allowing the elected branches of government to proceed with the construction of a modern welfare state. Congress's power to regulate interstate commerce, which had previously been deemed to exclude manufacturing, wages and working conditions, and other "indirect" effects on the exchange of goods and services, was now read broadly. This allowed Congress to regulate such areas as collective bargaining, industrial and agricultural production, and wage and hour restrictions. By 1942, Congress's reach over interstate commerce was read so expansively that it applied even to a farmer who grew grain to feed to his own livestock (*Wickard v. Filburn* 1942). The power to lay and collect taxes and spend for the general welfare was upheld as an independent grant of power, allowing Congress to establish and fund a social security system (*Helvering v. Davis* 1937). And the 10th Amendment to the Constitution was held no longer to constitute an independent check on Congress's power but was reduced to a mere "truism" (*U.S. v. Darby* 1941). In short, the Court now permitted an activist Congress great latitude, limited only by its ability to demonstrate a rational basis for its regulations. As Martin Shapiro (1990: 66) put it: "The New Deal Court had effectively announced the constitutional demise of federalism as a limit on the power of the national government."

Following World War II, the Court became a powerful nationalizing force of its own. It increasingly viewed its role as a defender of minority rights, as protector of civil liberties, and as a promoter of political equality. In the process, it ventured aggressively into spheres that had heretofore been the province of state policy making. In the words of Philip Kurland (1970: 59):

---

2 Clearly there are important exceptions to this rule. There have been twenty-seven amendments to the U.S. Constitution, including fifteen since the founding era. Many have dealt with expansion of suffrage or changes in the structure of government that could not be accomplished through interpretation. Nevertheless, the federal Constitution, at 7,800 words, remains much shorter than the median state constitution at 22,500 words – even after decades of state constitutional reform and simplification (see Gray/Jacob 1996: 257).

"The Warren Court stands in the great tradition of its predecessors in its efforts at transferring areas of governmental control from the states to the nation. Every one of its major constitutional developments falls in this category. The school desegregation cases, the criminal procedure cases, the reapportionment cases, all emphasize this single theme of restraint on state power."

Partly as a result of these constitutional developments, the contours of American federalism were altered dramatically from their pre-New Deal outlines. Between 1929 and 1980, federal expenditures rose from less than 3% of GNP to over 21% of GNP, and the federal share of government spending rose from 34% of state and local expenditures to 197% of state and local expenditures. During this same period, the number of federal grant programs went from approximately 30 to over 490, the number of federal regulatory agencies increased from 15 to 41, and the number of intergovernmental regulatory statutes grew from 0 to 37 (U.S. ACIR 1980: 78, 79, 112). Thus, by the 1960s and 1970s, some scholars went so far as to argue that "[i]n fact, if not in form, we live today under a national, not a federal, Constitution" (Magrath 1968: 64).

The Rediscovery of Federalism in the 1990s

Today, such assessments are being reassessed. Since 1991, a slim majority of the U.S. Supreme Court has been engaged in a concerted effort to restructure the post-New Deal balance of power and authority in the American federal system. In a series of rulings, a narrow Court majority has begun to constrict Congress's authority on a number of fronts, overturning all or portions of federal statutes that were deemed to:

- exceed Congress's authority to regulate interstate commerce;
- commandeer the policy making and administrative apparatus of state and local governments;
- infringe on state sovereign immunity; or
- exceed Congress's power to regulate state action under the 14th Amendment to the Constitution.

As Paul Gewirtz (Biskupic 1996: A-16) has observed: "Something very large is at work [...]. The judicial branch is [engaged in] an across-the-board restriction on national government power on every front and a bolstering of state sovereign authority."

Transition to the Rehnquist Era

These new cases follow in the wake of a transitional era between the expansive nationalism of the Warren Court and the contemporary Rehnquist Court. This transitional period, from the early 1970s to the late 1980s, was marked by inconsistency and indecision in the Court's federalism rulings. Nothing underscored this period of ambivalence more than the noted case of *National League of Cities [NLC] v. Usery* (1976). Here, the Court held that Congress's attempt to apply the wage and hour provisions of the Fair Labor Standards Act (FLSA) to state and local government employees was an unconstitutional violation of the 10th Amendment. Overturning an earlier case and challenging the reigning post-New Deal dictum that the 10th Amendment was merely "a truism," the Court held in *NLC* that the 10th Amendment protects the "integral government functions" of state and local governments:

Congress has sought to wield its power in a fashion that would impair the states' "ability to function effectively in a federal system. [...]. This exercise of congressional authority does not comport with the federal system of government embodied in the Constitution" (*NLC v. Usery* 1976: *152).[3]

This was a bold decision that attracted great attention at the time, since it seemed to portend a sharp turn from the Court's philosophy on the 10th Amendment. Yet this promise went unfulfilled as the Supreme Court declined to apply or extend its ruling in subsequent cases. Over the next several years, the Court rejected 10th Amendment challenges to federal surface mining regulations, energy conservation requirements, and age discrimination laws.[4]

Finally, in 1985, the Court reversed *National League of Cities* altogether. In *Garcia v. San Antonio Metropolitan Transit Authority*, the Court held that the wage and overtime provisions of the FLSA *could* be applied to state and local government employees. Most important, the new majority in *Garcia* rejected as "unsound in principle and unworkable in practice" the attempt in *NLC v. Usery* to carve out a sphere of state government autonomy based on the "'traditional,' 'integral,' or 'necessary' nature of governmental functions" (*Garcia v. San Antonio* 1985: *546-47). Instead, the Court now sided with legal scholars who had argued that the interests of state governments are protected through political representation in the elected branches of the federal government rather than by judicial circumscription (Wechsler 1954; Choper 1980). As Justice Blackmun argued for the Court's five member majority:

---

3 LEXIS pagination (*page #) is used throughout in citing current case law.

4 *Hodel v. Virginia Surface Mining and Reclamation Association*, 452 U.S. 264; *FERC v. Mississippi*, 456 U.S. 742; and *EEOC v. Wyoming*, 460 U.S. 742.

"The composition of the Federal government was designed in large part to protect the States from overreaching by Congress. [...]. States' sovereign interests [are] more properly protected by procedural safeguards inherent in the structure of the federal system than by judicially created limitations on federal power. [Any] substantive restraint on the exercise of Commerce Clause powers [must] be tailored to compensate for possible failings in the national political process rather than to dictate a 'sacred province of state autonomy.' [...]. The political process insures that laws that unduly burden the States will not be promulgated." (*Garcia*: *550-54)

Garcia was issued by a sharply divided Court in which the switch of a single Justice made the difference from the *NLC* decision a decade earlier. The four dissenting Justices chastised the majority's rejection of "the basic precepts of our federal system." Other observers questioned whether empirical evidence supported the Court's claim that state interests were adequately protected in the federal legislative process (Conlan 1990). Most tellingly, however, Chief Justice Rehnquist (*580) said in his dissent that he was "confident" the federalist principles that had been expressed in *National League of Cities* would "in time again command the support of the majority of this Court."

That prediction was not immediately realized. Three years after *Garcia* the Court reiterated its logic in a decision that overturned longstanding precedent and removed the federal income tax immunity for interest earned on state and local bonds.[5] But, beginning in 1991, the Rehnquist Court issued the first of what became a growing and nearly uninterrupted series of decisions that breathed life into the old concept of judicial dual federalism. These cases have touched on diverse issues from nuclear waste disposal to gun control to Indian gambling casinos, but they have all developed along two general themes. The first theme involves efforts to define a sphere of state sovereignty that is protected from federal regulation and intrusion. The second involves efforts to limit the scope of Congress's powers under Article I and the 14th Amendment.

Resurrecting State Sovereignty

In *New York v. United States* (1992), the Court began its recent quest to define a sphere of state institutional autonomy that lies beyond the reach of congressional authority. In this case, the Court overturned a portion of the Low Level Hazardous Waste Policy Amendments of 1985, declaring that "the Federal Government may not compel the states to enact or administer a federal regulatory program" (1992 U.S. 3693: *188).

This case involved a law in which Congress sought to encourage states to form interstate compacts for the disposal of low level radioactive waste. Congress provided a set of financial and regulatory incentives for states, or

5 *South Carolina v. Baker*, 485 U.S. 505 (1988). For an analysis, see Wrightson 1989.

groups of states, to dispose of such wastes that were generated within their borders. As a last resort, the law required states to "take title" and assume the costs and responsibility for all low level wastes generated within their borders if they had not established an acceptable disposal site by 1996. New York objected to this provision and sued.

In its decision, delivered by Justice O'Connor, the Court accepted the law's system of financial incentives to the states as "an unexceptional expression of Congress's power." It also upheld Congress's power to allow compact members and other compliant states to discriminate against non-compliant states. But the "take title" provision was deemed to be "of a different character:"

> "Congress may not simply commandeer the legislative processes of the States by directly compelling them to enact and enforce a federal regulatory program." (*Hodel v. Virginia Surface Mining & Reclamation Assn.*)" – "While Congress has substantial powers to govern the Nation directly, including in areas of intimate concern to the States, the Constitution has never been understood to confer upon Congress the ability to require the States to govern according to Congress' instructions." (*161-62)

This anti-commandeering theme was reiterated in the 1996 case of *Printz v. United States*. This case involved Congress's attempt, under the Brady Handgun Violence Prevention Act, to require that local law enforcement authorities conduct background checks of prospective gun purchasers. Once again, the Court declared that

> "[t]he Federal Government may neither issue directives requiring the States to address particular problems, nor command the States' officers, or those of their political subdivisions, to administer or enforce a federal regulatory program. It matters not whether policymaking is involved, and no case by case weighing of the burdens or benefits is necessary; such commands are fundamentally incompatible with our constitutional system of dual sovereignty." (1997 U.S. 2165: *935)

State Sovereign Immunity

New York and *Printz* were based in part on the 10th Amendment and in part on a broader structural and historical interpretation of the Constitution as a system of divided sovereignty. As these cases made clear, one attribute of state sovereignty involves judicial protection of states' legislative and administrative apparatus from federal usurpation. A related set of cases has sought to strengthen the concept of state sovereign immunity from private lawsuits. In particular, the Court has sought to restrict Congress's authority to make states liable to private rights of action under federal law.

In *Seminole Tribe of Florida v. Florida*, the Supreme Court voided provisions of the Indian Gaming Regulatory Act that authorized Indian Tribes to sue states in federal court if they failed to negotiate in good faith the establishment of a tribal-state compact to regulate Indian gambling within the state. A majority of the Court held that Congress lacked power under the Indian Commerce Clause to abrogate states' sovereign immunity under the 11th Amendment:

"The 11th Amendment prohibits Congress from making the State of Florida capable of being sued in Federal court. Even when the Constitution vests in Congress complete lawmaking authority over a particular area, the Eleventh Amendment prevents congressional authorization of suits by private parties against unconsenting states." (1996 U.S. 2165: *72, *76)

Seminole Tribe, which overturned an earlier Supreme Court decision granting Congress the power to abrogate State sovereign immunity under the interstate commerce clause,[6] was reinforced in the 1999 decisions, *Alden v. Maine*, *Florida v. College Savings Bank*, and *College Savings Bank v. Florida*. *Alden v. Maine* has attracted the most attention. It dealt with a group of state employees who were suing Maine under the federal Fair Labor Standards Act. They had first brought their suit in federal court, but after the Seminole Tribe decision they switched to the state court system, as authorized under the FLSA. Thus, in *Alden*, the Court was asked to consider whether Congress has the power under Article I to authorize private suits against the states *in their own courts*. This is a question not addressed in the language of the 11th Amendment.[7]

The Supreme Court's response was in keeping with its other recent decisions touching on state sovereignty. Writing for the majority, Justice Kennedy (*Alden, et. al., v. Maine*, 1999 U.S. 4374: *2246) wrote that, in the absence of explicit text, the answer could be found in the "structure and history" of the Constitution:

"We hold that the powers delegated to Congress [...] do not include the power to subject nonconsenting states to private suits for damages in state courts [...]. The Constitution's structure and history [...] make clear that States' immunity from suit is a fundamental aspect of the sovereignty they enjoyed before the Constitution's ratification and still retain today."

Despite the 11th Amendment's silence on the issue, he argued that "a congressional power to authorize suits against States in their own courts would be even more offensive to state sovereignty than a power to authorize suits in a federal forum" (*2246).

---

6 *Pennsylvania v. Union Gas Co.*, 491 U.S. 1 (1989).

7 The Amendment reads: "The judicial power of the United States shall not be construed to extend to any suit in law or equity, commenced or prosecuted against one of the United States by citizens of another state, or by citizens or subjects of any foreign state."

Limitations on Delegated Powers

The other important development in recent federalism jurisprudence involves so-called "internal" limitations on the scope of Congress's constitutional powers. Unlike the state autonomy and state immunity cases, where Congress's authority is circumscribed because it is deemed to invade a constitutionally protected sphere of state sovereignty, internal limits are inherent within the very powers delegated to Congress by the Constitution.

The most prominent of these cases was the 1995 decision in *U.S. v. Lopez* (1995 U.S. 2165), which involved a challenge to the Gun-Free School Zone Act of 1990. Alfonzo Lopez was convicted under the act for carrying a concealed handgun to his school, and his lawyers challenged the law for transcending the scope of Congress's powers under the Constitution. A majority of the Supreme Court agreed and reversed his conviction, holding that "the Act exceeds the authority of Congress 'to regulate Commerce [...] among the several States'" (*551). As was widely noted at the time, this marked the first occasion since the New Deal when the Court had invalidated a congressional statute for exceeding the Commerce power.

Writing for a sharply divided Court, Chief Justice Rehnquist argued that the decision was grounded in the constitutional "first principle" of enumerated powers. The law in question exceeded those powers because it "neither regulates a commercial activity nor contains a requirement that the possession be connected in any way to interstate commerce" (*551). According to Rehnquist, prior decisions of the Court had defined three categories of activities that Congress could regulate under the Commerce power: the channels of interstate commerce, such as roads and restaurants; the instrumentalities of commerce such as railroads; and activities with a substantial effect on interstate commerce. Historically, this last category has been the most controversial and difficult to define, but the Court declared that the Gun-Free School Zone Act had overstepped the boundaries, however vague:

"We do not doubt that Congress has authority under the Commerce Clause to regulate numerous commercial activities that substantially affect interstate commerce and also affect the educational process. That authority, though broad, does not include the authority to regulate each and every aspect of local schools." (*565)

A Devolution Revolution?

What should we make of this rediscovery of federalism on the High Court? Does it constitute a new judicial revolution on a par with that of the 1930s? Clearly, some observers – and participants – think so. Justice John Paul Stevens, reading his dissent in a 1999 sovereign immunity case from the bench, compared the Court's new doctrines to the "period of confusion and crisis [under] the Articles of Confederation" (Greenhouse 1999: 2). *New York Times* columnist Anthony Lewis (1999: 1) called the Court's slim federalist majority "a band of radical judicial activists determined to impose on the Constitution their notion of a proper system of government."

These predictions of sweeping change may ultimately prove to be correct, but for the time being they are too hasty. Although significant, this line of cases is not as far reaching as may first appear. Individually and collectively, these cases are subject to a number of constraints: doctrinal, logical, and political.

Doctrinal Limits

In terms of doctrine, many of the Court's recent rulings are too limited to constitute a true "anti-federalist revival" (Gunther/Sullivan 1997: 113). In *Lopez*, for example, the Chief Justice took pains to work around existing precedents, including *Wickard v. Filburn*, which he acknowledged represents "the most far reaching example of commerce Clause authority over intrastate activity" (*560). His opinion made no attempt to recreate past distinctions between manufacturing and commerce or other such discredited notions. Rather, he acknowledged that "where economic activity substantially affects interstate commerce, legislation regulating that activity will be sustained" (*560).

Indeed, only one Justice expressed a willingness to go farther and reopen settled law regarding the economic scope of the Commerce power. Justice Thomas, in a concurring opinion, stated that the Court took a "wrong turn" in the 1930s. "At an appropriate juncture," he wrote (*585), "I think we must modify our Commerce Clause jurisprudence." Significantly, not one other member of the Court joined him in this opinion.

In contrast, the essence of the Chief Justice's argument was to avoid reading the Commerce Clause so broadly that it constituted a general police power for the federal government (*Lopez*, *567). Even some liberal analysts and commentators have been untroubled by or supportive of that thrust. For example, Harvard University law professor Laurence Tribe has agreed that the Lopez decision was "probably right" (Taylor 1999: 2136) because to "permit Congress to regulate anything and everything that in any way relates to or affects commerce [would] essentially reject the principle of limited national authority embodied in [...] Constitution."

For many, the Court's rulings on state sovereign immunity have raised greater concerns than *Lopez*. It was this line of decisions that prompted Justice Steven's allusions to the Articles of Confederation, and it has incited similar objections from outside observers (Taylor 1999: 2137). Yet, even here, the Court's rulings have recognized limitations on the sovereign immunity doctrine. For example, the *Alden* decision does not extend immunity to municipalities or other local government jurisdictions, which employ the vast majority of state and local government employees. Nor does protection extend to individual state government employees, who remain subject to lawsuits in their individual capacities. The doctrine does not confer immunity from civil rights suits that are authorized under the 14th Amendment. And, finally, sovereign immunity does not absolve states from the obligation to comply with federal law. The *Alden* opinion (*2266) emphasized that

> "[a] State's constitutional privilege to assert its sovereign immunity in its own courts does not confer upon the State a concomitant right to disregard the Constitution or valid federal law. States and their officers are bound by obligations imposed by the Constitutional and federal statutes that comport with the constitutional design."

The federal government's power to enforce such laws directly was explicitly recognized by the Court. Although this constitutes a more costly and difficult enforcement option for the Congress than the strategy of providing private rights of action under federal law, it does provide an option for remedy in such cases.

A significant degree of judicial restraint has also been present in the Court's recent 10th Amendment rulings. As noted earlier, these rulings, such as *New York v. United States* and *Printz v. United States*, have attempted to define a sphere of state institutional autonomy into which the federal government may not intrude. In the words of *NLC v. Usery*, these rulings protect the "states as states," as cosovereign entities in the federal system. The federal government may not "commandeer" their policy making and administrative machinery.

But these new 10th Amendment rulings do not attempt to wall off a broader and more consequential sphere: the "traditional functions" of state and local governments, such as education and law enforcement. This was the approach that the pre-New Deal Court took in cases such as *Hammer v. Dagenhart* (1918), which struck down a federal ban on child labor, and *U.S. v. Butler*, which overturned the Agricultural Adjustment Act in 1936. But it is not the approach that has been adopted by the present Court. When the opportunity to do so presented itself in *Lopez*, the majority opinion chose to focus on the fuzzy outer limits of the Commerce power rather than attempt to resurrect a wall of functional separation through the 10th Amendment. Likewise, in *New York v. United States* (1992: *162), the majority acknowledged that "Congress has substantial power to govern the nation *directly*, including in areas of intimate concern to the States." Thus, the institutional focus of the Court's contemporary dual sovereignty doctrine defines a far smaller orbit of state autonomy than the old judicial concept of dual federalism, with its separate and distinct spheres of national and state governmental responsibility.

Conditional Grants and the Court's New Federalism

Far from restoring constitutional dual federalism, the contemporary Court continues to embrace the concept of "cooperative federalism" in its spending power decisions. The result has been to provide Congress with effective alternatives for accomplishing many of the same objectives that the Court precludes on other grounds.

In the 1930s, the Court settled the question of whether the welfare clause of the Constitution is an independent grant of power to the Congress. It is, said the Court, and it allows Congress to spend public funds, directly or through grants to state and local governments, on activities that it otherwise lacks authority to address. This laid a legal foundation for the dramatic post-New Deal expansion of federal grants-in-aid to state and local governments and to the rise of cooperative federalism. Equally important, the Court has also held that Congress is free to attach strings or limitations to the use of such federal grant funds.

Over time, the Supreme Court has consistently given Congress wide latitude in the types of conditions and requirements that it attaches to federal grant funds. This was most recently demonstrated in the 1987 case of *South Dakota v. Dole* (1987 U.S. 2871). Here the Rehnquist Court upheld, by a 7-2 decision, a congressional requirement that states raise their minimum drinking age to twenty-one. If they did not, they would suffer a loss in federal highway funds. South Dakota objected that this amounted to coercive federal interference into a domain of state responsibility, but the Court rejected the argument. Writing for the majority, Chief Justice Rehnquist (*210) argued that even "a perceived 10th Amendment limitation on congressional regulation of state affairs did not concomitantly limit the range of conditions legitimately placed on federal grants." Although the Chief Justice acknowledged that "the spending power is of course not unlimited," the restraints placed upon it are very broad. To a large extent, the Court continues to maintain, as it first did in *Massachusetts v. Mellon* (1923), that states may voluntarily agree to abide by highly restrictive grant conditions and that they are free to avoid such restraints by simply refusing to accept the grant.

Because the Rehnquist Court continues to accept spending power doctrines that give Congress the ability to regulate states through conditions of aid, in ways that it could not do directly, a major loophole exists in the Court's state autonomy exclusions. Justice O'Connor emphasized this in her dissent to *South Dakota v. Dole*. She acknowledged this point, as well, in her majority opinion in *New York v. United States*. Her opinion in that case (*166-67) upheld the provisions of the Low Level Radioactive Waste Amendments that were based on conditional incentives to the states, while it rejected the law's direct order that states "take title" of their radioactive wastes:

"Our cases have identified a variety of methods, short of outright coercion, by which Congress may urge a State to adopt a legislative program consistent with federal interests [...]. First, under Congress' spending power, Congress may attach conditions on the receipt of federal funds."

Similarly, had Congress made the Brady Bill's background check requirements, which were overturned in *Lopez*, a condition of existing federal aid to law enforcement rather than a simple mandate to police, it presumably would have been upheld by the Court.

Political Limits on the Court's New Federalism

In addition to the substantive, doctrinal limits embodied within its federalism decisions, the Rehnquist Court confronts significant political constraints on its devolutionary leanings. The most obvious of these is the narrow margin of the new federalist majority on the Court. Virtually all of the cases discussed in this paper, including *Lopez*, *Printz*, *City of Boerne*, *Seminole Tribe*, *Alden*, and *Florida v. College Savings Bank* were decided by narrow five to four margins. The same core of Justices (Rehnquist, O'Connor, Scalia, Kennedy, and Thomas) provided the majority in almost every case. Of the cases listed, only *New York v. U.S.* was decided by a marginally more comfortable six to three majority.

This pattern means that these decisions are highly vulnerable to erosion or reversal. A single member's change of heart, or the replacement of a single Justice in the majority block, can lead the Court to an abrupt u-turn in its philosophy. This is exactly what happened in 1985, when a single Justice – Harry Blackmun – changed his position from *National League of Cities v. Usery* ten years earlier. The Court reversed its 10th Amendment stand in *NLC* and replaced it with the highly permissive, nationalist doctrine laid out in *Garcia v. San Antonio*. Similarly, Justice Kennedy's defection from the federalist bloc in *U.S. Term Limits, Inc. v. Thornton* was likewise responsible for the nationalist outcome in that case. Considering the age and health of several current Justices on both sides of the recent federalism cases, the future of what might be termed the "Rehnquist restoration" will almost certainly depend on the appointments made by the next President of the United States. A Republican President could give the devolutionary trend on the Court a powerful boost, while a liberal Democrat might be able to stop it or roll it back.

There is another, less obvious but vitally important political constraint on the Court's federalist majority. This constraint is imposed by the absence of public support for a return to a strict system of dual federalism. Since the 1960s, it has been clear that large majorities of Americans support a broad range of federal policy initiatives in education, law enforcement, economic development, and other traditional state and local functions. This is true even among many Americans who can be classified as philosophical conservatives (Free/Cantril 1967; Cantril/Cantril 1999). The continuing strength of such views is evident in contemporary polls and levels of popular support for many of President Clinton's initiatives in these policy areas. Although public dissatisfaction with the national government reached serious levels in the mid-1990s, this pattern of support for cooperative federalism remains as firmly ingrained in the hearts of Americans as it does in the structure of domestic programs (Smith 1995).

Philosophical Constraints

Recent Court doctrines on federalism are rooted in a concept of dual sovereignty which, although it is not new, is inherently paradoxical and unstable. Sovereignty means "supremacy of authority or rule." Both historically and conceptually, it is a unitary and absolutist concept of government. Yet federalism, by its very nature, rests on the division of governmental powers between two or more levels of government. Thus, building a theory of federalism based on the concept of sovereignty – especially divided sovereignty – poses unavoidable problems (Riley 1973). In one recent case, for example, Justice Kennedy was reduced to arguing that states retain "the dignity, though not the full authority, of sovereignty" – a pale version of the concept indeed!

One traditional solution to this problem was merely to embrace it. Under the system of dual federalism, the powers of government were to be clearly divided between the national government and the states, and each level would be "supreme within its sphere." This concept found expression in many of the classic decisions of the Supreme Court during the 19th and early 20th centuries. One of the clearest statements was the 1859 decision of *Ableman v. Booth*, in which the Court declared:

> "The powers of the general government, and of the state, although both exist and are exercised within the same territorial limits, are yet separate and distinct sovereignties, acting separate and independent of each other, within their respective spheres."

Although this system did not solve the conceptual problem, and a source of higher authority in the Court or the Constitution had ultimately to be drawn upon to deal with conflicts between the spheres, it did help to manage the conflicts inherent in divided sovereignty and to reduce the amount of friction. But complete dual federalism was never practical nor fully practiced. Although scholars debate how well the concept ever described the realities of American federalism, there were important departures from the model even in the early 19th century (Elazar 1962). More importantly, the idea of a rigid division of governmental power and responsibilities between the federal government and the states has been thoroughly discarded in 20th century practice, and it would be tremendously difficult and unpopular to attempt a restoration. Nor, as our earlier discussion of 10th Amendment cases makes clear, does the current Court, Justice Thomas excepted, wish to do so. Even among the Court's new federalists, this is a "solution" with few advocates.

There is a second approach to addressing the problem of sovereignty in a federal system that has enjoyed support over the course of American history. This is the concept of popular sovereignty. As the name suggests, it is the people who hold sovereignty under this theory, not the federal or state governments. The people choose, through their Constitution, to divide the powers and functions of government between the nation and the states. But they retain the ultimate source of authority and can alter the arrangements from time to time as they see fit.

This theory resonates deeply with American political culture, and it has been present in some form from the nation's very beginning. As Madison (1937: 304-304) wrote in Federalist 46: "The Federal and State governments are, in fact, but different agents and trustees of the people, constituted with different powers, and designed with different purposes." A modern variation can be drawn from Samuel Beer (1993: 20):

> "My argument is that this curious arrangement of a constitutionally protected vertical division of power is an intentional and functional institution – not an historical accident or the upshot of mere compromise – of the self-governing American people as they seek over time to make and remake themselves as a nation."

For all its theoretical power and political energy, this model does not provide clear guidance to the Court in most instances when it is called upon to settle specific disputes arising under the Constitution. Accordingly, new federalists on the Court have been prone to fall back on a constricted version of dual federalism. Their decisions refer to "attributes of state sovereignty,"[8] the "Constitutional system of dual sovereignty,"[9] and, as noted, states' retention of "the dignity, though not the full authority, of sovereignty."[10]

On the one recent occasion when the Court did draw directly on the theory of popular sovereignty, it failed miserably to reach consensus about the implications of this theory for the federal system. In *U.S. Term Limits, Inc. v. Thornton* (1995 U.S. 3487), the Supreme Court grappled with the question of whether a state or its voters could impose term limits on members of Congress from that state. The majority held that only a constitutional amendment could impose such limits because the Constitution derives its authority from the people as a whole and "gives the representatives of all the people the final say in judging the qualifications of the representatives of any one state"

---

8 *New York v. United States*, *155.
9 *Printz v. United States*, *935.
10 *Alden v. Maine*, *2247.

(*65). In his dissent, which was joined by three other members of the Court, Justice Thomas (*111-112) argued that "nothing in the Constitution deprives the people of each state of the power to prescribe the eligibility requirements for the candidates who seek to represent them in Congress." He based this conclusion in part on a very different view of popular sovereignty: "The ultimate source of the Constitution's authority is the consent of the people of each individual State, not the consent of the undifferentiated people of the Nation as a whole." With such "dueling sovereignties" on the Court, even the concept of popular sovereignty has failed to quiet the contradictions inherent in melding the institution of federalism with doctrines of sovereignty. In his concurring opinion, Justice Kennedy – voting with the liberals in this case – observed that the task before the Court required it to "split the atom of sovereignty." The explosive potential of this metaphor speaks volumes about the philosophical tension that inhabits the Courts new federalist rulings.

The Supreme Court's Role in the Federal System

Beyond the particulars of the cases examined in this paper, these contemporary decisions pose a fundamental question about constitutional government. What is the Supreme Court's proper role in American federalism? At least five potential roles are candidates for the job, having been articulated at various times in the Court's history: Neutral Arbiter, Agent of the National Government, Advocate for the Powerless, Benign Neglect, and Balance Wheel of the Federal System. The role selected has important implications for the operation of American federalism, and the range of possibilities sheds light on the judiciary's role in any federal system.

Traditionally, the Supreme Court has been viewed as the neutral arbiter of the Constitution. Any federal system based upon divided powers has need of an umpire to decide and rule on conflicts that can arise between the institutional parties. As Philip Kurland (1970: 56) once put it: "one of the prime functions of the Supreme Court has been to act as 'umpire of the federal system,' to allocate or justify the assumption of power as between the nation and the states." In his magisterial work on American government, Lord Bryce said much the same thing at the turn of the last century:

> "By placing the Constitution above both the National and the State governments, it has referred the arbitrament of disputes between them to an independent body, charged with the interpretation of the Constitution, a body which is to be deemed not so much a third authority in the government as the living voice of the Constitution."[11]

11 Quoted in Kurland 1970: 56.

As Bryce notes, the Court's role as arbiter gives it a unique position in the system – not one arm of the national government but an "independent body [...] the living voice of the Constitution."

Not all observers accept whether the Supreme Court can act – or has acted – as a neutral party in the contest for power between the federal government and the states. Writing critically about the Court's role under Earl Warren, Kurland (57) rejected this "arbiter" model as "misleading:"

"The Court has not more achieved neutrality between the interests of state power and national power than would any umpire paid by one of the two contestants. The Court is and always has been an integral part of the central government."

As an arm of the national government, Kurland (58) argued that, over the long term, the Supreme Court must inevitably act as an agent of centralization:

"Of all the important functions [the Supreme Court] purports to perform, its essential role has been to act as a centripetal force, to modify the Constitution in order to sustain the enhancement of national authority and the despoliation of state power."

One problem with what might be called the "agent theory" of the Court is that one can readily point to long periods where the Supreme Court has either actively resisted or failed to promote such centralization. Except under Marshall, the Court has never adopted this as a self-conscious role for itself. But a third role that has been self-consciously adopted by the Court also tends to lead it toward centralization in the federal system. In his famous footnote in *United States v. Carolene Products Co.* (304 U.S. 144 [1938]), Justice Stone (Gunther/Sullivan 1997: 484) suggested that the Supreme Court has a special duty to protect minority rights that may be at risk in a majoritarian democracy:

"There may be a narrower scope for [...] the presumption of constitutionality when legislation appears on its face to be within a specific prohibition of the Constitution, such as those of the first ten Amendments, which are deemed equally specific when held to be embraced within the 14th. [...]. It is unnecessary to consider now whether legislation which restricts those political processes which can ordinarily be expected to bring about repeal of undesirable legislation, is to be subjected to more exacting judicial scrutiny under the general prohibitions of the 14th Amendment. [...]. Nor need we enquire whether similar considerations enter into the review of statutes directed at particular religious [...] or national [...] or racial minorities; whether prejudice against discrete and insular minorities may be a special condition, which tends seriously to curtail the operation of those political processes ordinarily to be relied upon."

Many have argued that the Warren Court adopted precisely such a role for itself. It is certainly true, as Martin Shapiro (1978: 181) has noted, that "[f]ew American politicians [...] would care to run on a platform of desegregation, pornography, abortion, and the 'coddling' of criminals" – all areas where the Court was the initiator of major policy innovations during the Warren era.

A fourth role for the Court in issues of federalism might be termed "benign neglect." This concept was clearly enunciated in *Garcia v. San Antonio*, when the Court declared: "States' sovereign interests [are] more properly protected by procedural safeguards inherent in the structure of the federal system than by judicially created limitations on federal power." As noted earlier, the premise of this position is that, given equal state representation in the Senate, the electoral college in presidential elections, and other expressions of federalism in the political institutions of the national government, the states have no need of judicial intervention on their behalf.

The first of the roles discussed above is intended to be neutral. The remaining three are biased toward centralization. A final role, and the one that best characterizes the Rehnquist Court's new federalism rulings, focuses on policing and maintaining the balance of power in the federal system. Conceivably, the Court could lean in either direction under this role, but after two generations of governmental centralization, the current Court has weighted its decisions in favor of the states.

There is little doubt that the current majority on the Court views its role as a stabilizer of the federal-state balance of power. As Justice Scalia has said, the Supreme Court has a duty to maintain a "healthy balance of power between the states and the federal government."[12] Likewise, Justice Kennedy (1995: *1642) defined the Court's role in similar terms in his concurrence in the *Lopez* decision: "while the intrusion on state sovereignty may not be as severe in this instance as in some of out recent Tenth Amendment cases, [...] [it] contradicts the federal balance the Framers designed and that this Court is obliged to enforce." Finally, Justice O'Connor has endorsed this role as well, while justifying the Court's leaning in the direction of the states:

"[The] Court has been increasingly generous in its interpretation of the commerce power of Congress, primarily to assure that the National Government would be able to deal with national economic problems. [...]. The Court [should] enforce affirmative limits on federal regulation of the States to complement the judicially crafted expansion of the interstate commerce power."[13]

Given the structure of the American Constitution, this is a natural, and perhaps necessary, role for the Court to play. In a system where "ambition must be made to counteract ambition," the Court's role might well include ensuring that no level of government becomes so powerful as to keep this mechanism from operating. Indeed, given the proclivity of all federal systems to become unbalanced over time, as they are tossed about by powerful centrifugal and centripetal forces, this may be a role that transcends the bounds of American federalism and needs to be performed in some manner in all federal systems that seek to endure.

---

12 Quoted in Savage 1997: 11.

13 Quoted in Lauricella 1997.

References

Beer, Samuel H. 1993: *To Make a Nation. The Rediscovery of American Federalism*, Cambridge: Harvard Belknap Press.
Biskupic, Joan 1996: "Justice Shifts Federal-State Power Balance: Rehnquist led Majority Determined to Restrict Washington's Authority," in: *The Washington Post*, March 29.
Cantril, Albert H./Cantril, Susan D. 1999: *Reading Mixed Signals. Ambivalence in American Public Opinion about Government*, Washington, D.C.: Woodrow Wilson Center Press.
Choper, Jesse 1980: *Judicial Review and the National Political Process*, Chicago: University of Chicago Press.
Conlan, Timothy J. 1990: "Politics and Governance: Conflicting Intergovernmental Trends in the 1990s?" in: *Annals of the American Academy of Political and Social Science* 509, 128-136.
—— 1998: *From New Federalism to Devolution. Twenty-five Years of Intergovernmental Reform*, Washington: Brookings Institution Press.
Elazar, Daniel 1962: *The American Partnership*, Chicago: University of Chicago Press.
Free, Lloyd A./Cantril, Hadley 1967: *The Political Beliefs of Americans. A Study of Public Opinion*, Rutgers: Rutgers UP.
Gray, Virginia/Jacob, Herbert [6]1996: *Politics in the American States*, Washington: CQ Press.
Greenhouse, Linda 1999: "States are Given New Legal Shield by Supreme Court," in: *The New York Times* (web ed.), June 24, 2.
Gunther, Gerald/Sullivan, Kathleen M. (eds.) [13]1997: *Constitutional Law*, Westbury: Foundation Press.
Hamilton, Alexander/Jay, John/Madison, James [1787] 1937: *The Federalist*, New York: Tudor Publishing.
Kettl, Donald 1999: "Governor Rehnquist," in: *Governing*, August, 10.
Kurland, Philip 1970: *Politics, the Constitution, and the Warren Court*, Chicago: University of Chicago Press.
Lacey, Michael J. 1999: "Federalism and National Planning: The Nineteenth Century Legacy," in: Robert Fishman (ed.), *The American Planning Tradition. Culture and Policy*, Baltimore/London: Johns Hopkins UP.
Lauricella, Peter A. 1997: "Comment: the Real 'Contract with America': The Original Intent of the Tenth Amendment and the Commerce Clause," in: *Albany Law Review* 60, 1377-1408.
Lewis, Anthony 1999: "The Supreme Power," in: *The New York Times* (web. ed.), June 29, 1.
Lowi, Theodore J. 1978: "Europeanization of America? From United States to United State," in: Theodore J. Lowi/Alan Stone (eds.), *Nationalizing Government. Public Policies in America*, Beverly Hills: Sage, 15-29.
Magrath, C. Peter 1968: "The Supreme Court and a National Constitution," in: Murray Stedman (ed.), *Modernizing American Government*, Englewood Cliffs: Prentice Hall, 63-83.

Riley, Patrick 1973: "The Origins of Federal Theory in International Relations Ideas," in: *Polity* 6 (Fall), 87-121.

Savage, David 1997: "High Court Bolsters States Rights," in: *State Legislatures* 23 (September), 11.

Shapiro, Martin 1978: "The Supreme Court: From Warren to Burger," in: Anthony King (ed.), *The New American Political System*, Washington: American Enterprise Institute Press, 179-211.

—— [2]1990: "The Supreme Court from Early Burger to Early Rehnquist," in: Anthony King (ed.), *The New American Political System*, Washington: American Enterprise Institute Press, 47-85.

Smith, Tom W. 1995: "Public Support for Spending, 1983-1994," in: *The Public Perspective* 6 (April/May), 3-5.

U.S. Advisory Commission on Intergovernmental Relations 1980: *A Crisis of Confidence and Competence*, A-77, Washington: Government Printing Office.

Wechsler, Herbert 1954: "The Political Safeguards of Federalism," in: *Columbia Law Review* 54, 543-560.

Wrightson, Margaret T. 1989: "The Road to South Carolina: Intergovernmental Tax Immunity and the Constitutional Status of Federalism," in: *Publius* 19, 39-55.

Young, James Sterling 1966: *The Washington Community, 1800-1828*, New York: Harcourt, Brace & World.

Abelman v. Booth, 21 Howard 506.

Alden, et al., v. Maine, 1999 U.S. 4374.

EEOC v. Wyoming, 460 U.S. 742.

FERC v. Mississipi, 456 U.S. 742.

Garcia v. San Antonio Metropolitan Transit Authority, et al., 1985 U.S. 48.

Helvering v. Davis, 301 U.S. 619 (1937).

Hodel v. Virginia Surface Mining and Reclamation Association, 452 U.S. 264.

National League of Cities, et al., v. Usery, 1976 U.S. 158.

New York v. United States, 112 S.Ct. 2408; 1992 U.S. 3693.

Pennsylvania v. Union Gas Co., 491 U.S. 1.

Printz v. United States, 1997 U.S. 4044.

Seminole Tribe of Florida v. Florida, et al., 1996 U.S. 2165.

South Carolina v. Baker, 485 U.S. 505.

South Dakota v. Dole, 1987 U.S. 2871.

United States v. Carolene Products Co., 304 U.S. 144.

United States v. Darby, 312 U.S. 100 (1941).

United States v. Lopez, 1995 U.S. 3039.

Non-Constitutional Reform and the Canadian Federation: The Only Game in Town

Harvey Lazar/John McLean

This paper surveys recent trends relating to constitutional reform and federalism within Canada. It does so mainly from the perspective of how these trends are impacting on the single most important fault line in the federation, namely, relations between mainly French-speaking Québec and the mainly English-speaking rest of Canada. There are, of course, a myriad of other angles from which one can examine the intersection between constitutional reform and federalism. These are left for another day.

The paper begins by dividing constitutional and other reforms to the federation into *formal* and *informal* components. It then examines the role of *top-down* and *bottom-up* processes of reform for both components. The paper is in effect organized as a 2x2 matrix, with the formal and informal reform components on one axis and bottom-up and top-down processes on the other. The paper examines what is happening in the four cells of the matrix, focusing mainly on their impact on the language fault line noted above.

The overarching theme of the paper is that the mainly top-down processes of *informal* constitutional change and *non-constitutional* change have been the principal instruments for reforming the Canadian federation in recent years.[1] They have been at the heart of federal and provincial government strategies for managing the federation since the public's rejection of the Charlottetown Accord in 1992, which was the last major effort at comprehensive constitutional reform in Canada. Together, they serve as the main vehicles for renewing and rebalancing the federation on behalf of Canadians generally but also with a view to proving the federation's worth to the people of Québec. Top-down comprehensive constitutional reform is, for the foreseeable future, off the agenda.[2] And bottom-up informal constitutional reform,

---

1 Henceforth, the two methods are lumped together here and referred to simply as non-constitutional reform methods.

2 Formal constitutional amendments that have a narrower purpose are not off the political agenda. Indeed, two have been passed in the last couple of years. Both required the support of Parliament and the province affected. The Constitution Amendment, 1997 (Québec), removed the province's requirement to provide denominational schools, facilitating the establishment of a linguistically-based system of education. A similar amendment, the Constitution Amendment, 1998 (Newfoundland Act), removed that

mainly through citizen initiated judicial activism, however functional it may be from the perspective of enhancing citizen rights and freedoms, appears to be destabilizing from the perspective of narrowing differences across Canada's language divide.

As for the remaining cell in our matrix, bottom-up formal constitutional change, this has arguably been the vehicle through which supporters of Québec sovereignty/secession have pressed their position. Given that their goal is ultimately a formal constitutional reform that will usher in a more sovereign Québec, whether inside or outside the Canadian political family, it is arguable that their activities can most usefully be classified in this way. To date, however, this approach has been unsuccessful in narrowing the differences between Québec and the rest of Canada. The same can also be said about the efforts of the Reform Party. It too has been a vehicle for bottom-up formal reforms but its efforts have been unhelpful in promoting reconciliation within Canada.

We recognize that dividing the change process between top-down and bottom-up oversimplifies reality. Some top-down initiatives may only occur when the public has made clear that it would welcome such action. Bottom-up pressures frequently have champions at the top.[3] For our purposes, however, we will use these simple categories recognizing that the real world is often more complex. We do so in the belief that they convey an important perspective on how change happens in Canada.

The essential question posed by a strategy based on non-constitutional reform is whether it can in fact narrow the political chasm across Canada's language solitudes. That it can meet substantive concerns about, for example, issues like fiscal autonomy or demands for decentralization, is obvious even if, as a political matter, there is dispute about the extent to which this is occurring. But there are also issues of identity – issues that are as much about symbolism as they are about "meat and potato" politics – that may be less easily satisfied via the non-constitutional route. Whether they prove eventually to be the Achilles heal of the current strategy remains the unwritten chapter of Canadian politics.

---

province's requirement to provide denominational schools and enabled the province to modernize its school system. These involved a mix of top-down and bottom-up approaches.

3 For a more thorough explanation of this point see Cairns 1995.

Top-Down Formal Constitutional Reform

It may be useful to set out what we mean by formal and informal constitutional reform.[4] The primary constitutional documents associated with the Constitution Act, 1982, and the Constitution Act, 1867, are the formal constitution. According to Hogg (1996: 9), however, "they [the primary documents] do not by any means include all of the rules of Canadian constitutional law. These rules have to be hunted down in a variety of places." Hogg (1996: 9-25) states that Canadian constitutional law also includes: Imperial statutes, Canadian statutes (the Canadian Bill of Rights, the Supreme Court of Canada Act, etc.), the case law that interprets the Constitution Acts and the other constitutional statutes, the common law, parliamentary privilege, Crown prerogative, and a host of conventions surrounding the operation of the constitution and the political system. Other constitutional scholars have used this same broad definition.[5] Therefore, a discussion of constitutional reform not only includes amendments to the primary constitutional documents themselves. It also includes changes to these other elements of the constitution.

One way of entering into a discussion of top-down formal constitutional reform, and its interaction with Canadian federalism, is to compare and contrast it with the American experience, both from the viewpoint of process and content. There are important *similarities* in this regard. In both countries, formal constitutional amendment is difficult. In both, the federal legislature (both houses) and a large majority of the provinces/states are required to amend the written constitution.[6] As a consequence, there have been few amendments to the two written constitutions. In the United States the constitution has been amended only twenty-seven times since 1789. The first ten amendments were made in 1791 and constitute the Bill of Rights. Only 17 amendments have been made since then.

---

4 Section 52(2) of the Constitution Act, 1982, states that:
"The Constitution of Canada includes
(a) the Canada Act, 1982, including this Act;
(b) the Acts and orders referred to in the schedule; and
(c) any amendment to any Act of order referred to in paragraph (a) or (b)."
However, most constitutional authorities recognize that the constitution consists of more than just the primary constitutional documents.

5 For example, see Smiley 1987: 28-32.

6 It should be noted that under s. 47 of the Constitution Act, 1982, the Senate alone cannot prevent an amendment. For the amendment formula of the Unites States Constitution see Article V of the Constitution of the United States of America. For the Canadian formula see Part V (ss. 38-49) of the Constitution Act, 1982.

In Canada there have been relatively few amendments to the Constitution as well. Canada was made a federation in 1867 through an Act of the British Parliament. Between 1867 and 1982, the formal amendment procedure for the Canadian constitution was by way of the British Parliament in London.[7] The Canadian constitution was amended 18 times by the British Parliament (this includes the 1982 amendment). Since then, there have been a few amendments but these have been restricted to issues in which the consent of the federal government and one province only was required.[8] But there have been no formal amendments since 1982 that have required the consent of both the federal government and more than one province. As a result of the Constitution Act, 1982, there are five main formulae for amending the Canadian constitution – formulae that vary according to the section of the constitution that is to be changed. What these formulae have in common, however, is that they provide that it is a single government, or groups of governments, that have the constitutional power to amend the Canadian constitution.[9] There is no constitutional requirement to consult the public, whether by referendum or otherwise.

Until 1982, there was even ambiguity regarding how many governments had to support an amendment in order for the British Government to be willing to pass amendments through Westminster. That is, the original 1867 BNA Act did not provide for a "domestic" amending formula. Certain sections of the BNA Act did authorize their own amendment. And either the provincial legislatures or the federal parliament acting on their own could amend other sections. But for all other matters, the only method for amendment was by the British Parliament (Reesor 1992: 94-100). The result was that there was ambiguity about the kind of provincial support required to amend the constitution formally, at least to the extent that such amendments affected the rights and powers of the provinces and federal government or the role and representation of provinces in national institutions. One result of this ambiguity was that it complicated not only the amendment process as such but also the politics surrounding that process.

---

7 Before the enactment of the Constitution Act, 1982, there was no "domestic" amending procedure for the Canadian constitution. However, it should be noted that certain sections of the constitution authorized their own amendment and that there was a procedure whereby the provincial legislatures and the federal government could amend certain sections of the constitution (see Reesor 1992: 94-96).

8 Since 1982 there have been several amendments that require the consent of the federal government and only one province. There has been one amendment made under the amending procedure requiring the consent of the federal government and at least seven of the provinces (making up 50 per cent of the population). This amendment was the Constitutional Amendment Proclamation, 1983, and it concerned the inclusion and specification of aboriginal rights in the Constitution Act, 1982. For further details on this amendment, and all others since 1982, see Hurley 1996: Chapter 5.

9 More precisely, it is the legislative bodies at the federal and provincial level that have the constitutional authority.

While the similarities between the U.S. and Canada relate to process, equally interesting are the *contrasts* between the two countries. And the one that is most relevant here is that before the enactment of the Charter of Rights and Freedoms in 1982, and even since then, the dominant subject of the *formal* process of constitutional amendment in Canada has been the substance of Canadian federalism itself. This includes the relative roles and powers of the two orders of government, the distribution of representation in the federal institutions among the provinces, the relative role of the two orders of government in appointing officials to federal institutions and so on. In contrast, in the United States, formal constitutional change has focused mainly on the evolution of American democracy and the rights of citizens in that democracy.

Three points need to be made regarding the process of formal constitutional reform in Canada. The first is that it has been overwhelmingly top-down. Given the formal role assigned to governments in amending Canada's formal constitution, this is perhaps not surprising. Still, the fact that it has been driven by political elites, involving negotiation and accommodation among them, has raised concerns over the last decade or so about the political legitimacy of the process.

Second, a cursory review of the last 60 years of Canadian history provides powerful support for the thesis that it has been the federation itself that has been at the heart of most efforts at formal constitutional change. What has been at stake are issues relating to the very terms of the federation pact, both symbolically and substantively. In the 1930s, the terms of reference of the Royal Commission on Dominion-Provincial Relations (popularly known as the Rowell-Sirois Commission) directed them to conduct "a re-examination of the economic and financial basis of Confederation and of the distribution of legislative powers in the light of the economic and social development of the last seventy years" (Canada 1940: 13). After World War Two attention shifted to finding an amending procedure for the constitution. The Constitutional Conference of 1950 was the first failed attempt to get agreement on an amending formula.[10] After a series of federal-provincial discussions on the amending formula in the early 1960s, it looked for a while that a deal had been struck that would stick. This was the so-called Fulton-Favreau Formula of 1964. However, in January 1966 Premier Lesage of Québec indicated to the Canadian Prime Minister that "the government of Québec has decided to delay indefinitely the proposal for constitutional amendment."[11]

10 There had been previous discussions about establishing an amending formula in 1927 and in 1935-1936 but with the possible exception of some meetings in 1936 the amending formula was not a major focus of government discussions. See Hurley 1996: 25-30.

11 *House of Commons Debates*, January 28, 1966, 421-423, as cited in Smiley 1972: 10.

The impetus for sustained constitutional negotiations began in the late 1960s as Québec's "quiet revolution" gained momentum.[12] In 1966, the Union Nationale was elected as the provincial government in Québec on the slogan "égalité ou indépendance" and for the first time confronted the federal government with the possibility of independence. The Union Nationale government also indicated that it would not give its consent to an amending formula or patriation until an agreement had been reached on a new division of powers that would provide Québec with greater autonomy (Gagnon/Montcalm 1990: 155-156). The position of the Québec government meant that the constitutional division of powers became almost a permanent feature of the constitutional debate. In 1967, the Ontario government initiated a series of intergovernmental conferences, the Confederation of Tomorrow Conference, in order to resume the discussion on the future of Québec in Canadian federalism. The series of conferences from 1967 to 1971 discussed a range of issues that included: fundamental constitutional rights, official languages, the distribution of powers, reform of institutions linked with federalism including the Senate and the Supreme Court, regional disparities, an amending procedure, and provisional arrangements and mechanisms of federal-provincial relations.[13] This series of intergovernmental meetings resulted in the 1971 Victoria Charter, which initially appeared to be acceptable to the Québec government. But Québec Premier Robert Bourassa subsequently announced that his government would not agree to the terms of the Charter.

Negotiations on the constitution continued throughout the 1970s. A Special Joint Committee of the federal Parliament (the Molgat/MacGuigan Committee 1970-72) conducted a comprehensive review of the constitution and covered many of the same areas as the Confederation of Tomorrow meetings (Canada 1972). The election of the secessionist Parti Québécois in Québec in 1976 prompted the federal government to establish a Task Force (The Pepin-Robarts Task Force) on National Unity. The Task Force undertook a comprehensive reassessment of the Constitution and issued a list of seventy-five recommendations covering issues that included language rights, the division of powers, the Supreme Court and the judicial system, Senate reform, electoral reform, and the amending formula (Task Force on Canadian Unity 1979: 11, 121-132). In this instance, it was Prime Minister Trudeau who quickly distanced himself from the very report he had commissioned.

In 1980, the Parti Québécois referendum on "sovereignty-association" attracted 40% of Québec voters. This level of support was obviously not sufficient to win the referendum but was large enough to convey the view that many Québécois were seeking change. Negotiations began anew. This time the subject of the negotiations concerned the amending formula, the division

12 For a full explanation of the constitutional demands made by Québec governments see Gagnon/Montcalm 1990: 150-170.

13 For a detailed account of the conference proceedings see Smiley 1972: 41-52.

of powers, and a preamble recognizing the distinct French-speaking society and the Charter of Rights and Freedoms. When these negotiations failed Prime Minister Trudeau announced his plan to seek a unilateral amendment of the Constitution. After a decision of the Supreme Court forced Trudeau back into negotiations with the provinces in 1981, he was able to negotiate an agreement with all of the provinces except Québec on what was to become the Constitution Act, 1982.[14] The National Assembly of Québec did not concur in the 1982 amendments then nor has it since then. The consensus view within Québec was that this historic constitutional package weakened its position in the federation, because it did not confirm Québécois veto over all constitutional changes affecting the province and because the new Charter of Rights and Freedoms was seen as elevating individual rights at the expense of collective rights that are so important to Québec (this is explained in greater detail below).

In 1984, a newly elected federal Progressive Conservative government under Brian Mulroney initiated another series of federal-provincial negotiations with a view to encouraging Québec to sign on to the Constitution of 1982. The result was first the Meech Lake Accord (1987). It secured the approval of the federal Parliament (including all parties in the House of Commons) and the legislatures of eight provinces representing close to 95% of the people of Canada. But in this instance the relevant amending formula required unanimity and the reform package failed. A major criticism of this effort was that it was "cooked up" by federal and provincial leaders meeting in private and that it was inappropriate for such important change to take place without a more transparent process (Simeon 1990: 30-32). In other words, while there was a widespread consensus among political elites that this Accord was in the public interest, there were important pockets of opposition across the country. There is little doubt that the provincial governments that declined to support the amendments (Newfoundland and Manitoba) were aware that they had political support in the country as a whole that exceeded their small share of the national population. And within a short time of the collapse of the Meech Lake Accord, it became conventional wisdom in some quarters to view that agreement as an example of the dark side of executive federalism – one marked by a serious democratic deficit (Brock 1991; Stein 1993).

A few years later, Prime Minister Mulroney tried again for a political reconciliation between the Government of Québec and the other governments. This time, trying to learn by the criticisms attached to the Meech Lake failure, the process was more transparent, with extensive opportunities for citizen involvement. The Charlottetown Accord (1992) covered many of the issues

---

14 It should be noted that the proposal for a Charter of Rights was always part of Trudeau's proposal to amend the Constitution but that for Trudeau the Charter was also an essential part of readjusting the federalism agreement (see Russell 1983; Cairns 1979).

that were central to earlier negotiations. These included: a redefinition of the amending formula, recognition of Québec as a "distinct society," provincial input into Supreme Court appointments, restrictions on the federal spending power, as well as Senate reform and commitments to the process of self-government. This time, a majority of the people in Québec and in the rest of Canada rejected the amendments in a politically decisive consultative referendum.

The failure of both Accords has meant that these issues remain as "unfinished business." The National Assembly of Québec has still not assented to the principal constitutional document that sets out the terms of Québécois participation in the Canadian family.

The third point regarding the process of formal constitutional reform is that the politics surrounding these efforts to amend the constitution, both the failed and successful efforts, have been a source of great tension in the federation, to the point of threatening its survival. Whether the failures or the success (in 1982) have been the larger sources of tension and instability is an open question.

The tensions that arise from attempts at "macro-constitutional change" are different in French-speaking Québec and the mainly English-speaking provinces. From the 1960s to the mid-1970s, Québec was the driving force behind constitutional negotiations. Moreover, much of the debate reflected the competing visions of nationalist and federalist francophones from Québec. From the perspective of the Government of Québec, the process of amendment was generally viewed with suspicion if it any way derogated, or might be seen as derogating, from Québec's constitutional powers, whether they be shifted to citizens, markets or other governments.[15] To the contrary, successive Québec governments demanded increased autonomy. As the only political territory in North America with a majority of French-speakers, the Government of Québec has been long convinced that Québécois' long-term survival as a distinct French language community in North America requires that the Québec state receives special constitutional powers as well as those it was originally assigned in 1867.[16]

Until the mid-1970s, the other provinces did not express any great dissatisfaction with the constitution but they did participate in constitutional negotiations that were aimed at accommodating Québec's constitutional requirements. However, by the mid-1970s pressures for constitutional reform also began emanating from English-speaking regions, especially the Western provinces. The concern for the Western provinces reflected the view that constitutional change too often reflected Québec's priorities and excluded

15 Nonetheless, the Government of Québec did agree to an amendment in 1940 which assigned to the federal government the authority to legislate on unemployment insurance.

16 For a list of Québec's historical constitutional demands see Gagnon/Montcalm 1990: 150-170; Rocher 1992.

other issues, such as the representation of other provinces in the House of Commons and in the Senate. These feelings were made worse by the Western provinces' weak representation in the federal government (this is partly due to the first past the post electoral system). Federal government programs, such as the National Energy Program, were perceived to be for the benefit of Ontario and Québec and at the expense of the Western provinces. Québec's constitutional demands for additional constitutional powers or "special status" were greeted with particular hostility because the Western provinces felt that Québec already had enough, or too much, influence over the political agenda of the federal government (Smiley 1972: 178-180). As already noted, the current formal constitution does not provide for the formal involvement of the public in the amendment process.

In summary, the process of formal constitutional change has been a top-down process driven mainly by elites, it has been focused on the federation pact, and has been associated with enhanced political tension in the country. The Meech Lake negotiating process highlighted a growing dissatisfaction among the public with that top-down process (Simeon 1990; Brock 1991; Stein 1993). Indeed, this dissatisfaction led to the inclusion of a public referendum process in the failed Charlottetown Accord. And it is unlikely that any future effort at major constitutional reform will be attempted without some substantial and symbolic way of including the public in the process (however, the formal written constitution still does not require such public involvement). The political need to involve the public in the process of amending the constitution formally, at least based on recent evidence, makes comprehensive constitutional change even more sensitive politically given the diversity of interests and viewpoints across the country and especially given the different perspectives of Québec residents relative to those elsewhere in Canada.[17]

One result is that there is now widespread belief among leaders within Canada about the need to avoid another big effort at formal constitutional reform lest once again it result in failure. Indeed, the spread of referendum requirements in a number of provinces as a precondition to provincial approval for such constitutional amendments adds to the concern. However, the lack of an amendment that will satisfy Québec means Québec remains a non-

---

17 As this chapter was being completed the federal government introduced new legislation that might be considered part of the federal government's attempt at constitutional reform (broadly conceived). In the case *Reference re Secession of Quebec* [1998] 2 S.C.R. 217 the Supreme Court of Canada stated that the federal government was under a legal obligation to negotiate with the government of Québec in a case where a referendum on a *clear* question resulted in a "clear expression by the people of Quebec of their will to secede from Canada" (para. 87). In December 1999 the federal government introduced Bill C-20 that specified the federal government's criteria for what it would consider a "clear" question. Consistent with the preceding analysis, this legislation is part of a top-down, elite driven strategy. Initial newspaper headlines and the political reaction to the Bill also indicate that it may not serve to narrow the Québec-rest of Canada divide.

signatory to the 1982 Constitution and hence a source of serious instability in the federation. Yet an effort to amend the constitution in a fashion that will meet Québec's concerns may be even more destabilizing given the apparent impatience with Québec's demands in other regions of the federation. This creates a dilemma for the future of the federation.

Bottom-Up Formal Constitutional Reform

It was noted at the outset of this paper that the approach would essentially be to view trends in constitutional reform and federalism through the prism of a 2x2 matrix, with formal and informal reform on one axis and the top-down and bottom-up on the other. The discussion above indicated that, formally, it is governments that are the constitutional actors in the formal amendment process. Constitutionally, no role is assigned to citizens in amending the constitution, as for example is the case in Australia and Switzerland.[18] There is no requirement constitutionally for a referendum although, as noted above, the absence of such a requirement is increasingly a political problem for Canada's elected leaders.

A bottom-up process aimed at eventually forcing formal constitutional change is one way of viewing the political efforts of the Québec sovereignty/secession movement, at least some of the time. To the extent that a substantial number of Québécois wish either political independence from the rest of Canada, or at least a significant increase in their constitutional autonomy, and that they are politically active in support of their cause, by definition they constitute a grassroots bottom-up movement. Indeed, to the extent that they pursue and achieve their goals using constitutional means, this will require formal amendments to Canada's written constitution and, in some circumstances, a new formal Québec constitution. In this sense, the activities of the Parti Québécois, the Bloc Québécois and their various affiliates and supporters can be characterized as an example of attempted bottom-up formal constitutional change.

Is this activity helping to reduce differences across the divide between Québec and other parts of Canada? The answer is surely not. Rather, it has come to symbolize the division more than anything else.

Bottom-up activity is not confined to Québec. As noted above, some provincial legislatures have passed legislation requiring their governments to consult the people through a referendum before approving a major constitu-

18 It is recognized that in Australia, citizens cannot initiate amendments through referenda whereas there is more scope for citizens in the Swiss case.

tional reform.[19] And as noted above, it is likely that no future federal government would attempt mega-constitutional reform without a referendum even though there is no formal constitutional requirement that it do so. Many commentators in Canada believe that accommodation between Québec and the rest of Canada will be more difficult as a result, since a referendum is more likely to inflame differences than to overcome them.

It is also arguable that the Reform Party movement in Canada reflects a bottom-up sentiment of rural Canada, especially west of the Ottawa River. The Reform Party has also sought constitutional change that establishes the equality of the provinces and more room for the use of direct (majoritarian) democracy. From a Québec-rest of Canada perspective, this too has further strained relations.

So whether top-down or bottom-up, formal constitutional change of a comprehensive type has been destabilizing. This brings us to the role played by informal attempts to reform the Canadian federation.

Bottom-Up Informal Constitutional Change

At the outset, we quoted Hogg to the effect that much of Canada's constitution can be found outside its primary constitutional documents. And historically, it is arguable that broadening and deepening of Canadian democracy came about in this way. Our principal focus here will be on the process of judicial review under the Charter of Rights and Freedoms.

We have characterized the process of substantive judicial review under the Charter as a bottom-up process because it is a process of constitutional reform that is not initiated by, or controlled by, political elites.[20] Despite having its origins in the top-down process of elite negotiations that led to the Constitution Act, 1982, the Charter has created an opportunity for citizens to initiate, and to some extent, control the process of constitutional reform by allowing them to challenge the substance of government legislation and policies. Examples of the bottom-up method existed before the adoption of the Charter in 1982 but these were relatively limited. Statutory measures such as the federal Bill of Rights, 1960, and various provincial human rights legisla-

---

19 In B.C. and Alberta the government is required to hold a referendum before a resolution authorizing amendment of the constitution. In Manitoba the government must hold public hearings. Canada, Québec and Newfoundland do not require a referendum to be held but they do have referendum procedures in place which may be used.

20 Of course it must be recognized that the Charter is itself the result of the one successful instance of the top-down process of constitutional reform. The use of the label "top-down" is meant to indicate the new process the Charter has introduced rather than a reference to its origins.

tion provided the opportunity for a bottom-up process of reform.[21] The extension of the franchise to women and aboriginal peoples along with the elimination of disqualification on the basis of race and religious discrimination might also be seen as examples of bottom-up reforms.[22] The significance of the Charter is that it provides citizens with a venue or process that allows them to become actively engaged in the process and substance of constitutional reform by challenging the substance of federal or provincial legislation and public policy through the courts.

The Charter has resulted in stronger protection of rights and liberties and also enjoys widespread public support – 72% of anglophones and 62% of francophones think the Charter is a good thing for Canada (Sniderman/Fletcher et al. 1996: 169). Despite its relative popularity the Charter has also generated tensions in the federation. Discussion of its effect on federalism will be divided in three broad and somewhat overlapping categories: the Charter's conflict with the principle of federalism, the Charter's effect on Québec, and the Charter's effect on the process of constitutional change. Each of the three themes will now be dealt with in greater detail. We deal first with the Charter's effect on the federal principle.

The Charter's Conflict with the Federal Principle

In 1980 the Trudeau Liberal government felt that two decades of centrifugal pressures from the provinces, especially from Québec, were seriously undermining the legitimacy of the federal government and the stability of Canadian federalism. In response to these pressures and because of his own promise of "renewed federalism" during the 1980 Québec referendum, Prime Minister Trudeau pursued two strategies. First, the federal government used its fiscal power to re-establish a role in setting national policies (Simeon/Robinson 1990: 289-295). Second, the patriation of the constitution and the inclusion of the Charter were a political response to the nationalist pressures from Québec and to the province building strategies of the provinces. The political purpose of the Charter was to counter the forces of Québec nationalism and foster national unity. Both centralizing strategies were seen as ways to compete with the provinces for citizens' loyalties and strengthen national unity. However, seventeen years after the enactment of the Charter it appears that Canada is at least as far from that goal as it was when Trudeau acted. There have been two more failed attempts at macro-

21 In practice the Bill of Rights, 1960, turned out to be of little significance in initiating law reform (see Hogg 1996: 602-603).

22 For details on the development of the franchise in Canada see Elections Canada 1997. We would remind readers that we have already acknowledged that the bottom-up/top-down dichotomy involves an oversimplification of reality.

constitutional change, the re-election of the Parti Québécois in 1994 and 1998 and a second and very close referendum on the future of Québec within Canada. Furthermore, there is the possibility of another referendum before the end of the current PQ's term as government in Québec. Clearly the Charter has not narrowed the chasm separating Québécois and other Canadians.

Scholars quickly recognized that one of the central purposes behind the 1982 Charter was to serve as an instrument of national unity. The early predictions of the effects of the Charter also anticipated that it would have a centralizing effect on Canadian federalism (Russell 1983: 30-54; Cairns 1979: 348-365; Brun 1985; Knopff/Morton 1985). The late 1960s and 1970s had been a period of intense centrifugal pressure – led by Québec nationalists. The Charter was seen as tool for re-asserting the role of the federal government in the minds of the public in an attempt to strengthen their Canadian identity. As LaSelva (1983: 384) and Mandel (1994: 129-131) have noted Trudeau's political writings of the 1960s showed his belief that the way to reconcile federal tensions was by establishing a "transcendent Canadian identity" through the entrenchment of a document similar to the Bill of Rights into the Canadian constitution (Trudeau 1968a, 1968b). The reason why Trudeau favoured the entrenchment of a Bill of Rights was because such a document would be binding on both federal and provincial governments and it would subject all Canadian law, no matter when enacted, to uniform *national* standards.[23] As Henri Brun (1985: 8) notes, "the simple fact that it [the Charter] contains national standards is [...] evidence of a measure of centralization." The purpose of establishing a national standard of rights that would apply to both levels of government was that citizens would now associate the protection of their "fundamental" rights with a federal, "national," or central institution. Writing in the same vein, Cairns recognized in 1979 (354) that "the consequence, and one very clear purpose [of the Charter] was to set limits to the diversities of treatment of Canadian citizens by provincial governments, and thus to strengthen Canadian as against provincial identities." This was also consistent with Russell's (1983: 41) early predictions about the nationalizing potential of the Charter:

> "In interpreting the Charter, the Supreme Court of Canada, at the top of the judicial structure, will set uniform national standards – often in policy areas which otherwise would be subject to diverse provincial standards."

An analysis by Peter Hogg in 1989 (250) reaffirmed the earlier predictions of Cairns and Russell. Hogg pointed out that most of the provisions in the Charter relate to individual not collective rights. These individual rights belong to every person in Canada, regardless of the province or territory in which they live. In other words, rights do not vary from one province to another: "Where guaranteed rights exist, there must be a single national

23 Brun 1985: 8. Hogg (1989: 249) also makes this point.

rule."[24] Therefore, according to Hogg, the Charter's guarantee of individual rights on a national basis "[...] is inconsistent with the diversity of treatment by regional [provincial] governments that is the value at the core of federalism."

Morton's (1995: 173) analysis of the Charter's effects further illustrates how the Charter conflicts with the principle of federalism by eroding the autonomy of provincial governments. According to Morton too much analysis of the Charter has focused on its role as an instrument of rights and not enough attention has been given to the role the Charter played in Prime Minister Trudeau's broader strategy of nation-building. Morton (1995: 178) claims that the Charter was "a deliberate strategy to overrule various provinces' restrictive and unfriendly treatment of official language minority groups." The entrenchment of minority language rights into the Charter meant that an area of policy that used to be the jurisdiction of the provinces was turned over to the courts. This meant that the Supreme Court (and other courts appointed by the federal government) would now be responsible for protecting minority rights and these institutions would be much more sensitive to minority language concerns than provincial legislatures.

According to Morton, interest groups have played a critical role in the centralizing effects of the Charter. The most important of these groups were the minority language groups because of their significance in establishing Trudeau's pan-Canadian strategy. The federal government provided money to minority language interest groups in Québec and the rest of the country through government departments and the Court Challenges Program. With financial support from the federal government these minority language interest groups were particularly successful in challenging various provincial language policies in Québec, Manitoba, Saskatchewan and Alberta. This strategy of providing money to interest groups to challenge provincial legislation was extended to other groups. Although the minority language groups remained the primary beneficiaries the same strategy was extended to other interest groups that included feminist and women's organizations, aboriginals, ethnic minorities, gays and lesbian groups, and civil libertarian organizations. Although these groups have not been as successful as the minority language groups in challenging provincial legislation the overall result has been the erosion of the provinces' policy autonomy (Morton 1995: 177-183). Recent cases, such as the *Vriend* case, further illustrate the provinces' continuing frustrations with the Charter.[25]

---

24 This analysis and quote are from Hogg 1989: 250.

25 [1998] 1 S.C.R. 493. Also see Morton 1996: 121-125; Alberta 1999 (in response to the Supreme Court's decision in the *Vriend* case). The only dissenting judgement in this case was written by Justice Major from Alberta.

The Charter versus Québec

The Charter has also had particular significance for Québec, as the only province that did not agree to the terms of the new constitutional settlement. This was particularly significant because the adoption of the Constitution Act, 1982, took place over Québec's opposition and despite Québec's claim that it had a veto on constitutional amendments (by convention):[26] "As such, it [the Charter] was the result of a procedure that directly contradicted the established French Canadian view of Canada and Québec's place within it" (McRoberts 1997: 181). Shortly after the Constitution Act was proclaimed law, the Government of Québec issued a symbolic rejection of the measure by enacting legislation that applied the Charter's "notwithstanding clause" (section 33) to all Québec provincial legislation.[27]

The Charter has resulted in conflicts with the Québec government because the language provisions of section 23 of the Charter, in particular, have had the effect of undermining the language policy of the Québec government. Bill 101 in Québec was the cornerstone of the Parti Québécois' language policy. Provisions of Bill 101 set restrictions on access to English language education. Section 23 of the Charter guarantees minority education language rights and made access to English language schools in Québec easier than Bill 101 contemplated. In one of its earliest Charter cases, the Supreme Court ruled in the 1984 *Protestant School Board* case[28] that the educational language provisions of Bill 101 violated section 23 of the Charter (and that the limitations on section 23 rights were not justified under section 1). Because the case involved the language rights of section 23, the Québec government could not make use of section 33 to override the decision of the Court.

It was not long before another Charter case challenged other provisions of Québec's language law. In addition to specifying language rights, Bill 101 required that public signs and commercial advertising be in French only. In 1988 the Supreme Court found in the *Ford* case[29] that Bill 101's restrictions on advertising were an unjustified limit on the Charter's guarantee of freedom of expression. The *Ford* and *Protestant* cases clearly illustrate that the Charter was serving to weaken the Québec government's ability to determine language and cultural policy – policy areas that were among the most important to the Québec government.[30] Scholars such as Hiebert, who argue that the

26 The Supreme Court of Canada later ruled that Québec did not have a veto over constitutional amendments (see *Re Objection by Québec to Resolution to Amend the Constitution* [1982] 2 S.C.R. 793).

27 For a clear statement of Québec nationalism's reaction to the 1982 constitutional patriation, including the Charter, see Laforest 1995.

28 [1984] 2 S.C.R. 66.

29 *Ford v. A.G. Québec*, [1988] 2 S.C.R. 712.

30 For a more detailed explanation of this argument see De Montigny 1997.

Charter is capable of accommodating the principles of federalism, also acknowledge that the Charter has seriously constrained the autonomy of Québec on issues of language and education (Hiebert 1996).

In short, the Charter has not fostered reconciliation between Québec and the rest of Canada. To this time, at least, its effect has been quite the opposite. Not surprisingly, the Supreme Court's decision in the *Ford* case outraged Québec francophones who saw Bill 101 as the symbolic and practical recognition of Québec as a predominantly French society. In reaction to the Supreme Court's decision in the *Ford* case, Bourassa's Liberal government responded by making use of section 33 and re-introduced the sign law in the form of Bill 178. The use of s. 33 resulted in a wave of protests among anglophones in Québec as well as in other parts of Canada. These events helped shape the political environment surrounding the ratification process for the Meech Lake Accord, including the attitudes in Newfoundland and Manitoba that were noted above. And they ultimately contributed to its collapse.

The Charter's Effect on the Process of Constitutional Change

In addition to affecting the legislative powers of the provinces, the Charter has also had an effect on the process of constitutional amendment that has contributed to further instability. As noted earlier, the arrival of the Charter has coincided with the growth of a number of significant interest groups. Some scholars have referred to this collection of interest groups as the "Court Party" (Morton/Knopff 1992, 2000) and others have used the label "Charter Canadians" (Cairns 1979, 1992). Whatever the label, citizens who were once passive observers of elites carrying on constitutional negotiations have been transformed into active rights bearers that want to play a role in the process (and content) of constitutional change.

Members of these interest groups were initially among the supporters of the Charter in 1981 and they have been among its primary beneficiaries since its enactment in 1982. Many of these groups played a leading role in opposition to the Meech Lake and Charlottetown Accords (Morton 1995: 184; Russell 1993: Chapters 9, 10, 11). They objected to the (top-down) process of formal constitutional reform that excluded them from constitutional negotiations. The same interest groups have also objected to the substance of the two Accords because both Accords would have weakened the Charter and threatened the source of their political influence (Cairns 1992; Morton 1995; McRoberts 1997: 185).

Before the Charter, governments dominated the process of constitutional change. Although there has been no formal change to the amending process, in practical political terms, the increasing influence of interest groups mobilized around the Charter and an expanded role for public participation have weakened the ability of provincial and federal governments to control the constitutional amending process: "The governments' historical monopoly on the constitutional amending process has been broken" (Morton 1995: 185). This has in turn weakened the ability of the provinces and the federal government to accommodate the constitutional demands of Québec. This is because the very interest groups that now play a more active role in the constitutional reform process also object to any proposals that may weaken the Charter in response to Québec's constitutional demands.

The Charter has also had another effect on constitutional reform. Trudeau's original strategy behind the Charter was that it would serve to strengthen national unity by creating a set of values and norms that would be shared by the entire Canadian community. According to Cairns, the Charter has had the effect of reinforcing the concepts of provincial equality and individual equality in English-speaking Canada, but not in Québec (Cairns 1991). This is not because Québec does not support respect for fundamental rights and freedoms.[31] The Charter has failed to take "root" in Québec because, in addition to being adopted against the objections of the Québec National Assembly and its consequences for Québec's legislative powers, the Charter's values of provincial and individual equality run contrary to Québec's historical demands for "special status" (asymmetrical constitutional powers), and it has undermined the ability of the Québec government to protect the status of the French language and culture.

In summary, judicial review has not only been important as a vehicle for strengthening individual rights and freedoms. It also appears to have helped to build a sense of political nationhood in Canada outside Québec. But it has not helped to narrow the differences between Québec and the rest of Canada. It is not that the Charter is unpopular in Québec as such. Rather, it is simply that, however much individuals in Québec may support the Charter, they are probably much more committed to the Québec state as the instrument best suited to protecting and advancing their rights and needs as a collectivity. To date, at least, bottom-up constitutional reform via the Charter has failed to serve the wider nation-building role that had been one of its original purposes. Indeed, by helping to sink the Meech Lake Accord, it arguably has had the opposite effect.

31 Support for rights is similar in English Canada and Québec (see Sniderman/Fletcher et al. 1996).

Top-Down Informal Reform

It may not always be clear when legislative change qualifies as constitutional. In this last substantive section, we examine the mainly top-down process that includes informal constitutional change in the sense referred to by Hogg. We also include the techniques of non-constitutional reform to the federation as they are a part of the informal approach. Indeed, most of our focus will be on the non-constitutional as it has been the centrepiece of recent efforts at federation management. Here we include political and administrative agreements between federal and provincial governments and legislative actions related to those agreements. Fiscal federalism, social and economic union, intergovernmental environmental and industrial development arrangements are examples of what we have in mind.

Although mega-constitutional reform has been on the political backburner since the collapse of the Charlottetown Accord in 1992, this by no means indicates that the federation is in gridlock. To the contrary, the ways in which the federal and provincial governments relate to one another have been undergoing a continuous evolution as governments have looked increasingly at mechanisms other than formal constitutional reform as the preferred means to reform and renew the federation.

The range of issues that have been subjected to intense federal-provincial dialogue is very large. It includes the rules governing internal trade, the framework for the making of social policy, arrangements to collaborate on the management of the environment, aboriginal issues, fiscal federalism, and a host of other items (Lazar 1998). In the last few years, for example, agreements have been reached to modify the financing of the Canada and Québec Pension Plans, to devolve labour market training from the federal to provincial governments, to create an integrated federal and provincial strategy for reducing child poverty and for facilitating the transition from welfare to work, for collaboration on meeting international commitments to reduce carbon emissions and to introduce more flexibility into federal-provincial arrangements for personal income tax harmonization.

Two characteristics are associated with the way in which the federation has been evolving recently. The first is that this new brand of federalism is, at one and the same time, both more collaborative and more disentangled. An excellent example of what we mean is to be found in the new Social Union Framework Agreement and in the new National Child Benefit that is effectively an element of the Framework Agreement (although negotiated prior to the framework itself). In the Social Union Framework Agreement (SUFA), the two orders of government (except Québec) have committed to "work more closely together" to meet the needs of Canadians. The governments have committed to undertaking joint planning, to share information on social trends, problems and priorities, and to work together to identify priorities for collaborative action. The governments have also recognized that the actions of one government may have an impact on other governments and therefore committed to giving advance notice prior to implementing a major change in social policy. A Ministerial Council has been established to oversee this process. The Framework Agreement also has put some new limits, however modest they may be, on the federal government's freedom to use its spending power in the areas of provincial legislative competence. Of particular note is that these restrictions on Ottawa are somewhat tougher in relation to jointly financed programs, that is, programs where Ottawa seeks to reach its objectives by contributing to provincial programs, than in cases where Ottawa makes payments directly to citizens as a part of its social policy. In the former case, while there is no formal opting out procedure, de facto, there is the equivalent of one. In the latter case of transfers to citizens, there is no provision for a province to opt out and receive the cash that would have otherwise been expended on its residents.

At the same time, the SUFA calls on governments to clarify the relative roles and responsibilities of each order of government. It thus anticipates that, within the joint planning framework, each order of government will be responsible for designing and implementing its own measures. Further, by clarifying roles and responsibilities, it suggests that Canada's social union can be strengthened by enhancing each government's accountability to its own constituents. Note that the SUFA entails no changes to the constitution. Although it has a dispute settlement mechanism, it is not a binding mechanism. The SUFA is a political agreement that respects the sovereignty of both orders of government.

The National Child Benefit is an interesting example of these broad concepts in practice. The two orders of government jointly agreed that a reduction of child poverty and an improvement in transitions from welfare to work were high priority. To do this, the federal government agreed to increase its financial transfers to families with children. In turn, this allowed provincial governments to reduce their welfare payments to poor families with children. The provinces would no longer top up their welfare payments because the family had children. Thus, a family that was on welfare would lose less of its combined federal and provincial government payments if one or both spouses went to work because the federal payment for children (not being part of welfare) would not be eroded as a result of their return to work.[32] The financial incentive to work was thus improved. For their part, the provinces committed to using the money that they would save because of lower welfare

32 In fact, the benefit is income tested and does erode but at much higher income levels than was the case when these benefits were a part of provincial welfare.

payments for child-related benefits or services. Individual provinces were entirely free to make re-investment decisions to reflect their own priorities (which might include programs for early childhood development, child-care, child welfare services and so on). Each order of government would design and deliver its own programs, and be publicly accountable for the results, within the collaborative framework. Thus, at the level of the framework there is collaboration. At the level of program design, governments act independently of one another.[33]

The Agreement on Internal Trade is similar in important respects. It reflects the commitment of both orders of government to reduce internal barriers to economic mobility. In particular, it involves commitments by all governments to remove laws, regulations or practices in one province that discriminate against out-of-province persons or businesses. It also commits governments to more than "negative integration" by calling for the elimination or harmonization of regulations (e.g., standards) to facilitate interprovincial business activity and free movement of labour. Like the Social Union Framework Agreement, the Agreement on Internal Trade is a political agreement. It too has dispute settlement mechanisms but again it is not legally binding. Both orders of government have agreed to collaborate to remove barriers to investment, to labour mobility, to allow free competition for government-determined contracts (procurement) and so on. Each order of government is responsible for acting on its commitments. But all have agreed politically, including Québec, to collaborate in this endeavour. While the Agreement has deadlines for meeting the various commitments, in practice they are only as good as the political good will of the signatory governments.

The sheer volume of federal-provincial activity is so great that it is always possible for an observer to select several examples that would illustrate a different pattern than the one referred to above. For example, the federal government's Millennium Scholarship Fund initiative is difficult to reconcile with the federal-provincial agreement on roles and responsibilities in the social area. Under this program, announced in the 1998 federal budget, the federal government is proposing to pay worthy post-secondary students to help them finance their education. This is a use of the federal spending power in what would otherwise be provincial jurisdiction. For many provinces, this was an example of federal unilateralism (notwithstanding that Ottawa undertook to work with them to ensure harmonious delivery). It certainly runs counter to the spirit that underlies the subsequent SUFA. From a federalism perspective, an important question regarding the Millennium Scholarship Fund is whether, in its unilateral features, it was an aberration in the new federal-provincial relations. In our interpretation of recent trends, the Millen-

33 This raw statement ignores the huge amount of negotiating effort by federal and provincial officials that went into this agreement and similar ones. These can involve not only political factors but a host of substantial administrative matters.

nium Scholarship Fund is best viewed as an aberration that is inconsistent with the newly emerging pattern for the federation. The October 1999 federal proposals for a Children's Agenda, for example, were made conditional on federal-provincial agreement.

In many senses, the trend towards domestic intergovernmental collaboration may be inevitable. Just as national governments the world over are increasingly finding it necessary to collaborate with other national governments in order to manage an increasingly globalized world – economically, environmentally, culturally and so on – interdependence among governments within a national order is likely to grow. For example, the Kyoto Agreement to reduce greenhouse gas emissions reflects the pressures of the international agenda. Canadians cannot deal with this issue without extensive collaboration between both orders of governments (as well as between governments and the private sector).

At the same time, within these framework arrangements, disentanglement is taking place. And each order of government is seen to be politically accountable for getting results.

The second characteristic of this new federalism is that while the Government of Québec sometimes chooses to sign on to these new intergovernmental agreements, it often decides not to do so.[34] The result is a growing de facto asymmetry in the new federation. When Québec does not sign, this is typically because Québec governments see the collaborative element in the above-mentioned strategy as a thinly veiled assertion of federal government paramountcy. Québec governments have long questioned the political legitimacy, if not the constitutional validity, of the federal government's spending power (Coleman 1984: 64-74; Simeon/Robinson 1990: 140-150). Québec argues that what appears to be collaboration is in fact the intrusion of an arrogant and centralizing federal government into areas that are the legislative competence of the province.

From the viewpoint of reconciliation across Canada's language divide, this paper has argued that most of the techniques of reducing political instability in the federation have been counterproductive. We have suggested that the only game in town has been top-down non-constitutional renewal. This raises the question how effective it has been in lowering the tensions within the country. Has it been effective in helping to bridge the gaps within Canada? Elsewhere, one of us has argued that this strategy has been helpful in improving policy effectiveness and in changing the nature of the federation. In this view, the federation was marked by an absence of *hierarchy* and con-

34 In those intergovernmental agreements that Québec has not signed, the accompanying federal-provincial Ministerial press statement typically includes a brief reference from the Québec minister that the Government of Québec shares similar objectives to those which underlie the agreement but that it is not participating because it believes that the subject of the agreement is better managed by the Québec government alone.

siderable *independence* among orders of government in the interwar years (a classical form of federalism). In the postwar years, there was a trend toward both *hierarchy* and *interdependence* that may have reached its peak in the 1970s or early 1980s. In any case, the current trend appears to be increasingly *non-hierarchical* but with growing *interdependence*. (In this regard, the Charter is viewed as an important exception to this trend [Lazar 1998]).

Has this strategy helped to promote reconciliation across the Québec-rest of Canada chasm? Such a conclusion would be premature. But it has helped cool the differences. The policy successes it has helped to achieve, for example, eliminating the public sector deficit in Canada, the Agreement on Internal Trade, the SUFA and the National Child Benefit are to its credit.

Since much of this activity has taken place without Québec's signature, it has also had the effect of fostering de facto asymmetry in the federation. This has the advantage of allowing the other provinces to push ahead with what they wish to do without being "held back" by a Québec that sees more disadvantages than advantages in such collaboration. And by allowing the other provinces to act in this way, it also helps to dispel the notion that Québec controls the national agenda. Over time, this may help to make other provinces more open to Québec's aspirations and agenda although it is clearly too soon to reach such a conclusion. A less positive spin on these same developments would focus on the fact that they may also represent a growing willingness of the rest of Canada to accept a Québec in growing isolation from the rest of the country.

In any event, as a bare minimum, the non-constitutional approach has served to buy time for the federation, while the bitter emotions attached to the failures of the Meech Lake and Charlottetown Accords have been allowed to ease. And it may also be an essential feature on any more formal political reconciliation between Québec and other partners on the Canadian federation. In terms of an ultimate modus vivendi between Canada outside Québec and Québec, one provincial premier speaks often of the 80/20 solution. The 80% he alludes to is non-constitutional reform.

Non-constitutional reform, as a strategy for facilitating reconciliation, suffers from two deficiencies. Like top-down formal constitutional reform, it lacks transparency, being built so heavily on federal-provincial diplomacy, which largely happens behind closed doors. To date, however, Canadians have been much less concerned about the democratic deficit in non-constitutional reform matters than they have become in matters of comprehensive constitutional reform.[35] This could change at some future time. What has worked to its favour, at least to now, has been the essentially technocratic

35 The issue of the democratic deficit in matters of non-constitutional reform is receiving growing attention by governments. Improving this situation is likely to require many small changes in behaviour, by governments and other political actors. A single "silver bullet" is most unlikely to be discovered.

nature of many of these programs, as illustrated by Allan Maslove's contribution to this volume. The issues of non-constitutional reform lack emotional symbolism. They are opaque. They are often boring. But they are also the stuff of that part of government that touches the real economic and social life of Canadians. If the federation functions better in these areas, Canadians have less reason to question the political underpinnings of their society.

Its second deficiency is that this approach cannot, almost by definition, respond to Québec's demand for greater constitutional recognition of its nationhood – a recognition that would contain both symbolic and substantive elements. This takes us back to Peter Russell's admonitions regarding the pitfalls of comprehensive constitutional reform, which we argued above have been damaging to relations between Québec and the rest of Canada.

Conclusion

This paper has explored the formal and informal approaches to achieving reconciliation in Canada's federation, from both a top-down and bottom-up perspective. While there are advantages and disadvantages to each, from the single perspective of this paper, three of the four have been functioning in a counterproductive way. To be sure, some of these approaches have important victories to their credit on issues unrelated to the issue of reconciliation. But from the Québec-rest of Canada vantage point they are not working well. If anything, they are making things worse.

Formal constitutional reform in Canada has been heavily concerned with the symbols and substance of the Canadian federation pact. Many reform efforts have failed. In recent decades, one major reform has been adopted. Both the failed and successful reforms have been destabilizing for the federation. They have not managed to bridge the gap between the majority French-speaking opinion in Québec and the majority English-speaking opinion elsewhere in Canada regarding the appropriate relationship between federal and provincial orders of government and between francophone Québécois as a national group and other Canadians. Moreover, the process has been top-down and has, until recently, excluded the voting public. The result has been to discredit the process in some eyes. Many Québécois distrust the constitutional development process because it has failed to deliver what they want. Many other Canadians mistrust it because the process itself is seen as flawed.

Bottom-up formal constitutional change is mainly in the hands of those who would either end the federation (mainly in Québec) or make it even less acceptable to Québécois to remain (mainly in the Reform Party). Thus, it is adding to the strain in the country.

Judicial review was analyzed as a technique of bottom-up informal change. It has come to play a growing role in the constitutional process since the early 1980s. It has empowered groups that previously had felt disenfranchised and, to that extent, has served as a counterweight to the criticism that formal constitutional change is a top-down process. But it has not helped, and could in fact be hindering, the building of bridges across the language divide.

For federation reform, the informal top-down approach has been increasingly relied on. Its record has been mixed, although when seen through a rearview mirror rather than the cut and thrust of daily debate, it has introduced much needed flexibility into federation leadership and management. It does not and probably cannot deal with the symbolic aspects of Québec's drive for greater recognition as a distinct society and nation with a distinct set of needs. Indeed, this weakness is also its strength since it allows other substantive issues to be addressed without opening old wounds unduly. Like formal constitutional reform, it is an elite driven process. It suffers from a democratic deficit. But to date, unlike on constitutional matters, the public has not been greatly troubled by this shortcoming. In any case, in terms of federation management, for the foreseeable future, non-constitutional reform is the only game in town.

References

Alberta, Government of 1999: *Government Empowers Albertans on Use of Notwithstanding Clause*, Edmonton.

Brock, Kathy 1991: "The Politics of Process," in: Douglas M. Brown (ed.), *Canada: The State of the Federation 1991*, Kingston: Institute of Intergovernmental Relations, 57-87.

Brun, Henri 1985: "The Charter of Rights and Freedoms as an Instrument of Social Development," in: Clare Beckton/Wayne Mackay (eds.), *The Courts and the Charter*, Toronto: University of Toronto Press, 1-33.

Cairns, Alan C. 1979: "Recent Federalist Constitutional Proposals: A Review Essay," in: *Canadian Public Policy* 5, 3, 348-365.

—— 1991: "Constitutional Change and the Three Equalities," in: Douglas M. Brown/Ron Watts (eds.), *Options for a New Canada*, Toronto: University of Toronto Press, 77-100.

—— 1992: *Charter versus Federalism. The Dilemmas of Constitutional Reform*, Montreal/Kingston: McGill-Queen's UP.

—— 1995: "The Embedded State: State-Society Relations in Canada," in: Douglas Williams (ed.), *Reconfigurations. Canadian Citizenship and Constitutional Change*, Toronto: McClelland & Stewart, 31-61.

——/Williams, Douglas E. (eds.) 1991: *Disruptions. Constitutional Struggles, from the Charter to Meech Lake*, Toronto: McClelland & Stewart.

Canada, Royal Commission on Dominion-Provincial Relations 1940: *Report of the Royal Commission on Dominion-Provincial Relations*, Ottawa: J.O. Patenaude I.S.O. printer to the King.

Canada, Special Joint Committee of the Senate and of the House of Commons on the Constitution of Canada 1972: *Final Report*, Ottawa: Queen's Printer.

Coleman, William D. 1984: *The Independence Movement in Québec, 1945-1980*, Toronto: University of Toronto Press.

De Montigny, Yves 1997: "The Impact (Real or Apprehended) of the Canadian Charter of Rights and Freedoms on the Legislative Authority of Québec," in: David Schneiderman/Kate Sutherland (eds.), *Charting the Consequences. The Impact of Charter Rights on Canadian Law and Politics*, Toronto: University of Toronto Press, 3-33.

Elections Canada 1997: *History of the Vote in Canada*, Ottawa: Canada Communication Group.

Gagnon, Alain-G./Montcalm, Mary Beth 1989: *Québec. Beyond the Quiet Revolution*, Scarborough: Nelson Canada.

Hiebert, Janet 1996: *Limiting Rights. The Dilemma of Judicial Review*, Montreal/Kingston: McGill-Queen's UP.

Hogg, Peter W. 1989: "Federalism Fights the Charter of Rights," in: David P. Shugarman/Reg Whitaker (eds.), *Federalism and Political Community. Essays in Honour of Donald Smiley*, Peterborough: Broadview Press, 249-266.

—— 1996: *Constitutional Law of Canada*, Toronto: Carswell.

Hurley, James Ross 1996: *Amending Canada's Constitution. History, Processes, Problems, and Prospects*, Ottawa: Canada Communication Group.

Knopff, Rainer/Morton, F.L. 1985: "Nation-Building and the Canadian Charter of Rights and Freedoms," in: Alan C. Cairns/Cynthia Williams (eds.), *Constitutionalism, Citizenship, and Society in Canada*, Toronto: University of Toronto Press, 133-182.

Laforest, Guy 1995: *Trudeau and the End of a Canadian Dream*, Montreal/Kingston: McGill-Queen's UP.

LaSelva, Samuel V. 1983: "Only in Canada: Reflections on the Charter's Notwithstanding Clause," in: *Dalhousie Review* 63, 383-397.

Lazar, Harvey (ed.) 1998: *Non-Constitutional Renewal* (Canada: The State of the Federation 1997), Kingston: Institute of Intergovernmental Relations.

Mandel, Michael 1994: *The Charter of Rights and the Legalization of Politics in Canada*, Toronto: Thompson Educational Publishing.

McRoberts, Kenneth 1997: *Misconceiving Canada*, Toronto: Oxford UP.

Morton, F.L. 1995: "The Effects of the Charter of Rights on Canadian Federalism," in: *Publius: The Journal of Federalism* 25, 3, 173-188.

—— 1996: "Canada's Judge Bork: Has the Counter-Revolution Begun?" in: *Constitutional Forum* 7, 4, 121-125.

——/Knopff, Rainer 1992: "The Supreme Court as the Vanguard of the Intelligentsia: The Charter Movement as Postmaterial Politics," in: Janet Ajzenstat (ed.), *Canadian Constitutionalism 1971-1991*, Ottawa: Canadian Study of Parliament Group, 57-80.

——/—— 2000: *The Charter Revolution and the Court Party*, Peterborough: Broadview Press.

Reesor, Bayard 1992: *The Canadian Constitution in Historical Perspective*, Scarborough: Prentice-Hall.

Rocher, François 1992: "Québec's Historical Agenda," in: Duncan Cameron/Miriam Catherine Smith (eds.), *Constitutional Politics*, Toronto: Lorimer, 23-36.

Russell, Peter 1983: "The Political Purposes of the Canadian Charter," in: *Canadian Bar Review* 61, 30-54.

—— 1993: *Constitutional Odyssey. Can Canadians Become a Sovereign People?* Toronto: University of Toronto Press.

Simeon, Richard 1990: "Why Did Meech Lake Fail?" in: Ronald L. Watts/Douglas M. Brown (eds.), *Canada: The State of the Federation 1990*, Kingston: Institute of Intergovernmental Relations, 15-40.

——/Robinson, Ian 1990: *State, Society and the Development of Canadian Federalism*, Toronto: University of Toronto Press.

Smiley, Donald V. 1972: *Canada in Question. Federalism in the Seventies*, Toronto: McGraw-Hill Ryerson.

—— 1987: *The Federal Condition in Canada*, Toronto: McGraw-Hill Ryerson.

Sniderman, Paul M./Fletcher, Joseph F. et al. 1996: *The Clash of Rights. Liberty, Equality, and Legitimacy in Pluralist Democracy*, New Haven: Yale UP.

Stein, Michael B. 1993: "Tensions in the Canadian Constitutional Process: Elite Negotiations, Referendums and Interest Group Consultations, 1980-1992," in: Ronald L. Watts/Douglas M. Brown (eds.), *Canada: The State of the Federation 1993*, Kingston: Institute of Intergovernmental Relations, 87-116.

Task Force on Canadian Unity 1979: *A Future Together. Observations and Recommendations*, Ottawa: Queen's Printer.

Trudeau, Pierre Elliott 1968a: "A Constitutional Declaration of Rights," in: *Federalism and the French Canadians*, Toronto: Macmillan, 52-60.

—— 1968b: "Québec and the Constitutional Problem," in: *Federalism and the French Canadians,* Toronto: Macmillan, 3-51.

3. Budgeting and Constitutional Politics

Regulation, Taxation or Inaction? Budgetary Politics, Institutional Reform and American "Judicialism"

Markus M. Müller

To the foreign observer, budgeting in the United States is a fascinating puzzle. Both the legislative and the executive branches of the federal government are not only substantially involved, but represent a confusing multitude of actors at work at different points in time, partly vested with veto powers. While executive predominance in many European countries, including Germany, is due both to the constitutional mode of assigning budgetary authority and to long-standing practice, the power of the United States President in budgetary affairs (which to call "predominance" one would certainly hesitate) is based on legislatively delegated authority and the institutional significance of an office whose public presence is particularly high. Accordingly, it is usually the President to set the budgetary agenda, leaving congressional committees, and all the heterogeneous interests represented therein, with the trouble to react to a document that shapes public expectation considerably. The kinds of collective action problems in Congress have often been discussed, both in theory and empirically. In sum, it is hardly surprising that the specific characteristics of the American political system as a whole create a quite unique budgetary process, which is nevertheless comparable to the German process with regard to the role of both the executive and the legislative branches.

However, there is another particularity from a German point of view; the history of federal budgeting in the United States seems largely a struggle for institutional improvement. Due to a constitutional provision, which – in accordance with the European tradition – grants budgetary authority to Congress, the distinct American system of "separated institutions sharing powers" had to learn to live with the ebb and flow of power between executive and legislative branches in budgetary policies. Such a constitutional arrangement might work as long as governmental tasks, income and outlays are relatively small and easily manageable. However, as soon as the scope of government activity grows, the system becomes increasingly dysfunctional. That is, the United States budget is a budget passed by Congress, which ultimately bears responsibility for it; but the legislative branch is certainly unable to draft a budget without knowing what and how the executive spends.

Until 1974, when Congress created the Congressional Budget Office (CBO) to deliver independent budgetary information and material necessary to draft a budget, legislators had to base their decision substantially on what was presented to them by the executive. The very mode of constitutional distribution of roles in the budgetary process (i.e., budget authority lies with Congress, but just like any other bill, the various acts the annual budget is incorporated in is subject to the presidential veto power) has generated a certain dichotomy between both branches, which often leads to even greater emphasis on the respective interests and political goals. And still, in a way, budgetary politics is a game between the executive and the legislative branches, both needing the other one to get their policies through. While this is challenging enough for any system of representative government, the extreme heterogeneity of Congress and the relative lack of party discipline when it comes to spending (interim phases of higher discipline tend to break down rather quickly) add yet another dimension of complexity to the problem.

Hardly surprising, American budgetary politics has been permanently accompanied by efforts to find a new balance between the branches (and their diverse actors) involved. Some might argue they were not successful, at least until the end of the 20th century. However, this history of institutional, quite often merely procedural, change in budgeting seems to have accelerated as the debt problem grew. Especially since the Gramm-Rudman-Hollings legislation in the mid-1980s, a range of institutional modifications has been added to a budget process whose complexity always seemed to be matchless.

This is, of course, not to argue that rising deficits represent an external challenge to budgeting. On the contrary, budgetary politics and its very institutional foundation in the U.S. polity have often been considered a major cause for the deficit problem, and rightly so. The logic of decision-making in Congress provides for both incentives to spend more and more money and disincentives to cover costs within the boundaries set by tax revenues: separate decisions on appropriations (spending) and taxation, diversification of the appropriation bill formulation in different committees, congressional rules of formal legislation (allowing for the need to decide on "packages"), the logic of behavior of congressmen and women, etc. Some of these features have been tackled, but others still prevail.

Politics has realized the dysfunctionalities built into the budgetary process. However, not all of them were directly provoked by the constitution. On the contrary, major institutional arrangements for decision-making within Congress, such as the appropriations committee system, are mere outcomes of budget process reform, which had already started in the 19th century.[1] Therefore, the constitution itself bears responsibility vis-à-vis budgetary

---

1 For an overview, see Müller 1997; Sturm/Müller 1999: 90-122.

dysfunctionalities only with regard to two aspects. First, the above-mentioned mode of assigning budgetary competence in principle (which, of course, stands in full accordance with the logic of the whole framework of a presidential system) and second, maybe even more importantly, underdetermining a political process whose impact on almost all policies cannot be overestimated.

I will not argue that reform efforts of Congress lie at the bottom of the problem. Rather, they have to be understood in their historical context. Some of them were inevitable, even from today's point of view. Such landmark events were the 1921 Budget Act, introducing the "presidential budget" as a kind of budgetary agenda for Congress to start from – this is the beginning of presidential power in budgeting based on a legislative act; the 1974 Budget and Impoundment Control Act, recapturing budgetary powers given away so easily in 1921 while putting the budgetary process in a strict time frame; maybe even the 1985 Gramm-Rudman-Hollings legislation, providing for an independently managed "across the board" cut automatism ("sequestration"), which was ruled out by the Supreme Court in 1986;[2] and several more incremental changes such as the PAYGO rule and other procedural barriers to tax-uncovered spending in the 1990s.

The latest of this series of attempts to improve the budgetary process has been the Line Item Veto Act of 1997, which again was ruled out by the Supreme Court in 1998. Congress does, however, not give up. In 1999, a new version of the (unconstitutional) Line Item Veto Act of 1997 was introduced in Congress and it remains to be seen how the courts will deal with this kind of "inventing around" the barriers set by the Supreme Court.

It seems all too easy to understand the history of American budgetary reform as one which is *solely* driven by "efficiency" concerns. Of course, the dysfunctionalities are obvious. Profits, i.e. spending specified to respective constituencies, are so to speak "privatized," while costs, i.e. deficits and interests to be paid thereon, are "socialized" and put off to an unknown future. The institutional flaws go, however, beyond this more general description of the problem, concerning almost all stages of the budgetary process. Since the 1974 watershed event of budgeting legislation – and maybe the 1985 semi-important sequestration idea –, institutional improvements have followed a piecemeal approach. I do not argue that the latter was totally insufficient. On the contrary, the easing of the budget problem in America in the late 1990s may be partly attributed to incremental procedural improvements – even though economic prosperity has made the larger contribution.

While institutional dysfunctionalities have been tackled – successfully to a certain extent –, it seems shortsighted to reduce one's understanding of budgetary reform to a mere remedy of several institutional illnesses. Rather,

2 *Bowsher v. Synar*, 478 U.S. 714 (1986).

budgeting has always confronted a major normative barrier: the widespread conviction that the federal government should neither spend nor interfere with people's life in whatever way. It is the "small government" doctrine which sharply distinguishes the normative background of central government in basically all European countries from the American case. While one must not generalize this distinct position (which certainly is rivaled by a more positive view of federal activity with regard to both social and economic issues), it plays a significant role in debating budget policies and institutional improvements. Several reform proposals, which, if they do not succeed in Congress, are often ignored in debating budget politics, display this important strand of, as I should say, "ideological budgeting."

First, there have been several attempts to add a Balanced Budget Amendment to the U.S. Constitution.[3] While efforts date back to Jefferson, the movement has gained speed in the 1990s, when a whole series of amendments were introduced in Congress. Although neither one made it through Congress, it seems rewarding to analyze their content. It reveals that the movement was less concerned with balancing spending and revenue than with keeping the spending side at a certain level, while outlawing both deficits and tax increases.[4] The Balanced Budget Amendment as a normative concept is a good example for "ideological budgeting" due also to another reason: while Gramm-Rudman-Hollings provided for an institutional cure, i.e., the automatic across-the-board cut, exercised by a fairly independent and neutral institution (the General Accounting Office), most Balanced Budget Amendment versions in the 1990s did not provide for any concrete approach to achieving the goal. It seems that their sponsors were less concerned with the details than with making a popular statement to the people.

Second, the 1990s also saw new interest in what has been called "regulatory budgeting."[5] The idea materialized (once more) in the Regulatory Accountability Act, proposed by Representative Lamar Smith, a Republican from Texas, brought into the 104th Congress.[6] It would have required the President to submit an annual regulatory budget to Congress, which estimates costs to be imposed by the various programs and regulatory agencies. Each year Congress would have had to approve the regulatory budget the same way it approves appropriations. The rationale behind this is that Congress and the executive branch would thus be pressured to reduce the regulatory burden. Notwithstanding the long list of problems involved in practice,[7] the very concept of regulatory budgeting is only superficially concerned with

3 For an overview of how the idea of balanced budgets evolved in America in the course of the centuries, see Savage 1990.

4 For details, see Müller 1997.

5 See, for instance, the special issue of *Policy Sciences* 31 (1998).

6 For an overview of respective reform proposals, see also Shanahan 1997.

7 See, for example, Meyers 1998.

efficiency. Rather, it reveals a substantial, structural doubt about the legitimacy of state action, except in cases of greater good for the sectors of economy and society involved. To put it differently, where government intends to shape economic or social outcomes which do not involve a calculable net benefit to the regulated, it is wrong. Governmental "visions" of what society or economy should be like are not welcome in this logic.

Therefore, I argue that reform proposals tackling budgeting and the budget process, including the wider context of alternative government action, should be considered with regard to both their ability to solve institutional flaws and their degree of ideological bias as to the extent of legitimate government activity. While I would consider the Balanced Budget Amendment proposals as well as the Regulatory Budgeting proposal as more ideologically grounded, the most recent attempt to grant the President a line item veto as well as the older idea of Gramm-Rudman-Hollings to add the sequestration procedure to the budget process seem to me more concerned with overcoming mere institutional problems, caused by the constitutional setting. Interestingly enough, the latter have both been ruled out by the Supreme Court, referring to a somewhat formalistic argumentation.

In *Bowsher v. Synar*, the Supreme Court ruled out sequestration, as it was vested in the General Accounting Office, an agent of Congress.[8] As sequestration is, however, a matter of "executing a law," the Court argued that it has to be performed by the executive branch. In the 1987 reformed Gramm-Rudman-Hollings Act, sequestration was transferred to the Office of Management and Budgeting, the central budgetary clearing-house of the President. Now, however, the "bad idea whose time has come" (sequestration) was transformed into a toothless tiger, because OMB is not an independent and politically neutral government agency. Of course, neutrality of contra-spending enforcement is not a sufficient prerequisite for budgetary discipline. And with regard to the 1987 reformed sequestration procedure, it may well be argued that both Congress and the President had already lost interest in a serious attempt to bring back the annual deficit in a tight time frame (of five years, as prescribed by the act). However, politics was never given a chance to experiment institutionally.[9]

The Line Item Veto Act of 1997 aimed at outsmarting the logic of congressional budget-making, too. It authorized the President to cancel parts of discretionary spending, any items of new direct spending or any limited tax benefit. Although the law provided for a congressional counter-instrument, the "disapproval bill," to prevent the President's cancellations to become effective, it is clear that in fact a two-thirds majority is required to stop the

8 For a critique of the decision, see Elliott 1987.

9 This is also in essence the criticism put forward by Elliott (1987), i.e., we do not know what could have been achieved had the Supreme Court affirmed the 1985 Gramm-Rudman-Hollings version.

President; after all, the disapproval bill is subject to the presentment clause of Art. I, § 7 of the constitution and hence, might be vetoed by the President. That means in turn that the line item veto is ultimately protected by the constitutional veto power of the President.

When the United States District Court for the District of Columbia held the Line Item Veto Act unconstitutional, it was feared that a new era of the "non-delegation doctrine" was about to come. As this point is indeed crucial for debating the line item veto, I shall shed some light on the context.

Congress had voluntarily passed on the line-item veto power to the President; however, the law may be repealed by any other act. Ultimately, if Congress does not like the way the law works, it can certainly stop the President, whose veto on a repeal of the act could be overridden by a two-thirds majority.[10] If this is so, the line-item veto authority, delegated by the legislative branch to the executive, is surely no more "dangerous" than any regulatory competence, transferred in numerous congressional laws to the executive. This in turn means that if Congress surpassed the borderline in the case of the line item veto, it had already strongly violated the rationale in the past. After all, Congress has widely used the means of de facto delegation of jurisdiction with regard to economic or social regulation. Sometimes, independent regulatory commissions are given enormous discretion vis-à-vis implementing regulatory policies, bound only by more or less broadly defined goals; sometimes the presidential administration is empowered. Delegation of originally legislative competence "by law" to executive offices, independent or not, has, in any case, been standing practice since the beginning of the 20th century at the latest. Why should this be constitutional and delegation of a rather specified budgetary power not? Therefore, it seems rather convincing that denying the constitutionality of the Line Item Veto Act implies a certain challenge to "delegation" in general, hence to the "regulatory state" in the United States as developed in the course of the past decades.

However, the Supreme Court's majority avoided any such reference in its fairly safe 6 to 3 vote, including the wider issue of "balance of powers."[11] Rather, it grounded its decision on the violation of the presentment clause. That is, the Court focused on the concrete cancellation undertaken by the President in the case at stake, rather than considering the Line Item Veto Act as an abstract legal entity. Again, the Court took a fairly formalistic road. The judicial branch seems unwilling to let Congress and President try out new ways of dealing with the problems caused by the very inability of the system to "form a government" as Cutler (1980) once claimed.

10 Whether this is possible in view of voters' opinion vis-à-vis the usage of the line item veto by the President is, of course, another question. But it is a political and not a constitutional issue.

11 See *Clinton v. City of New York, et al.*, 524 U.S. 417 (1998).

However, while large parts of the majority opinion as well as concurring and dissenting opinions are devoted to the formal issue of "standing," the dissenting opinions by Justices Scalia and Breyer, both delivered separately, are interesting for two reasons. First, as Scalia and Breyer argue, the issue at stake is not the presentment clause, but non-delegation. Both Justices hold that American history is full of instances of delegation, and that even a non-delegation doctrine, as pursued by the Court for a while, does not outlaw governmental interlocking. Justice Breyer seems more open to experimentation as he concludes his dissenting opinion:

"In sum, I recognize that the Act before us is novel. In a sense, it skirts a constitutional edge. But that edge has to do with means, not ends. The means chosen do not amount literally to the enactment, repeal, or amendment of a law. Nor, for that matter, do they amount literally to the 'line item veto' that the Act's title announces. Those means do not violate any basic Separation of Powers principle. They do not improperly shift the constitutionally foreseen balance of power from Congress to the President. Nor, since they comply with Separation of Powers principles, do they threaten the liberties of individual citizens. They represent an experiment that may, or may not, help representative government work better. The Constitution, in my view, authorizes Congress and the President to try novel methods in this way. Consequently, with respect, I dissent."[12]

Second, Breyer's opinion is worth reading for it might be understood as pointing to a remedy for designing a *constitutional* line item veto. He starts up with a description of the historical situation when the founding fathers wrote the constitution. At that time, Justice Breyer argues, Congress could substantially, if not formally, give the President the power to select among appropriations by embodying each in a separate bill, each one subject to a separate presidential veto. Senators Robb and Hollings, sponsoring a proposed Separate Enrollment and Line Item Veto Act in 1999, seem to have read this part. The idea behind the proposal, as introduced in the Senate in January 1999, seems to be that "spending items" should be disaggregated and treated as a separate bill (s. 4). By obligating House and Senate committees to report only sufficiently detailed "items," Robb and Holling's proposal lays the foundation for imitating Breyer's historical reference. If the law succeeds it will have the same effect as the 1997 Line Item Veto Act by applying procedure-centered, yet fairly uncontestable new means.

I think both Gramm-Rudman-Hollings and the 1997 Line Item Veto Act, including subsequent court rulings *and* congressional reactions, display a feature of American budgetary policy that is sharply distinguished from Germany. The judiciary in Germany has interfered in budgeting, yet mostly by mandating spending on certain issues or imposing (other) budgetary costs. For example, the German Federal Constitutional Court has ordered higher spending for families, referring to the "welfare state principle" in the German

12 *Clinton v. City of New York*, 524 U.S. 417 (1998); J. Breyer, dissenting, available at http://supct.law.cornell.edu/supct/html/97-1374.ZD.html.

Basic Law, and has also ruled out certain taxes, such as "property tax" (*Vermögensteuer*), as it is considered an instance of excessive taxation where income tax has already been applied.

Procedural or institutional issues in general are, however, not on the Court's agenda – due to obvious reasons; the budget process on the federal level in Germany follows a substantially different logic than in America. Moreover, where budgetary politics might be subject to litigation, opposition parties tend to hesitate to challenge a specific budget in court;[13] after all, the next election might bring the plaintiff to government. In that sense, leaving certain budgetary questions untouched by the Federal Constitutional Court saves discretion for both the parties in government and those waiting to get there.

In both countries, the budget process is highly determined by law, yet the United States system still leaves room for fundamental changes, such as the 1921 and 1974 Budget Reform Acts, Gramm-Rudman-Hollings in 1985 or the introduction of a line item veto. Maybe, Germany displays once more a higher degree of "legalism," sticking with the established rules and norms for the better or for the worse. The United States then, however, shows a considerably higher degree of "judicialism," where new budgetary rules and norms are very likely to reach the courts soon. Moreover, what is particularly characteristic about the two cases referred to here is the de facto judicial activism with regard to institutional adaptation to cure constitutional inefficiencies. Interestingly enough, a vote for or against the line item veto in the Supreme Court, for instance, did not always correlate with a presumed conservative or liberal attitude of the respective judge. Quite obviously, "social liberalism" has not only to be set apart from "economic liberalism," but also from "politico-institutional liberalism." The latter describes the degree to which judges are likely to let politics try out new institutional arrangements to overcome dysfunctionalities, caused or at least furthered by the very process of decision-making as set up by the constitution.

Nevertheless, as both Gramm-Rudman-Hollings and the Line Item Veto Act of 1997 illustrate, American politicians do not give up once the Court has spoken. Rather, if failed in the Court, proponents of reform stick with their project, often inventing around the Court's holding by institutional imagination. The latter seems impossible in Germany. Except for party finance, where the self-interest of political parties unleashes enormous creative power

---

13 A telling example is the challenge of one of the last budgets of the Social-Liberal Coalition before the 1982 *Wende*. The issue was to what extent the government is free to determine what a "situation of economic instability" is. This is relevant because only if this requirement, as laid down in a constitutional clause, is met, running a deficit in the federal budget is permitted. When the case came before the Court, the former complainant, the CDU party, was already in government. As the new government coalition referred to the above clause itself, it had little interest in a narrow, court-imposed definition.

to work around court restrictions, legislators tend to believe in the higher wisdom of the Constitutional Court. Maybe it takes the experience of about 200 years of constitutional court ruling for the legislative branch to develop a more mature attitude towards the judiciary.

References

Breyer, J. [1998]: Dissenting Opinion, at http://supct.law.cornell.edu/supct/html/97-1374.ZD.html.
Cutler, Lloyd N. 1980: "To Form a Government," in: *Foreign Affairs* 59, 1, 126-143.
Elliott, E. Donald 1987: "Regulating the Deficit after Bowsher v. Synar," in: *Yale Journal on Regulation* 4, 317-361.
Meyers, Roy T. 1998: "Regulating Budgeting: A Bad Idea Whose Time Has Come?" in: *Policy Sciences* 31, 371-385.
Müller, Markus M. 1997: *Haushaltsausgleich durch Verfassungspolitik? Die Diskussion um ein Balanced Budget Amendment in den USA*, Berlin: Logos.
Savage, James D. 1990: *Balanced Budgets and American Politics*, Ithaca/London: Cornell UP.
Shanahan, John 1997: "Regulating the Regulators," in: *Regulation* 20, 1.
Sturm, Roland/Müller, Markus M. 1999: *Public Deficits. A Comparative Study of Their Economic and Political Consequences in Britain, Canada, Germany and the United States*, London/New York: Longman.

Bowsher v. Synar, 478 U.S. 714 (1986).
Clinton v. City of New York, et al., 524 U.S. 417 (1998).

Canadian Federal Budgeting: Imaginative Responses and Troublesome Confusions

Allan Maslove

As any reader of Wildavsky knows, budgets and budgeting can be studied on many levels. In this paper, we focus on structures and process issues in Canadian government budgets particularly as they pertain to federal arrangements. The argument to be developed is that Canadian government budgets are in many ways quintessentially Canadian; they reflect the larger compromises struck within a government and within the federation, often in imaginative ways, and sometimes along the way they create confusion.

Canadian government budgeting is a balancing act. The budgeting process, as the budget itself, attempts to strike balances between political and economic goals, between communication and secrecy, between preserving stability and effecting change, and between recognizing the decentralized nature of the federation and promoting national objectives.

Among western industrialized countries, the Canadian federation is one of the most decentralized. This conclusion emerges, for example, when one examines the shares of revenues collected by or available to the central and provincial governments. Total provincial own revenues rose from 56% of federal revenues in 1965/66 to over 90% today. After transfers are taken into account, total provincial revenues have exceeded federal revenues since the mid-1970s.

This trend to decentralization was reflected in and facilitated by the federal-provincial fiscal arrangements, many of which developed during the same period. During the 1960s and 1970s especially, many of the modern components of this system were enacted, relating to both taxation and grants or transfer payments from the federal to the provincial governments.

Taxation

In the area of taxation, with one important exception, the federal government and the provinces have developed a highly harmonized system. The centerpiece is the set of Tax Collection Agreements signed by Ottawa and the provinces in the field of income taxation. The current system dates from 1962. While both levels of government levy personal and corporate income taxes, under the terms of the Agreements Ottawa collects personal income tax for nine of the ten provinces (as well as for itself) and corporate income tax for seven of the ten. In order to participate in the Agreements and have their taxes collected (at no charge) by the federal government, provinces agree to adopt the federal definition of the tax base, to abide by protocols for the interprovincial allocation of income, and to assess their taxes as percentages of the federal tax ("tax on tax" system).

The "tax on tax" model is about to be replaced with a "tax on base" system, in which each province would have the ability to determine its own rate schedule. This step which preserves the core of harmonization – a common income tax base and allocation measures for all jurisdictions – creates more discretionary room for both the provinces and the federal government. What the provinces gain is clear – the policy room that comes with the power to set unique tax rate schedules. The federal government is also liberated in that it is no longer constrained by taking account of the effects of its tax rate policy decisions on provincial budgets. While some might argue the federal government never concerned itself with such matters in any event, this decoupling (and extra measure of decentralization that it represents) is, at least, of political consequence.

This system results in efficiencies both narrowly and broadly defined. Administration and compliance costs are saved. Since Ottawa provides all the collection services (including audit and enforcement), provincial governments do not have to incur any administrative costs; on the compliance side, taxpayers can pay their taxes to both governments by filing one tax form rather than two. Similarly, withholding is simplified for employers. More broadly, and more importantly, efficiencies are gained through the harmonization that the collection agreements require. The harmonization of income taxes contributes to a more efficient operation of the national economy in that both interprovincial tax barriers and tax competition are limited. In particular the uncoordinated taxation of income that could otherwise occur, and which has occurred previously in Canada, is prevented.[1]

In other tax fields – excises (tobacco, alcohol, and motor fuels) and payroll taxes – both orders of government assess levies with little or no formal coordination, but with considerable informal coordination. But the one major tax field that both levels of government jointly occupy without harmonization is the general taxation of consumption.

---

1 It should be noted that even the provinces that are not part of the Tax Collection Agreements, Québec in the case of personal, and Québec, Ontario and Alberta in the case of corporate income taxation, have instituted regimes that very closely parallel the federal system.

The provinces have long been in the general sales tax field with taxes levied at the retail level on a wide range of goods (with some considerable variation across provinces) but on few if any services. In 1991 the federal government replaced a tax levied at the manufacturers' level on a narrow range of goods, with a Goods and Services Tax (GST) levied on most goods and services[2] on a value-added basis. As a result of the GST, both levels of government now tax final consumption, but the bases are not consistent, the operation of the taxes differs, and accounting procedures and reporting requirements differ, all of which greatly increase compliance costs. To illustrate, retailers can be faced with distinguishing among commodities that are taxed by both levels of government, by the federal government only, by the provincial government only, or not at all. Complications in the implementation of the GST itself further aggravate the situation. While the federal government, for political and economic reasons, would very much prefer one harmonized tax on the GST model, co-ordinating with the provinces has thus far been slow and difficult.[3]

The Federal Spending Power

It is on the expenditure side of the budget that the federal balances are most complex. A central underpinning of much of this structure is the doctrine of the federal spending power. The federal spending power is one of the more imaginative, and, especially in recent years, one of the more controversial, inventions of Canadian federalism. From one perspective it is an innovative and positive mechanism to address a national need that strengthens the federal system. From another it is an unwelcome federal intervention into the jurisdiction of the provinces that undermines the federal system.

The origins of the spending power lie in the original constitution of 1867. The Fathers of Confederation clearly set out to construct a centralized federation in which the federal government would be dominant and sufficiently strong (financially and jurisdictionally) to undertake the large scale investments and the regulatory measures required to build a national economy (see Winer/Maslove 1996; Boothe 1996). Thus, to the federal government they allocated the major economic development levers (as they were then perceived) and broad authority to levy taxes. The provincial governments were left with functions that were clearly local or regional in nature

---

2 Important categories of non-taxed items include food for home consumption, prescription medicines and medical devices, and rental housing.

3 Québec, somewhat ironically, was the first province to partially harmonize its sales tax with the GST. Since 1997 the federal GST is fully harmonized with three of the Atlantic provinces.

and which were, in nineteenth century Canada, of minor importance on the public agenda. These included the areas of health, social assistance and education, all of which are now major areas of public spending, but all of which were then activities largely undertaken by charities and churches with little state intervention or assistance.

In the first half of this century, the role and scope of the public sector began to change dramatically. The areas of government activity that began to grow most rapidly in fiscal terms were precisely those assigned to the provinces in the constitution. Demands for new and expanded public programs in health, education and social welfare grew rapidly. As governments responded to these demands two pressures began to emerge. On the one hand a vertical fiscal imbalance began to develop, with the provinces having the most rapidly growing expenditure responsibilities while the federal government held the keys to the most productive and growing revenue sources. A clearly perceived need to rebalance federal-provincial finances resulted.

Secondly, as these social fields became more prominent on the public agenda, there also developed a sense that there was a broader national interest at play that was not always clearly represented in provincial decisions. In the jargon of economics, there were externalities across provinces.

It was in this context that the federal spending power mechanism was developed to serve the interests of both orders of government. The provinces gain access to revenues well beyond what they could raise from their own sources and the federal government develops a presence in areas of important public concern that are under provincial jurisdiction.

The essence of the spending power is that while the federal government cannot regulate provincial government activities in their areas of jurisdiction, the federal Parliament has the power to authorize the spending of money whenever and however it wishes. The federal spending power thus involves federal payments to the provinces which deliver programs in their areas of jurisdiction that meet criteria established by the federal government. Historically, these arrangements have characterized social program areas such as health care and social welfare.

The result has been to create a federal system on the expenditure side of the budget which is somewhat more interrelated and complex than one would expect based on a reading of the written constitution. This spending power underlies much of the history of intergovernmental transfers which are discussed below.

Intergovernmental Transfers

One of the largest categories of spending in the federal budget is the grants or transfers made to the provinces under a number of programs. It is in the grants system where Canadian fiscal federalism has developed its most sophisticated and textured arrangements. Consequently, it is worth taking some time to trace their development and current state of play. It is also in this area where much of the current stress and confusion exist.

While transfer payments from the central to the provincial governments existed earlier, it is in the postwar period that these arrangements became major features of Canadian fiscal federalism. The formal rationales for these grants are primarily three. First, Canada is characterized by considerable variations in income, wealth and employment rates from region to region. While there is no compelling economic reason why these regional disparities are contained within provincial borders, over the years the provincial governments have emerged as the representatives of the regional economies, and as a result, the national policies to address these regional disparities have often been developed in the forum of federal-provincial arrangements.

Second, federal to provincial transfers have been instituted to address inter-regional (interprovincial) spillovers or externalities related to the delivery of public services by provincial governments, primarily in social policy areas. Most often, these arguments were expressed in terms of federal involvement in support of the national interest or in pursuit of national goals. The clear implication was that provincial governments, left to themselves, would design social programs that would in some aspects pursue provincial rather than national interests. For example, measures that inhibited the mobility of people between provinces would introduce inefficiencies into the labour market.

Third, as noted above, without fairly extensive transfers from the federal to the provincial levels, a problem of vertical fiscal imbalance would exist. While transfers are not the only way of addressing this problem (over the years there have been significant reallocations of taxing room from the federal to the provincial levels), they certainly have been important in the Canadian context. Without adjustments to fiscal structures, of which increasing transfers have been a major component, the provinces would clearly have been unable to meet the growing demands for public services in fields such as education and health.

While these formal rationales are relevant and important,[4] it is also interesting to note some of the political factors which fostered and indeed which were advanced by these developments. During World War II, "temporary" arrangements were arrived at to allow the federal government to increase its access to income tax revenues to meet the wartime emergency. The development of an extensive program of fiscal transfers to the provinces provided a rationale for the federal government to hang on to these revenue sources after the War rather than return them to the provinces. Further, transfer programs opened the door for the federal government to become involved in the growing areas of social policy which otherwise might have been the occasion for a major expansion of public programs from which the federal government would have been largely excluded. In the event, it was in this period that the doctrine of the federal spending power was most aggressively developed, thus permitting the federal government to maintain its relevance by playing a (sometimes leading) role in these growing areas of national importance. Finally, it is not coincidental that these arrangements emerged in an era before the provincial governments were as sophisticated and as assertive as they now are. It is highly unlikely that this extensive array of transfers and federal involvement would have developed if the provinces had been as protective of their jurisdictions as they have become over the past two decades.

Whatever explanation one prefers, it is clear that the system of intergovernmental grants was, for the most part, put in place in the postwar period of economic expansion. It was part of and facilitated the development of the programs of the welfare state. This fruitful period of social programming was very much a product of the strong economic growth of the time. It was a period of joint federal-provincial forging and financing of programs, though not without conflict (especially with respect to the development of Medicare) (see Perry 1989).

Several transfer programs emerged. In 1957, building on an earlier program of grants, the federal government first began to make formal fiscal equalization payments to the less well off provinces. In 1982, the principle of equalization was written into the constitution. The explicit purpose of this program is to redistribute regionally to the less well off provinces to "ensure that provincial governments have sufficient revenues to provide reasonably comparable levels of public services at reasonably comparable levels of taxation."[5] Over the years, there have been occasions when adjustments to equalization were required, most notably after the dramatic petroleum price increases of the 1970s significantly changed the interprovincial balance of revenues. But, unlike the transfer programs summarized below, the fiscal equalization program has been remarkably free of difficulty and is supported by both recipient and non-recipient provinces.

---

4 For example, arguments such as these are made quite explicitly in Trudeau 1969.

5 Constitution Act 1982, section 36 (2).

Several essential points about the fiscal equalization program should be noted. First, the program is one of unconditional cash transfers from the federal government to the recipient provinces. Second, the transfers are based on complex measures of fiscal capacity (involving 32 separate revenue sources) only; they do not depend on actual levels of taxation levied by the recipient provinces[6] nor on any differences that might exist in the per unit cost of delivery of services. Finally, the program equalizes below average provinces up to the average; it does not equalize down.

Also emerging out of earlier programs, in 1966 the Canada Assistance Plan (CAP) began, under which the federal government agreed to reimburse provincial governments for about 50% of their eligible expenditures on social welfare. To receive funds, the provincial governments were required to structure their social assistance programs to meet several conditions. These included: eligibility for assistance determined on the basis of need only, the prohibition of minimum residency requirements, and the establishment of an appeals process (Torjman 1994).

The CAP was one of the most directive of the federal initiatives with the provinces in that the transfer was both conditional and matching. In 1990, the federal government introduced legislation to restrain the growth of CAP payments to the three non-equalization receiving provinces: Ontario, Alberta and British Columbia. In the following years, the share of eligible social assistance payments reimbursed to these provinces fell markedly. Though CAP continued to function well in many respects, this restraint measure undermined the transfer program and contributed to its demise and replacement in 1996, thirty years after it began. But to pursue this story further, it is first necessary to sketch, in a little more detail, the history of the third major fiscal arrangement.

By the late 1960s, Canada had developed a system of comprehensive public hospital and medical insurance.[7] Health care is primarily under provincial jurisdiction in Canada; however through the conditional grant programs developed in the late 1950s and 1960s, the federal government paid essentially 50% of provincial costs on eligible hospital and medical care programs. By the mid-1970s the federal government was becoming increasingly concerned that a growing portion of its annual expenditures was tied up in health care grants to the provinces over which it had no effective budgetary control. High rates of inflation contributed to this expenditure growth pressure. At the same time, federal revenues were becoming less buoyant.

On the other side, provincial dissatisfaction with the existing arrangements mainly focused on the degree of federal intrusion into provincial affairs. In part this was a continuation of some original provincial opposition to

---

6 The equalization formula includes a measure of "average tax rate." A province may be in a position to affect its transfer indirectly if changes in its tax rate affect the national average.

7 This discussion draws on Maslove 1995.

Medicare; in part it reflected increased assertiveness on the part of provincial governments of their constitutional powers. The nature of the argument that was enunciated more explicitly was that the shared cost arrangements distorted provincial priorities, both between health care in general and other provincial areas of responsibility, and within the health care field between services that were subsidized by the federal program and those that were not.

Thus, mutual dissatisfaction with the status quo, though for quite different reasons, led to the federal-provincial negotiations that resulted in the Established Programs Financing (EPF) arrangements of 1977[8] which replaced the separate federal grant programs for hospital insurance, Medicare and post-secondary education. The federal EPF transfer to the provinces was composed of two parts. First, the federal government withdrew from a portion of the Personal and Corporate Income Tax, creating room for the provinces to raise their income tax rates. The tax transfer amounted to 13.5 Personal and one Corporate Income Tax points,[9] equalized according to the general equalization formula. The second portion, the cash transfer, was an equal per capita payment to each province. The two components each amounted to approximately 50% of the federal contributions to the three "established" programs in 1975/76. A federal cash payment for extended health care was added to the EPF cash transfer. The cash grant was to grow in future years in accordance with provincial population and GDP (three year moving average). The tax room taken over by the provinces would generate more revenue over time; it was expected that this growth would also approximate the growth rate of GDP. This arrangement was popularly referred to as "block funding."

The important changes incorporated in EPF were seen differently by the provinces and Ottawa, just as their dissatisfactions with the previous arrangements differed. From the federal perspective, the major innovation was that its cash grant would no longer be determined by provincial spending on health and education. Federal transfers, which were now tied to GNP growth, would henceforth increase roughly in step with federal revenues which were also closely related to economic growth. Moreover, the provinces would now have a stronger incentive to control costs in these programs because they were no longer spending "50-cent dollars."[10]

---

8 Formally, passed by Parliament as the Federal-Provincial Fiscal Arrangements and Established Programs Financing Act.

9 This amount included points previously transferred to the provinces with respect to post-secondary education and a revenue guarantee portion to protect the revenues of the provincial governments necessitated by the income tax reform of 1971.

10 This often repeated phrase overstated the actual situation in that the replaced grants were more closely tied to national average expenditures than they were to the expenditures within any one province. However, a large province could noticeably affect the national average through its own expenditure levels. The elimination of the "50-cent dollar" arrangement did appear to be consequential. There was a clear downward shift in the

From the provincial perspective, the meddling and conditions imposed by Ottawa were greatly diminished. Further, they were free to allocate the EPF funds according to their own priorities; the division of the EPF transfer into health and education components was purely a federal fiction.

Satisfaction with the new arrangement, at least on Ottawa's part, was short-lived. The tax room Ottawa had vacated in favour of the provinces did not generate as much revenue for them as predicted at the outset, and, as a result, under transitional arrangements Ottawa found itself providing larger cash transfers than anticipated. Further, the federal government was dissatisfied with the relatively little visibility[11] and credit it was receiving for the relatively large financial commitment to the program. For Ottawa, this was the downside of the block funding arrangement that broke the link between provincial spending on health care (and post-secondary education) and the size of the federal grant.

The principal argument that the federal government advanced publicly was somewhat different, however. This was the argument that the provinces had not lived up to the spirit of the EPF agreement, because, relative to the grant amounts, they did not maintain their spending levels in the notionally associated programs, particularly post-secondary education. In fact, the provinces were simply taking advantage of the increased flexibility EPF offered to adjust their spending priorities.

In 1982, when the EPF arrangement was renewed, the federal government sought to limit further its financial exposure through an alteration in the formula. This change, which to many observers first appeared as a technical adjustment without great significance, has proved to be – in combination with subsequent events – of great consequence. Rather than separate determinations of the tax point transfer and the cash transfer (the latter being an equal per capita amount for all provinces), the revised EPF was based on a single equal per capita entitlement. From this entitlement was subtracted the revenue generated by the original tax point transfer; the cash transfer equalled the remainder. Each province thus receives a different (per capita) amount in cash, depending on the amount of revenue it generates from the tax points.

The import of this change soon became apparent, as the federal government entered into a long period of expenditure restraint from which the EPF cash transfer did not escape. In 1983/84 and 1984/85, the growth escalator for the portion of the total entitlement the government notionally designated as being for post-secondary education was limited to 6% and 5% respec-

provincial health care spending trend lines after 1977 (Maslove: unpublished research results).

11 While "visibility" is difficult to measure, it was clear that federal officials felt that the government's perceived presence in the health care field suffered as a result of the move to block funding.

tively. In the May 1985 budget the escalator for the full EPF entitlement was reduced from the GDP growth rate to GDP minus two percentage points beginning in 1986/87. In the April 1989 budget the escalator was reduced by another percentage point beginning in 1990/91. In the budget of February 1990 the escalator was frozen for two years (1990/91 and 1991/92) and limited to GDP minus three thereafter. Ultimately this freeze was extended through to 1995/96.[12]

This succession of restraints and freezes applied to the total entitlement of each province. Therefore, when the (generally) growing revenues from the designated tax points were subtracted, the residual cash payment to the provinces declined each year. By 1995, most independent estimates suggested that shortly after the turn of the century the cash transfer would begin to disappear entirely, the precise year varying somewhat by province.

Why did this shrinking cash transfer matter? During this period, in 1984, the Canada Health Act was passed (replacing the Hospital Insurance and Diagnostic Services Act and the Medical Care Act) which enunciated five principles or criteria that provincial health systems must meet in order to receive the full EPF cash transfer. These are:

- accessibility – reasonable access to health care without financial or other barriers;
- comprehensiveness – all medically necessary services are covered;
- universality – all legal residents of a province (after three months residency) must be covered;
- portability – residents are entitled to coverage when temporarily absent from their province or when moving between provinces;
- public administration – health plans must be administered by an agency of the province on a non-profit basis.

To uphold the accessibility principle, the federal government had the authority to reduce the cash transfer to a province on a dollar-for-dollar basis for any amount that the province allowed physicians to bill their patients or that hospitals charged in the form of user fees for medical services. Unspecified authority also exists for the federal government to withhold cash for violations of the other CHA principles as well. The inconsistency between the CHA and the declining EPF cash was readily apparent. As the cash transfer dwindled, the power that Ottawa had to uphold[13] the terms of the Canada Health Act dwindled with it. At some point even before the cash transfer

12 The restraints and freezes were applied to the per capita entitlements. Therefore, the total entitlement continued to grow at the same rate as population growth, generally about one percent annually.

13 Enforcement in this context refers to the leverage Ottawa has by virtue of its spending power. The federal government has no direct constitutional authority to regulate provincial health care systems.

reached zero the amount involved would not have been sufficient to deter a province that wished to allow user fees or to take some other action counter to the CHA.[14]

The cuts listed above, the interprovincial inequities they created, and Ottawa's rapidly eroding political authority that resulted, prompted the federal government to announce in 1995 the creation of the Canada Health and Social Transfer (CHST) beginning in 1996/97. Initially the CHST combined the cash transfers under the EPF and CAP programs into one block grant. The immediate benefit to Ottawa was that it has more cash directly available to maintain its support of the Canada Health Act. A major short run problem was thereby solved. However, the CHST did not address other issues, perhaps the most important of which was the issue of interprovincial equity. In fact, the CHST simply lumped the CAP inequity and the EPF inequity together.

The cash transfer to the provinces under the CHST continued to decline until it was stabilized in 1998/99. The government scheduled increases in the grant for a five-year period beginning with the 1999/2000 fiscal year. The increase is also structured to move back towards equal per capita grants to the provinces, thereby partially addressing a major grievance of several provinces.

Fiscal Tensions

As this overview illustrates, over roughly the last decade and a half, the federal government unilaterally and repeatedly altered the structure of the grant programs and reduced the amounts transferred to the provinces. Beginning in the mid-1980s the federal government began to restrain the transfers payable under the Established Programs Financing Arrangements (EPF) relative to what the EPF formula required and relative to what the provinces anticipated. The EPF was the most important expression of the federal spending power; it was the largest such transfer program and was used to pursue federal goals in the field of health care. The manner in which this was done was essentially by adjusting the formula to produce the amount that the federal government, particularly the Department of Finance, was prepared to pay. In the process,

14 Recognizing the dilemma, in December 1999 Parliament passed legislation authorizing the federal government to withhold other money owed to a province when the so-called health component of the EPF cash transfer runs out or is no longer adequate. This measure has never become relevant, but if Ottawa ever resorts to this legislation, there is little doubt that its legality will be challenged by the provinces. Even if upheld in the courts, this measure would prove so damaging to federal-provincial relations in a broad range of fields that it is difficult to conceive it being viable.

not only were federal payments to the provinces restrained, but various inequities emerged in what the individual provinces received. During the same period the CAP program was also restrained. Ultimately the two were combined into the new CHST.

The series of restraint measures created further ambiguities in addition to those already inherent in the EPF program. While the existence of a transfer "formula" is meant to suggest stability and certainty, in fact the program was manipulated as frequently as any ordinary spending program as the federal government repeatedly adjusted the formula.

Perhaps the most serious consequence of this episode was that it undermined the moral and political authority of the federal government to be a legitimate participant in the provision of health care through establishing and maintaining national objectives. Even more unsettling, provincial governments and other critics began to argue that Ottawa should largely abandon all social policy fields, renounce the spending power and vacate further tax room in favour of the provincial governments. The provinces, argued the critics, were quite capable, given sufficient revenue-raising room, to run their own social services *and* to preserve national goals through interprovincial collaboration.

This change would represent a significant step towards further decentralization of the federation. This prospect must be viewed in the context of the ongoing contest with the sovereigntist movement in Québec, and the general preference for a smaller federal government expressed by small-c conservative parties. Towards the end of this period, the provinces had become quite strident in their arguments for federal withdrawal.

Not all forces are in the direction of greater decentralization, though. The Supreme Court has consistently supported a doctrine of an unfettered spending power, though the occasions when it has been at issue are infrequent. The most notable case in which the Court's views were expressed arose out of the restraint imposed on CAP by the federal government in 1990. The act of Parliament which authorized Ottawa to enter into cost-sharing agreements with the provinces was amended in 1990 to limit the growth of the total transfer to the three "have" provinces. The Government of British Columbia challenged the legislation and pursued its challenge to the Supreme Court. The Court upheld the validity of Ottawa's actions. It ruled that the Plan (and its financing formula) was an act of Parliament and as such could unilaterally be amended by Parliament. To hold otherwise would be to rule that the Plan as originally passed constrained future parliaments, and that would have been unconstitutional. The Court reaffirmed the authority of Parliament to legislate changes to cost-sharing programs and ruled that cutting expenditures in a shared-cost program, like the act of spending itself, did not constitute regulation of provinces in their areas of jurisdiction. Constitutionally, then, the federal spending power remains intact.

The recent (February 1999) conclusion of the Social Union Agreement marks an interesting development in this story. Signed by Ottawa and all the provinces except Québec, the Agreement constrains Ottawa's ability to introduce new social programs that directly involve the provinces as partners. However, before accepting this as an unambiguous step towards further decentralization, we should note that (notwithstanding a commitment to inform and consult) Ottawa's ability to introduce purely federal programs in social fields is not limited. Moreover, the Social Union Agreement represents a de facto acceptance by the nine signatory provinces of Ottawa's right to spend in areas of provincial jurisdiction. Thus, the federal spending power remains.

Another possible source of resistance to decentralizing and restricting federal budgetary action is the force, unfocussed as it often is, of public sentiment. While the arguments for decentralization, including the restriction of the spending power, are strongly expressed by many politicians, academics and media commentators, it is less clear that there is broad public support for the federal government's withdrawal. Further, now that Ottawa is entering a post-deficit period and seems to have renewed interest in social program spending, public support for a continuing federal presence in social policy is likely to become firmer.

Thus, there exists a measure of uncertainty and tension in one of the most important areas of federal budgeting. On the one hand, the invention of the spending power doctrine and the system of intergovernmental grants that has developed in Canada over several decades is an imaginative and creative response to fiscal and program challenges that have developed. On the other hand, aspects of the arrangements have been characterized by confusion and blurred lines of accountability. More recently, federal government actions have contributed to fundamental questions being raised about the future of federal budgetary involvement and the spending power. The next several years are likely to be characterized by further tension as the provincial governments continue to push for more unconditional resources and the federal government attempts to re-establish itself as a key player in social policy. Beyond saying that any return to conditional, cost-sharing formats is highly unlikely, the shape of federal-provincial fiscal arrangements and, therefore, the federal budget is difficult to predict.

References

Boothe, Paul (ed.) 1996: *Reforming Fiscal Federalism for Global Competition. A Canada-Australia Comparison*, Edmonton: University of Alberta Press.

Maslove, Allan M. 1995: "National Goals and the Federal Role in Health Care," in: *Canadian Health Action. Building on the Legacy*, vol. 4, Ottawa: National Forum on Health.

Perry, J. Harvey 1989: *A Fiscal History of Canada – The Postwar Years*, Toronto: Canadian Tax Foundation.

Torjman, Sherri 1994: "Is CAP in Need of Assistance?" in: Keith Banting/Ken Battle (eds.), *A New Social Vision for Canada?* Kingston: Queen's School of Policy Studies, 99-113.

Trudeau, Pierre E. 1969: "Federal-Provincial Grants and the Spending Power of Parliament," Ottawa: Government of Canada.

Winer, Stanley L./Maslove, Allan M. 1996: "Fiscal Federalism in Australia and Canada: A Brief Comparison of Constitutional Frameworks, Structural Features of Existing Fiscal Systems and Fiscal Institutions," in: Boothe (ed.), 45-85.

4. Minorities and Constitutional Politics

Race, Gender, Sexual Orientation – Minorities and the Supreme Court

Michael Dreyer

When the Supreme Court Justices returned to their marble tower after the summer recess in order to open the term 1999/2000, they were greeted not only by a new docket, but also by a Tom Toles cartoon which depicted them on the bench, wearing not their accustomed black robes, but instead white, Klan-like hoods. They were probably less than thrilled by the unfriendly reference to their recent decisions regarding minority rights and their striking down electoral districts with majorities of minority voters.[1] Unfair as it may seem, there is little doubt that the fate of minorities at the Supreme Court has changed quite a bit over the course of the Rehnquist years, especially during the 90s. This paper will take a closer look at some of these changes, and at the preceding years as well. The main focus will be on the Supreme Court, but the other branches of government and their contribution to constitutional reform will be looked at as well, at least in passing. First, however, we have to have a look at the minorities in question.

The definition of minorities is one of the few areas with a broad agreement that transcends the boundaries of disciplines. Social science and international law basically take the same approach with regard to definitions. The relevant portion of the International Covenant on Civil and Political Rights of 1966 states in Art. 26 that "the law shall prohibit any discrimination and guarantee to all persons equal and effective protection against discrimination on any ground such as race, colour, sex, language, religion, political or other opinion, national or social origin, property, birth or other status."[2] At the same time Arnold Rose wrote in the *International Encyclopedia of the Social Sciences* that a minority is "a group of people – differentiated from others in the same society by race, nationality, religion or language – who [...] think of themselves as a differentiated group."[3]

---

1 It would have been even more devastating (and unfair) if Toles had incorporated the current ideological division of the Supreme Court by just depicting the five Justices which are a reliable conservative majority with the infamous outfits.

2 The Covenant's text can be found, inter alia, in Sohn 1986.

3 Rose 1968: 365. For a more contemporary, but substantially identical definition see Laponce 1991.

These definitions take care to add an aspect of social constructivism and of voluntarism to the idea of "minority." You are rarely "just" born into a minority, it takes a psychological effort as well to actively belong to a particular minority. This aspect of voluntarism at the same time points to the fact that minorities do not necessarily have to be a minority in numbers. In fact, even a majority in numbers might just as well become a sociological minority if a dominant culture or group prevents their full participation in society by some legal or political or social devices. Case in point for this are women, who form a majority of the population in most countries, without having achieved legal equality, let alone actual equality, in quite a few societies – providing a classic case of a dominant group versus a less privileged one.

The United States, of course, is the quintessential society of minorities. From its very beginning it has seen mass immigration of people from as diverse a cultural, ethnic, religious, and racial background as could possibly be fathomed. While most of these immigrants actually chose to come to a new world of hope and opportunity, a significant number of people were forcefully imported under less promising circumstances. The most enduring "American dilemma,"[4] the ongoing divide between black and white Americans, stems from these beginnings.

While the travails of the enslaved blacks constitute, of course, the most egregious breach of the American promise of freedom and equality, not all minorities were welcomed with Jeffersonian splendor. A history of immigration in the United States displays all types of reaction, welcome and rejection, Miss Liberty and Know-Nothings, integration and separation and oppression.

Separatism does not always originate with the dominant culture. Time and again minority groups have found it necessary to assert their uniqueness by severing ties with the dominant culture as far as possible. But separatists, as a rule, do not tend to look for civil rights via the political processes they have shunned.

Instead, it is minorities looking for equality and integration which appeal to the political and even more, given their minority status, to the judicial process in their pursuits. "Equality" is an elusive term, in the realm of constitutional law no less than in political philosophy. In a narrow sense it can point to legal, formal equality, as the words of the equal protection clause of the 14th Amendment seem to indicate. In a broader sense it means something approaching real equality, somehow along the lines drawn by John Rawls with his second principle of Justice in his landmark *Theory of Justice* (1971: 65 and passim).

This paper will take a closer look at three American minorities, namely, black Americans, women, and gays and lesbians. These three groups are

---

4 Of course, a lot has changed since Gunnar Myrdal's (1944) classic *An American Dilemma: The Negro Problem and Modern Democracy*. But the basic dilemma has remained.

different from each other in outlook, history, composition, and in the form of oppression they had to endure. One might assume, therefore, that they might have looked for different remedies for their ailments, and that different paths may have led them to that goal. At the same time, these groups can be reasonably well defined against the rest of society. They all live under the same set of constitutional rules – which is not the case with Native Americans, whose highly complicated and diverse legal situation must lead to their exclusion from consideration in this paper. The same conclusion has to be drawn with regard to another minority group which usually plays a major role in research projects, namely, religious minorities. There is no longer (if indeed there ever was) a dominant religious group among the American denominations. The Jeffersonian "wall of separation" in the First Amendment interpretation of the Supreme Court adds to this. With regard to the three minorities in question, I will propose ten theses, which shall be discussed separately.

Thesis 1: There is a close relationship between societal change and legal equality, meaning the end of legal discrimination, for any minority. Legal and constitutional change, achieved via Congress or via the courts, can influence the views of society at large. A changing society, on the other hand, can result in forcing the branches of government into action.

The first thesis does not claim to present anything new and original. The relationship between the political process and society is fairly obvious in any democratic society, let alone in the United States. At the same time, however, it is worth keeping in mind that this relationship actually exists and shapes the situation for any minority looking for some legal and attitudinal change. Even change sought through the courts in the long run needs some backup from society in order to become a reality of everyday life. On the other hand, if the courts refuse to tackle change for which society is ripe, then there will be other venues. This will work differently for different minorities, as we shall subsequently see. The closer look at the three selected minorities shall begin with the first to seek redress from the judicial process.

Thesis 2: The road to legal equality for blacks had to go through the Supreme Court. Neither a Congress dominated by long-serving Southern Democrats nor a basically indifferent Eisenhower administration were willing or able to deliver the kind of constitutional change required.

There is no doubt that the 1954 decision of *Brown v. Board of Education* was a seminal decision, a landmark in every way. This is not just hindsight, but the sentiment of the contemporaries as well.[5] Perhaps the clearest, if also

---

5 A comprehensive account of the decision and the surrounding controversy can be found in Kluger 1975. For the development up to *Brown* see Howard 1999, especially chapter 8.

least charitable expression of that sentiment was given by Justice Felix Frankfurter, when he remarked upon the news of Chief Justice Fred Vinson's death that this was his first indication that there is a God (see Schwartz 1993: 286). Vinson's death opened the path to Earl Warren's appointment as the new Chief Justice, to a re-argument of the case, and finally to a unanimous Supreme Court under the guidance of its master negotiator Warren, whose performance surpassed the lackluster Vinson's immediately. During his stewardship the Court's deliberations on the *Brown* case had produced anything but unanimity. It was only Warren's persuasive power which led the reluctant Justices to join the bandwagon.

While the sweeping and encompassing language of *Brown* as well as its unanimity did come as a surprise, it was by no means an abrupt and total departure from previous holdings as it may seem from today's vintage point. It was, rather, a bold leap forward on a path which had already been entered upon by the Court and by the previous administrations some time ago. In 1941 President Franklin Delano Roosevelt ended racial discrimination with regard to federal employment, and in 1948 his successor, Harry S. Truman, not only boldly integrated the army, but even based his reelection effort on a civil rights platform, which led to a third party candidate with the backing of Southern Democrats.[6] But these were federal actions, which in and by themselves had little bearing on the states where the bulk of discrimination, legal and otherwise, occurred.

The Supreme Court slowly tackled this problem, beginning in 1938 with the arguably most famous footnote in its history, "Footnote 4" by Justice (and soon to be Chief Justice) Harlan Fiske Stone in an unrelated case.[7] Justice Stone hinted that race might be a "suspect class" under the 14th Amendment's equal protection clause, which would then apply to the states as well. This was tantamount to inviting further lawsuits in order to check the Court's willingness to travel that path further along the line. These lawsuits came along rapidly, and the Court began applying the *Plessy* doctrine of "separate, but equal" with a growing emphasis on "equal." While none of these decisions went all the way to directly overturn *Plessy*, taken together they nevertheless pointed that way. Table 1 demonstrates the narrowing of "separateness" under *Plessy*. It also shows a pattern which can be seen both before and after *Brown*: the Court tried hard to maintain a united front with opinions

6 The integration order was Executive Order 9981. Truman was somewhat forced to adopt the civil rights platform by then Minneapolis mayor Hubert H. Humphrey at the Democratic convention. But he wholeheartedly embraced it afterwards. Cf. Hamby 1995: 4481.

7 *United States v. Carolene Products Co.*, 304 U.S. 144 (1938), Footnote 4. For Europeans without the benefit of an extensive library, easy access to current and most historical decisions is provided by several excellent websites; e.g. supct.law.cornell.edu/supct/ or www.findlaw.com/casecode/supreme.html.

Table 1: Segregation Cases

Case	Citation	Vote	Opinion	Content
Plessy v. Ferguson	163 U.S. 537 (1896)	7:1	Brown	Establishes "separate but equal" doctrine
Missouri ex rel. Gaines v. Canada	305 U.S. 337 (1938)	6:2	Hughes	Opens white law school in absence of a black school
Smith v. Allwright	321 U.S. 649 (1944)	8:1	Reed	Voids "white primary" by Southern Democrats
Morgan v. Virginia	328 U.S. 373 (1946)	7:1	Reed	Voids segregation in interstate transportation
Sipuel v. Board of Regents	332 U.S. 631 (1948)	per curiam	-	Opens white law school in absence of a black school
Shelley v. Kraemer	334 U.S. 1 (1948)	6:0	Vinson	Racially restrictive covenants are not enforceble
Sweatt v. Painter	339 U.S. 629 (1950)	9:0	Vinson	"Separate but equal" unattainable in higher education
McLaurin v. Oklahoma State Regents for Higher Education	339 U.S. 637 (1950)	9:0	Vinson	Voids segregation of blacks admitted to grad schools
Terry v. Adams	345 U.S. 461 (1953)	8:1	Black	Voids "white primaries" conducted by "private" club
Brown v. Board of Education I	347 U.S. 483 (1954)	9:0	Warren	Overrules *Plessy* for primary education (merits)
Bolling v. Sharpe	347 U.S. 500 (1954)	9:0	Warren	Overrules *Plessy* for primary education in D.C.
Brown v. Board of Education II	349 U.S. 294 (1955)	9:0	Warren	Implements Brown I "with all deliberate speed" (relief)
Gayle v. Browder	352 U.S. 903 (1956)	per curiam	-	Voids segregation in buses (*Plessy* overruled)
Cooper v. Aaron	358 U.S. 1 (1958)	9:0	Warren	Immediate desegregation of Little Rock High School
Burton v. Wilmington Parking Authority	365 U.S. 715 (1961)	6:3	Clark	Voids segregation in private restaurant in public building
Johnson v. Virginia	373 U.S. 61 (1963)	per curiam	-	Voids segregation in public buildings
Watson v. Memphis	373 U.S. 526 (1963)	9:0	Goldberg	Voids segregation in public recreational areas
Heart of Atlanta Motel v. United States	379 U.S. 241 (1964)	9:0	Clark	Commerce Clause covers Civil Rights Act of 1964
Loving v. Virginia	388 U.S. 1 (1967)	9:0	Warren	Voids law prohibiting interracial marriage
Swann v. Charlotte-Mecklenburg Board of Education	402 U.S. 1 (1971)	9:0	Burger	Busing as tool for desegregation

Note: Decisions "per curiam" are delivered by the Court without an authored opinion.

written either by the Chief Justice or by a Justice who could boast Southern roots.[8]

Brown had an enormous symbolic meaning, but for the time being little else. It was loaded with shortcomings which sprang from three different sources. The first of these was homegrown. The Court had divided the decision on the merits (*Brown* I) from the decision on relief (*Brown* II). While the first was as clear as could be, the latter proved to be quite murky. The formula of *Brown* II, "with all deliberate speed," could be understood to allow a generous time frame for implementation. While the Supreme Court undoubtedly expected this time frame to be met pretty soon, Southern politicians thought more along the lines of the second coming of Christ. The second problem was the less than enthusiastic enforcement of *Brown* and the rapidly succeeding string of decisions by the Eisenhower administration. The picture of Little Rock 1957, with the National Guard enforcing the law of the land, is highly misleading. This was an isolated occasion, which cannot be taken to show the administration's commitment. In fact, President Eisenhower did not use the resources of his office to encourage Southern compliance with *Brown* and the subsequent decisions. The highly critical remarks both from Chief Justice Warren[9] and from the President's predecessor in that office[10] show an uncommon level of anger and frustration at the executive's inactivity. The third problem was, of course, Southern resistance to the decision. Most states decided to fight *Brown* all the way, and in view of a complacent federal administration, they were remarkably successful at that. A decade after *Brown*, integration in Southern schools had only marginally increased. It was only the Kennedy and especially the Johnson administration's determination which changed that picture. Integration was on a rise only in the 1960s, despite the Supreme Court's efforts a full decade before that.

---

8 The idea behind this strategy met with little success. The South did not react any more friendly to anti-segregation opinions by Justices from the South.

9 "With his popularity, if Eisenhower had said that black children were still being discriminated against long after the adoption of the Thirteenth, Fourteenth, and Fifteenth Amendments, that the Supreme Court of the land had now declared it unconstitutional to continue such cruel practices, and that it should be the duty of every good citizen to help rectify more than eighty years of wrongdoing by honoring that decision – if he had said something to this effect, we would have been relieved, in my opinion, of many of the racial problems which have continued to plague us. But he never even stated that he thought the decision was right until after he had left the White House." (Warren 1977: 291)

10 "If you just give people a chance to be decent, they will be. If the fella that succeeded me had just given people a little leadership, there wouldn't have been all that difficulty over desegregating the schools, but he didn't do it. He didn't use the powers of the office of the President to uphold a ruling of the Supreme Court of the United States, and I never did understand that" (Miller 1974: 278). Truman's language is earthier, but the sentiment is the same.

The Justices' commitment remained strong after the *Brown* decision. Subsequent decisions convey a growing sense of urgency (and disappointment), and in *Cooper v. Aaron* the Court took the unprecedented step of having its unanimous decision signed not only by its author, once again the Chief Justice, but by all nine Justices. It is hard to think of a more dramatic way for the Court to convey its order that integration must come, and that it must come *immediately*.

On the other hand, however, the story of segregation cases of the 1950s provides one of the best illustrations for Alexander Hamilton's famous dictum in Federalist # 78 that the Supreme Court commands neither the sword nor the purse, and that it is thus dependent on the cooperation of the political branches of government. This cooperation was not forthcoming for a long time after *Brown*.

In any case, all the Court could grant was the constitutional rejection of legal barriers to race integration. This is not equality in a meaningful Rawlsian sense of justice. Relief had to be sought elsewhere, and this leads to the next thesis.

Thesis 3: The Supreme Court could provide legal equality, but nothing coming close to really equal chances. For this the President and Congress had to step in, and in the 1960s they finally did exactly this by establishing affirmative action programs (EEOC 1961) and enacting laws (CRA 1964, VRA 1965).

In 1961 President Kennedy chose the highly symbolic act to address racial inequality in the very first Executive Order he signed as the newly inaugurated President. EO 10952 established the Equal Employment Opportunity Commission (EEOC) and thus committed the administration to affirmative action. President Kennedy, however, was less successful in persuading Congress to join forces with him. An unholy alliance of Southern Democrats and Republicans wielded enough power, assisted by the seniority system, to render the administration's efforts moot. It did not help that the young President was not the most skillful negotiator when it came to dealing with Congress.

All of this changed when the former Senate Majority Leader, Lyndon B. Johnson, became President. Making good use of his connections to the hill he cajoled Congress into passing the Civil Rights Act (1964), and after his triumphant election in 1964, also the Voting Rights Act (1965). In that same year Executive Order 11246 made the Labor Department oversee the whole variety of affirmative action programs.

Starting in the 1960s, one can depict the movement with regard to affirmative action as sort of a curve. After all sorts of programs were started in the 1960s, they reached their high point in the 1970s, with President Nixon's "Philadelphia Plan" of 1970 going as far as prescribing numerical goals and a timetable for racial integration. In 1972 the EEOA was founded with the intent to vigorously enforce these programs. The end of that decade, however, also saw the first genuine backlash for affirmative action, when the Supreme Court in its *Bakke* decision upheld the claim of a white man, who alleged reverse discrimination under the 14th Amendment and under the CRA of 1964. The 1980s ended, with the Reagan administration, all executive support of affirmative action, and the 1990s effectively ended most of these programs, when the Supreme Court required a "strict scrutiny" test for them. For all practical purposes, "strict scrutiny" means that the government will lose its case. The levels of scrutiny can be demonstrated most easily by a table.

Table 2: Levels of Scrutiny

Level	Constitutional test	Burden of proof	Classes
Strict scrutiny	"Closely" related to a "compelling" governmental interest ("least intrusive" means of regulation)	Legislation is presumed unconstitutional unless government shows otherwise	Race, religion, regulation of aliens ("suspect class")
Heightened (intermediate) scrutiny	"Substantially" related to an "important" governmental interest	No presumptions	Gender, illegitimacy
Ordinary scrutiny	"Reasonably" related to a "legitimate" governmental interest	Legislation is presumed constitutional unless plaintiff shows otherwise	Wealth, age, disabilities, sexual orientation

An important role in this was played by Clarence Thomas, first as the Reagan appointed chairman of the EEOC, since 1991 as the youngest Supreme Court Justice in a long time. In his administrative position he directed public policy (and public funds) away from affirmative action, in his judicial role he could find these programs outright unconstitutional. Basically the same curve, although a bit less symmetrical, can be observed in another area, which leads to thesis 4.

Thesis 4: Voting rights and the apportionment of districts are closely related in a non-proportional electoral system. The Supreme Court enforced equality in the 1960s, hesitated about race-conscious apportionment in the 1970s and 1980s, and struck down these districts in the 1990s, thus returning to supposedly colorblind equality.

The Supreme Court started to tackle black voting rights cases almost simultaneously with the segregation cases. As early as the 1940s and 1950s the Supreme Court struck down repeatedly all forms of "white only" elections, which were prevalent throughout the South – usually not just on a factual basis, but even legally. The 1960s brought the equal apportionment cases, which opened the path to voting equality for all Americans, without any special focus on black voters. The unconstitutionality of anti-black gerry-

Table 3: Affirmative Action Cases

Case	Citation	Vote	Opinion	Content
Regents of University of California v. Bakke	438 U.S. 265 (1978)	5:4	Powell	Strikes down med school set-asides, upholds affirmative action
United Steelworkers of America v. Weber	443 U.S. 193 (1979)	5:2	Brennan	Upholds private (corporate) affirmative action plan
Fullilove v. Klutznick	448 U.S. 448 (1980)	6:3	Burger	Upholds minority set-aside in federal public works program (ISc)
Wygant v. Jackson Board of Education	476 U.S. 267 (1986)	5:4	Powell	Strikes down modification of seniority for teachers (SSc)
Local 28 of Sheet Metal Workers ... v. EEOC	478 U.S. 421 (1986)	6:3	Brennan	Upholds quotas as remedies for past discrimination
Richmond v. J.A. Croson Co.	488 U.S. 469 (1989)	6:3	O'Connor	Overrules *Fullilove* for states. First application of SSc
Metro Broadcasting, Inc. v. FCC	497 U.S. 597 (1990)	5:4	Brennan	Upholds federal preference of minority owned station (Isc)
Adarand Constructors, Inc. v. Pena	515 U.S. 200 (1995)	5:4	O'Connor	SSc required for all racial classifications

Note: Osc: ordinary scrutiny; ISc: intermediate (heightened) scrutiny; SSc: strict scrutiny.

mandering and the corresponding constitutionality of pro-black and pro-minority, race-conscious districting provided the focal points of the 1970s. Plaintiffs had to show "discriminatory intent" to get their way in court. When the Supreme Court changed this to mere "discriminatory effect" in the 1980s, the high mark was reached – and the backlash came swiftly and completely. Under the leadership of Justice O'Connor the Court has applied its strict-scrutiny test to *all* race-conscious districting throughout the 1990s, consistently with the same 5:4 majority of Justices.

These cases have undone the political interpretation of the amended Voting Rights Act of 1982, which was a strange alliance of black Democrats and the Bush administration, calling for the establishment of minority-majority districts.[11] Both groups benefitted from this approach for different reasons: black politicians cherished the prospect of safe districts, while conservative Republicans delighted in the white (and presumably less Democratic) districts surrounding and outnumbering the pockets of minority strength.

In the light of these interests it is not quite clear whether the effects of the recent Supreme Court decisions will be as conservative as most observers

11 This policy has been questioned by some black academics. Cf. Thernstrom 1987; Guinier 1994.

Table 4: Voting Rights (Redistricting) Cases

Case	Citation	Vote	Opinion	Content
Colegrove v. Green	328 U.S. 549 (1946)	4:3	Frankfurter	No involvement in apportionment ("political thicket")
Gomillion v. Lightfoot	364 U.S. 339 (1960)	9:0	Frankfurter	Strikes down racial gerrymandering to exclude blacks
Baker v. Carr	369 U.S. 186 (1962)	6:2	Brennan	Overrules Colegrove, orders reapportionment
Reynolds v. Sims	377 U.S. 533 (1964)	8:1	Warren	"One person, one vote"
Wright v. Rockefeller	376 U.S. 52 (1964)	7:2	Black	Court does not intervene against racial gerrymandering, concentrating black voters in one district
Allen v. State Board of Elections	393 U.S. 544 (1969)	5:4	Warren	"Voting" (VRA 1965) can include new districting lines
United Jewish Organizations of Williamsburgh v. Carey	430 U.S. 144 (1977)	7:1	White	Upholds pro-black racial quota in reapportionment.
City of Mobile v. Bolden	446 U.S. 55 (1980)	6:3	Stewart	Upholds at-large election with discriminatory effect, but not intent
Rogers v. Lodge	458 U.S. 613 (1982)	6:3	White	Strikes down at-large election due to discriminatory intent
Thornburg v. Gingles	478 U.S. 30 (1986)	(9:0)	Brennan	Strikes down multi-member district due to discrim. effect; requires majority-minority districts (= VRA 1982)
Shaw v. Reno	509 U.S. 630 (1993)	5:4	O'Connor	Strikes down "bizarre" districts and racial gerrymandering (SSc)
Miller v. Johnson	515 U.S. 900 (1995)	5:4	Kennedy	Strikes down racial gerrymandering in compact district (SSc)
Lawyer v. Department of Justice	No. 95-2024 (1997)	5:4	Souter	Upholds majority-black district; race was not deciding factor
Hunt v. Cromartie	No. 98-85 (1999)	9:0	Thomas	Strikes down summary disposition of supposed racial districting by District Court

Note: Osc: ordinary scrutiny; ISc: intermediate (heightened) scrutiny; SSc: strict scrutiny. VRA: Voting Rights Act of 1965; amended 1975 and 1982 (overruling *Bolden*).

assumed.[12] Granted, the reliable "color-blind" 5:4 majority is composed entirely of conservative Justices. But the judicial outcomes of these rulings still remain to be seen, as future cases will further test the evolving nature of the Court's jurisprudence.[13] It is clearly going over the line to assert, as some commentators have done, that the strict-scrutiny test for race conscious districting amounts to the return of Jim Crow laws. But it is a marked shift from the decisions the Court has quite consistently taken during the four preceding decades.

While the Supreme Court historically has been the driving branch of government with regard to black equality, this has not been uniformly the case when one takes a closer look at other groups who claimed discrimination. In fact, its role in the black civil rights struggle becomes quite exceptional when regarded against that backdrop.

Thesis 5: Contrary to blacks, women took a very different path to change and equality. First society developed a new look at work, families, and gender relations. Then Congress included women in its non-discriminatory legislation in the 1960s, and only then the Supreme Court came around and departed from its dismal historical record with regard to gender equality. If anything, the Supreme Court provided a roadblock for women's rights for almost a century.

The turning point for Supreme Court protection of gender equality is the case of *Reed v. Reed* in 1971. Before that year "the Supreme Court never met a gender distinction it did not like" (Seymour 1998: 67). The table demonstrates this fact.

It is rather a series of legislative activities which instead paved the way to legal gender equality. Starting with the Equal Pay Act of 1963 and the inclusion of gender discrimination in the CRA protection of 1964, Congress passed a multitude of laws aiming in that direction. This includes the proposed, but ultimately failed Equal Rights Amendment to the constitution, which was passed by Congress with the support of President Nixon in 1972, as well as the 1974 Equal Credit Opportunity Act and the 1980 Science and Engineering Equal Opportunities Act. Accompanying these laws was the successful emergence of an organized women's movement. 1966 saw the founding of NOW, the National Organization of Women, as part of the 1960s new social movements. This seems to be a rather late date for an organization

---

12 E.g. "A Dinosaur Ruling," *New York Times* (6/30/1993), which criticizes *Shaw v. Reno*. A sharp "mainstream" liberal critique of the Court's agenda can be found in Rosen 1996.

13 The docket for the term 1999/2000 contained the case of *Rice v. Cayetano* (No. 98-818), which tested voting restrictions for non-native Hawaiians in certain elections; cf. Greenhouse 1999. The decision came down with an unexpectedly broad 7:2 majority that was based on Fifteenth Amendment arguments and struck down the restrictions; cf. Greenhouse 2000.

Table 5: Gender Cases

Case	Citation	Vote	Opinion	Content
Bradwell v. Illinois	83 U.S. (16 Wall.) 162 (1872)	8:1	Miller	Access to Illinois bar denied for woman
Minor v. Happersett	88 U.S. (21 Wall.) 162 (1874)	9:0	Waite	14th Am. does not confer the right to vote to women
Muller v. Oregon	208 U.S. 412 (1908)	9:0	Brewer	10 h. max. work day due to inferior strength of women upheld
Adkins v. Children's Hospital	261 U.S. 525 (1923)	5:3	Sutherland	Strikes down minimum wage for women, due to 19th Am.
Goesart v. Cleary	335 U.S. 464 (1948)	5:3	Frankfurter	Upholds restrictions on female bartenders
Hoyt v. Florida	368 U.S. 57 (1961)	9:0	Harlan	All-male jury and gender specific jury selection do not deny equal protection
Reed v. Reed	404 U.S. 71 (1971)	7:0	Burger	Ends gender discrimination in estate administration (Osc)
Frontiero v. Richardson	411 U.S. 677 (1973)	8:1	Brennan	Ends difference in benefits for male/female soldiers (OSc/ SSc)
Taylor v. Louisiana	419 U.S. 522 (1975)	8:1	White	Overrules Hoyt; strikes down exclusion of women from jury
Stanton v. Stanton	421 U.S. 7 (1975)	8:1	Blackmun	Strikes down differences (3 yrs. less for girls) in child support
Craig v. Boren	429 U.S. 190 (1976)	7:2	Brennan	Ends gender based drinking age diff.; first use of Isc
Miss. University for Women v. Hogan	548 U.S. 718 (1982)	5:4	O'Connor	Opens access to nursing school for male applicant
J.E.B. v. Alabama ex rel. T.B.	511 U.S. 127 (1994)	6:3	Blackmun	Peremptory gender-based jury challenges are unconstitutional
United States v. Virginia et al.	518 U.S. 515 (1996)	7:1	Ginsburg	Opens access to VMI for female applicant

Note: Osc: ordinary scrutiny; ISc: intermediate (heightened) scrutiny; SSc: strict scrutiny.

like this. A partial explanation lies in the limited reach of earlier incarnations of the women's movement. Despite the rather early gathering of prospective women's rights advocates at Seneca Falls in 1848, women pretty soon concentrated their reform work on the abolition of slavery, and especially after the Civil War had disposed of this topic, on prohibition. Both were social movements with far-reaching consequences, to be sure. But these consequences did not deal explicitly with women's rights, and after both goals were achieved, there was a certain lack of purpose that remained. The same goes for the suffrage movement, which swung into full gear around the turn of the century and dissembled after the 19th Amendment granted its desired goal in 1920.[14]

Where was the Supreme Court in all of this? Not just on the sidelines, but in fact actively working against the tides.[15] The earliest cases were remarkable not only for the near unanimity with which the Court denied equal rights to women, but also for the legal reasoning advanced both in *Bradwell* and in *Minor*. In both cases the lawyers for the women argued with the 14th Amendment, but curiously enough *not* along the lines of the equal protection clause (which nowadays is the vehicle of choice). Instead they employed the privileges and immunities clause, which, for all practical purposes, had been "slaughtered" in 1873 by an extremely narrow interpretation in an unrelated case, never to be resurrected again.[16] The plaintiffs thus took the unfortunate action of relying on a constitutional clause which the Supreme Court had decided *not* to use any longer. It is, however, quite unlikely that an advocacy along the lines of the equal protection clause would have been more successful.

Subsequent cases demonstrate the truth of Seymour's statement referred to above. Women had to wait until the 1970s, that is, until society and Congress had done their part, before the Supreme Court came around. Starting in 1971, a rapid succession of cases explored the new doctrine of equality. This leads to the next thesis:

Thesis 6: The cases starting in 1971 are less concerned with special (or even with equal) rights specifically for women, but rather with gender equality. Several of the most important cases in fact have men as the immediate beneficiaries.

The reason for this is actually quite simple. It is politically easier to generate support for equality measures when it can be demonstrated that gender equality does not mean any "undue" preference (as goes the main argument against affirmative action), but that it benefits *both* sexes. The Court has

---

14 David A. J. Richards (1998) has argued that the roots of modern "Second Wave Feminism" are to be found in the abolitionist movement, and that "Suffrage Feminism" belongs to a different tradition.

15 For the general background cf. O'Connor 1992, which contains plenty of reference literature.

16 On the group of cases, which is usually called the *Slaughterhouse Cases*, 16 Wall. (83 U.S.) 36 (1873), see e.g. Currie 1985: 342-51.

often used this device of politically shrewd maneuvering in cases involving minorities.[17] The gender cases did not elevate, as the women's groups had hoped, gender as a "suspect class" to the level of strict scrutiny, but it did not leave it with "ordinary scrutiny" either. Instead, the Court developed a new test for this middle ground, which was appropriately called "intermediate scrutiny" and which made it difficult, but not virtually impossible to demonstrate the reasonableness of gender distinctions.

At the turn of the century gender *equality* does not seem to be an important *legal* issue any more, as the Supreme Court has consistently removed all remaining barriers one by one.[18] The last important case, the VMI case of 1996, opened a formerly all male military institution to female applicants – it is hard to see, intermediate scrutiny or not, which type of gender exclusion can be upheld in the future if military-style education cannot be exempted. It must have been an especially sweet victory for the author of the opinion, Justice Ginsburg, to drive the final nail into the coffin. As a young lawyer, she had been the advocate in several of the cases which brought gender equality on the Supreme Court's agenda, and it was only fitting that she would be the Justice to finally close that chapter as well.

The argument around equality or, as the opponents claim, special treatment, is also very much part of the public and constitutional debate surrounding the last minority to look at.

Thesis 7: The starting point for gays and (to a somewhat different degree) lesbians is quite different from both blacks and women. White male homosexuals could choose to stay hidden in the closet and try to belong to the majority group. If found out, however, the legal situation became at once much worse than that for blacks or for women. The Supreme Court did absolutely nothing to change that.

One major difference, as far as legalities are concerned, must be the point of departure: whatever the problems of oppression for blacks and women may have been in the 20th century, it was never *illegal* just to be black or to be a woman. Neither was it illegal just to be homosexual, but up to 1961 homosexual conduct was illegal in all American states. In that year Illinois adopted a new penal code based on the recommendations of the American Law Institute which decriminalized consensual same-sex activities among adults. Even today there are 16 states which have sodomy laws on the books, with penalties going up to life imprisonment.[19] One has to add, however, that none of

---

17 The case which upheld the constitutionality of the Wisconsin hate crimes law featured a white victim and a black aggressor; *Wisconsin v. Mitchell*, 508 U.S. 476 (1993).

18 Affirmative action for women has come under much less criticism than plans which benefit racial minorities. Cf. Riddick/Riddick 1996. For a comparative perspective see also Stefan Sechting 1998.

19 This is the case in Idaho. The Idaho law pertains both to heterosexual and homosexual

these laws are actually enforced any more. Nevertheless, they are indicative of a certain legal atmosphere, and they may have a bearing in other cases like child custody cases. Two states, Massachusetts and Minnesota, allow themselves the luxury of keeping the sodomy laws in the penal code while, at the same time, enforcing far-reaching and generous gay rights laws.

The executive branch was not much different from this legal situation. With Executive Order 10405 the incoming Eisenhower administration made "sexual perversion" a ground for dismissal from federal civil employment in April 1953, regardless of any actual activity, of the person involved and of the sensitivity of the position in question.[20] During all of this, there was not one case before the Supreme Court which took up the issue, let alone provide relief from these forms of discrimination. So how did the changes come about?

Thesis 8: The road to legal equality (which is far from completed today) was started through the executive political process, after gays and lesbians started to vote (and to contribute money to campaigns) in a more concentrated and openly recognizable way, thus changing them into an attractive constituency. This was to a large degree a result of the gay community's immense politicization after the first years of the Aids crisis and the corresponding silence of the Reagan administration. The Supreme Court did not help along the way, but served as a catalyst in its own fashion with Bowers v. Hardwick *(1986).*

The seminal year in this respect is clearly 1992, when presidential candidates Paul Tsongas, the liberal former Senator from Massachusetts, and Bill Clinton calculated that getting the financial and electoral support of the gay community would be worth risking the alienation of more conservative and traditional voters. This led to an unprecedented wooing of gay voters and of gay interest groups, who in turn "delivered" the goods and raised copious amounts of money for Bill Clinton. Exit polls have shown that gay and lesbian voters supported the democratic ticket both in 1992 and in 1996 with a unanimity which was only matched by the black community. This unanimity, of course, was bolstered immensely not just by the affirming actions of the Democratic standard bearers, but also by the marked contrast provided for in the Republican platform, which showed both in 1992 and in 1996 the gay-bashing spirit of Pat Buchanan.

After the election of 1992 the support was rewarded by several highly visible appointments, both within the domestic administration and within the

---

sodomy, as do the laws in Massachusetts (up to 20 years), Virginia (5-20 years), and North Carolina (10 years). Oklahoma (10 years) covers same-sex sodomy exclusively. Cf. www.lambdalegal.org.

20 Cf. D'Emilio 1983: 43-47. The number of people dismissed for sexual deviancy probably exceeded the number of those dismissed for their supposed or real communist beliefs.

state department. In 1998 Executive Order 13097 explicitly banned all federal employment discrimination against gays and lesbians; quite a change from President Eisenhower's Executive Order of 1953! But these were rather symbolic gestures. The appointment of a successful entrepreneur, Democratic fund-raiser and former law school dean as ambassador to Luxembourg, after all, does not really affect possible discrimination at home.[21] And the more meaningful measures of the Clinton administration have all failed miserably. The attempt to "lift the ban" in the military resulted in the meager and hardly satisfactory (to *any* side in the dispute!) "don't ask, don't tell" policy, which in turn resulted in *more* discharges from the armed forces than during the preceding Republican administrations.[22] In 1996 President Clinton signed the Defense of Marriage Act and thereby made it clear that he was not willing to spend any political capital on his gay and lesbian constituents, obviously and correctly calculating that the Buchananite Republican agenda would not provide a viable alternative for them, come November.

While the administration's record is decidedly checkered, it is still visible that there is at least a certain willingness, which is more than can be said for Congress. To this very day Congress has not done anything to ease the situation for gays and lesbians, and after the Gingrich revolution of 1994 the Republican majorities in both chambers made any progress in that respect illusionary. Recently Senate majority leader Trent Lott (R-Miss.) equated homosexuality with kleptomania and alcoholism. It is only logical that a Hate Crimes Prevention Bill, which would have included gays and lesbians, and which somehow had passed the Senate in 1999, met its demise in the House. Legislation both in 1975 (amendments to the CRA) and in 1994 (Employment Non-Discrimination Act) excluded sexual orientation from its lists.

The courts, as mentioned earlier, have had a mixed record with regard to this minority. The problem already commences with the preliminary task of how to frame the questions at hand. Various cases in the area of anti-gay discrimination have been built up along the lines of free speech doctrines of the First Amendment, of the equal protection clause or of the due process clause, both of the 14th Amendment and of the privacy doctrine, which derives from that amendment as well. Sexual privacy has been affirmed by the Supreme Court as early as 1967 in its famous *Griswold* decision, but only, at that time, for heterosexual married couples. That doctrine still has to spill over.

The very variety of approaches by the parties in lawsuits is a clear indication that there is a scarcity of cases so far by which the Supreme Court has defined and refined the proper legal doctrines governing sexual orientation.

---

21 The appointment of openly gay James C. Hormel had been blocked by Republican Senators when President Clinton resorted to a recess appointment; cf. "Finally, Mr. Hormel Gets the Job," *New York Times* (6/5/1999).

22 Cf. Myers 1999. See also Schmitt 1999.

In fact, there have been only two cases so far which can really be regarded as fundamental.

The first one, *Bowers v. Hardwick* (1986), is widely regarded as the "Dred Scott case" of the gay community. In its decision the Supreme Court narrowly upheld the constitutionality of Georgia's sodomy law. The language of the law was gender neutral, but Justice White's opinion showed a clear anti-gay bias.[23]

The second one, *Romer v. Evans* (1996), struck down an amendment to the Colorado state constitution which forbade any local gay rights ordinances. The decision employed sweeping language, but this language and the biting dissent by Justice Scalia which invoked a presumably raging "Kulturkampf"[24] notwithstanding, it was not really a correction and overruling of *Hardwick*. The lower courts did not use it as such, as the subsequent cases have demonstrated, and in fact the majority opinion did not even *mention* the earlier *Hardwick* decision – a deliberate omission, which was exposed in Justice Scalia's dissent as avoiding the issue. The same can be said for another aspect of Justice Kennedy's majority opinion: by finding that Colorado's amendment did not even meet the lowest possible "rational basis test," he was able to frame the opinion within the limits of ordinary scrutiny, thus avoiding the issue of whether sexual orientation should be elevated to intermediate scrutiny, and hence receive the same level of protection as gender discrimination.[25]

In the wake of *Evans*, lower courts have responded differently to sexual orientation discrimination suits, and it does not take much power of prophecy to assume that in future cases the Supreme Court will be called upon to clarify the legal issues. In fact, for an overview of gay rights cases it is still necessary to rely heavily on non-binding lower court decisions to give a full picture.

Only as a footnote it may be added that the various responses of state courts and lower federal courts also raise issues of federalism, most of which center around the constitutionality of the 1996 Defense of Marriage Act (DOMA), which has provoked a barrage of legal articles, taking all possible differing positions.[26] Since no state has yet allowed same-sex marriage, the test on the DOMA has still to come. However, the most recent ruling of the

---

23 There are numerous discussions of *Hardwick* from a legal point of view; several American law reviews at one time or another have devoted an entire issue to this case. As an overview of the issues at stake see Halley 1993. The theoretical impacts are discussed at some length in Kaplan 1997.

24 A positive assessment of Justice Scalia's dissent can be found in Duncan 1997.

25 For a critical analysis see Papadopoulos 1997. It has been argued that *Evans* implicitly went beyond ordinary scrutiny; see Rogers 1997. The courts have not subscribed to that theory.

26 On the issue of federalism cf. Rothstein 1997. In the same vein argues Shuki-Kunze 1998. In favor of the DOMA's constitutionality see Crane 1998.

Table 6: Gay Rights Cases

Case	Citation	Vote	Opinion	Content
Griswold v. Connecticut	381 U.S. 479 (1965)	7:2	Douglas	First pronunciation of (sexual) privacy
Bowers v. Hardwick	478 U.S. 186 (1986)	5:4	White	No right to privacy for homosexual conduct
Gay Rights Coalition of Georgetown University Law Center v. Georgetown University	536 A.2d 1 (D.C. 1987) (en banc)	5:2 and 5:2	Judge Mack (lead opinion)	Private religious university has to give equal access to gay student group, but does not have to recognize it
Commonwealth v. Wasson	842 S.W.2d 487 (Ky. 1992)	4:3	Justice Leibson	KY S.Ct. strikes down state sodomy law, using equal protection argument
Hurley v. Irish-American Gay, Lesbian & Bisexual Group of Boston	515 U.S. 557 (1995)	9:0	Souter	St. Patrick's Day Parade organizers are allowed to exclude gay group
Romer v. Evans	517 U.S. 620 (1996)	6:3	Kennedy	State ban against gay rights ordinances violates equal protection (rational basis test)
Baehr v. Miike	1996 WL 694235 (Haw. Cir. Ct.)	-	Judge Chang	Ban against same-sex marriage violates state constitutional right to equal protection (SSc)
Shahar v. Bowers	114 F.3d 1097 (11th Cir. 1997) (en banc)	8:4	Judge Edmondson	Atty. Gen. of Georgia has the right to withdraw job offer after learning of her planned lesbian wedding
Oncale v. Sundowner Offshore Services, Inc.	118 S.Ct. 998 (1998)	9:0	Scalia	Title VII of CRA (1965) forbids same-sex harassment
Brause v. Bureau of Vital Statistics	1998 WL 88743 (Alaska Sup. Ct.)	-	Judge Michalski	Strikes down Alaska ban of same-sex marriages, which violates state constitutional right to privacy (SSc)
Powell v. Georgia	No. S98 A0755 (Georgia S.Ct.)	6:1	Chief Justice Benham	Strikes down Georgia sodomy law, which violates state constitutional right to privacy (SSc)
Able v. United States	155 F.3d 628 (2nd Cir. 1998)	3:0	Judge Walker	"Don't ask, don't tell" does not violate equal protection (OSc); District Ct. reversed

Note: Osc: ordinary scrutiny; ISc: intermediate (heightened) scrutiny; SSc: strict scrutiny.

Vermont Supreme Court has set the stage for most interesting future confrontations.[27]

As a second historical footnote it may be noted that the Georgia Supreme Court in 1998 struck down Georgia's sodomy law as a violation of the state constitutional right to privacy – twelve years after the United States Supreme Court found nothing wrong with that law in regard to the U.S. constitution.[28] Two final theses will serve to sum up the differing findings for the different minorities this paper looked at.

Thesis 9: While blacks, women, and gays certainly tried all available ways to achieve legal and political equality, there are clearly three different ways and three different waves recognizable. The most positive response came from the Supreme Court to blacks in the 1950s, from Congress to women in the 1960s, and from the executive branch to gays in the 1990s.

This should not come as a surprise. A final table lists a number of "firsts," and the ways and means by which equality was achieved, if at all. One should not read too much into this rather crude compilation, but a few rules of thumb can be derived from it nevertheless. Women, as a rule, fared better (and earlier) on the purely political front, while blacks did much better with the judicial process. This is also true when it comes to positions in Congress and in the administration. The first woman was elected to Congress at a time when women did not even enjoy a nationwide right to vote. The first black Congressman, on the other hand, had to wait quite a bit longer – that is, if one discounts the reconstruction era black Congressmen from the defeated Southern states, who owed their positions to a large degree to the protection of union troops. Compared to these two groups, gays and lesbians still have a long way to go. What, finally, has been the Supreme Court's role in this?

Thesis 10: The Supreme Court was less instrumental in ending discrimination than one might think after the Brown *fanfare in 1954, at least when one looks beyond the plight of the black minority. For this, a change in personnel, a change in time, or a change in judicial philosophy may be responsible.*

Even a social scientist who is trained to look for structural explanations can hardly overlook the fact that in a court of last resort with nine members who

---

27 *Baker v. Vermont* (No. 98-032) can be found at dol.state.vt.us/gopher_root3/supct/current/98-032.op. Cf. Goldberg 1999. Then-Republican presidential candidate Gary Bauer called this decision an act of terrorism; "Bauer Likens ruling on Gay Couples to Terrorism," *New York Times* (12/28/1999).

28 It should be noted that the same year 1998 fittingly enough saw the end of Attorney General Bowers' political career. He had to abandon his bid for the Republican nomination for governor when he had to admit to adultery, which under Georgia law is criminal as well.

Table 7: Breakthroughs to Equality

Achievement	Blacks	Women	Gays and Lesbians
Voting equality	1870 (15th Am.) 1965 (VRA)	1920 (19th Am.)	not applicable
Federal employment equality	1941 (Executive Order)	1963 (Equal Pay Act)	1998 (Executive Order)
Equality in Armed Services	1948 (Executive Order)	1973 (Frontiero v. Richardson)	- [1993, statutory law]
Anti-Discrimination Law	1964 (CRA)	1964 (CRA)	- (Died 1999 in House)
Marital equality	1967 (Loving v. Virginia)	1973 (Frontiero v. Richardson)	- (Cases pending)
Major organization	1909 NAACP	1966 NOW	1973 NG(L)TF
First in Congress	1928 Oscar DePriest (R-Ill); first from north	1916 Jeannette Rankin (R-Mont.)	1984 Gerry Studds (D-Mass.); re-elected after outing
First in Federal Administration	1966 Robert C. Weaver, Sec. of Housing	1933 Frances Perkins, Sec. of Labor	1993 Roberta Achtenberg, Asst. Sec. of Housing

are appointed for life, the personality of this small group matters immensely and any change in personnel is bound to change the often delicate balances on the Court. This can be affected by the personal relations between the Justices, by their political and judicial philosophies, but also by their background prior to the elevation to the Supreme Court. It is reasonable to assume that different paths to the Court can inspire different worldviews once the Justices assume the bench. A comparison between, on the one hand, the Vinson and Warren Courts in their years of growing activism, and, on the other hand, the current Rehnquist Court, can provide some insight.

Once again, this should not be overestimated. But it is a fact that of the 18 Justices on the Vinson and Warren Courts up to 1962[29] no less than eight had served in some elective office, as compared to only one on the current Court. Only seven of the earlier Justices had prior judicial experiences, and most of them were appointed by President Eisenhower after the "Warren debacle."[30] In the current Court, all of the Justices had some sort of judicial experience beforehand.[31] It is reasonable to assume that Justices with prior

29 1962 has been chosen as a cutoff date, as it marked the retirement of Justice Frankfurter, who had been the leader of the more conservative wing of the Court. Currie (1990) quite appropriately devoted two different chapters to the Warren Court, namely, "The First Warren Court" (377), and "The Real Warren Court" (415), using 1962 as the dividing line.

30 After his presidency had ended, Eisenhower referred to "my two biggest mistakes – and they are both on the Supreme Court," by which he meant Chief Justice Warren and Justice William Brennan. The remark is quoted in Abraham 1992: 7.

31 The Chief Justice's judicial experience has been his service as an Associate Justice of the

Table 8: Experience of Justices Prior to Service on the Supreme Court, Vinson Court and Warren Court (1946-1962)

Justice	S.Ct.	Elective	Administrative	Judicial	Last Position
Black	FDR 1937	U.S. Senator			U.S. Senator
Reed	FDR 1938	KY House	U.S. Sol. General		U.S. Soll. General
Frankfurter	FDR 1939				Professor
Douglas	FDR 1939		Sec. & Exch. Comm.		Sec. & Exch. Comm.
Murphy	FDR 1940	MI Governor	U.S. Attorney General		U.S. Atty. General
R. Jackson	FDR 1941		U.S. Attorney General		U.S. Atty. General
W. Rutledge	FDR 1943			U.S. Appeals Ct.	U.S. Appeals Court
Burton	HST 1945	U.S. Senator			U.S. Senator
VINSON	HST 1946	U.S. House	U.S. Sec. of Treasury	U.S. Appeals Ct.	U.S. Sec. of Treasury
Clark	HST 1949		U.S. Attorney General		U.S. Atty. General
Minton	HST 1949	U.S. Senator		U.S. Appeals Ct.	U.S. Appeals Court
WARREN	DDE 1953	CA Governor			CA Governor
Harlan II	DDE 1955			U.S. Appeals Ct.	U.S. Appeals Court
Brennan	DDE 1957			N.J. S. Ct.	N.J. S. Ct.
Whittaker	DDE 1957			U.S. Appeals Ct.	U.S. Appeals Court
Stewart	DDE 1959	City Council		U.S. Appeals Ct.	U.S. Appeals Court
B. White	JFK 1962		U.S. Dep. Atty. Gen.		U.S. Dep. Atty. Gen.
Goldberg	JFK 1962		U.S. Sec. of Labor		U.S. Sec. of Labor

Note: Highest position attained.

political experience might be more open to political arguments in their new arena as well, and thus be more inclined to act as a means to step in where the political process has failed to address the grievances. This is what happened in the 1940s and 1950s, when the Court acted on behalf of the black minority.

Supreme Court from 1972 on.

Table 9: Experience of Justices Prior to Service on the Supreme Court, Rehnquist Court (1999)

Justice	S.Ct.	Elective	Administrative	Judicial	Last Position
Stevens	GF 1975			U.S. Appeals Court	U.S. Appeals Court
O'Connor	RR 1981	Ariz. Senate		Ariz. Appeals Court	Ariz. Appeals Court
Rehnquist	RR 1986		U.S. Asst. Atty. Gen.	S.Ct. Ass. Just.	S.Ct. Ass. Just.
Scalia	RR 1986		U.S. Asst. Atty. Gen.	U.S. Appeals Court	U.S. Appeals Court
Kennedy	RR 1987			U.S. Appeals Court	U.S. Appeals Court
Souter	GB 1990		NH Atty. Gen.	U.S. Appeals Court	U.S. Appeals Court
Thomas	GB 1991			U.S. Appeals Court	U.S. Appeals Court
Ginsburg	WC 1993			U.S. Appeals Court	U.S. Appeals Court
Breyer	WC 1994			U.S. Appeals Court	U.S. Appeals Court

Note: Highest position attained.

Today's Court has a different outlook. The Justices have a different professional background, but they also tend to have a much more conservative judicial worldview. The Court has not refrained from tackling political questions, but it has cloaked its decisions in the rhetoric of "original intent," which is hardly supportive to new minority claims.

Four Justices of the Supreme Court usually vote together on the liberal side of most issues where there is an ideological disagreement on the Court;[32] namely, Justices Stevens, Souter, Ginsburg, and Breyer. On the other hand, Chief Justice Rehnquist and Justices Scalia and Thomas are almost always to be found on the conservative side of these issues. And Justices O'Connor and Kennedy are somewhat of an enigma, holding the balance of power between these two clearly defined groups. As a rule both Justice O'Connor and Justice Kennedy can be expected to vote with the conservative wing of the Court and thus provide the Chief Justice with a small, but rather reliable majority. This has been the case with some recent and highly controversial decisions in the areas of affirmative action, apportionment, and in states rights cases which are covered elsewhere in this volume.[33] All of these cases led to slim 5:4

32 On the other hand, the number of unanimous decisions is at an all time high for a modern Court. During the last few terms it had repeatedly come close to the 50% mark.

33 See in this volume the article by Timothy Conlan, who gives a cautious analysis of these cases.

conservative victories, and all of these majority opinions employed very broad language.

But these two votes cannot be taken for granted. Both Justices were part of the *Romer v. Evans* majority, and both voted to uphold abortion rights in *Planned Parenthood v. Casey* (1992),[34] the last major abortion case. Justice Kennedy's reluctant concurring opinion in the flag burning case of *Texas v. Johnson* (1989)[35] offers a clue to his jurisprudence: it has a somewhat libertarian streak, which sets him apart from such all-out conservatives as the Chief Justice and his main allies. This libertarian streak allows him to vote in favor of ending discrimination against individuals and classes of citizens who are singled out (as in his opinion in *Romer v. Evans*), while at the same time striking down anything smacking of group rights (as in the affirmative action and in the redistricting cases).

It is highly probable that the next President will have the chance to fill at least three positions on the Supreme Court, as the Chief Justice (born in 1924) and Justices Stevens (born 1920) and O'Connor (born 1930) are widely expected to retire. In this respect President Clinton had little luck during his two terms in the White House. Of all the Presidents who served the full eight years in office, only President Madison appointed as few Justices (namely, two) as Clinton did, and only President Monroe appointed even less (namely, one). All the others, and most of the one-term Presidents as well, had a better chance to impress their judicial philosophy on the Court. It is quite possible, then, that the entire outlook of the Court will change, and with that the close decisions might change as well. A Democratic President could have a lasting impact with their appointment. A Republican President, on the other hand, could strengthen today's conservative majority on the Court for the foreseeable future. This brings us to a final remark on minorities and constitutional change through constitutional jurisprudence at the Supreme Court. While the gender rights cases seem to be pretty much settled by now, affirmative action, reapportionment and the meaning of equality for the black minority are as much open for interpretation as ever. And waiting around the corner are the issues of equal rights for gays and lesbians in areas like marriage law, armed services, employment, and a host of other problems, which have not even scratched the surface of the Supreme Court cases to come.

---

34 *Planned Parenthood of Southeastern PA v. Casey*, 505 U.S. 833 (1992). For the role of *stare decisis* in this see Spaeth/Segal 1999: 1-8.

35 *Texas v. Johnson*, 491 U.S. 397 (1989), at 420-1. The remarks in his brief concurrence clearly showed his pain: "The case before us illustrates better than most that the judicial power is often difficult in its exercise. We cannot here ask another Branch to share responsibility, as when the argument is made that a statute is flawed or incomplete. For we are presented with a clear and simple statute to be judged against a pure command of the Constitution. The outcome can be laid at no door but ours. The hard fact is that sometimes we must make decisions we do not like. We make them because they are right, right in the sense that the law and the Constitution, as we see them, compel the result."

References

Abraham, Henry J. [3]1992: *Justices and Presidents. A Political History of Appointments to the Supreme Court*, New York/Oxford: Oxford UP.
Crane, Daniel A. 1998: *The Original Understanding of the "Effects Clause" of Article IV, Section 1 and Implications for the Defense of Marriage Act*, 6 Geor. Mason L. Rev. 307.
Currie, David P. 1985: *The Constitution in the Supreme Court. The First Hundred Years 1789-1888*, Chicago/London: University of Chicago Press.
—— 1990: *The Constitution in the Supreme Court. The Second Century 1888-1986*, Chicago/London: University of Chicago Press.
D'Emilio, John 1983: *Sexual Politics, Sexual Communities. The Making of a Homosexual Minority in the United States, 1940-1970*, Chicago/London: University of Chicago Press.
Duncan, Richard F. 1997: *Wigstock and the Kulturkampf. Supreme Court Storytelling, the Culture War, and Romer v. Evans*, 72 Notre Dame L. Rev. 345.
Goldberg, Carey 1999: "Redefining a Marriage Made New in Vermont," in: *New York Times*, December 26.
Greenhouse, Linda 1999: "Justices to Weigh Race Barrier in Hawaiian Voting," in: *New York Times*, March 23.
—— 2000: "Justices Reject a Voting Provision for Descendants of Original Hawaiians," in: *New York Times*, March 24.
Guinier, Lani 1994: *The Tyranny of the Majority. Fundamental Fairness in Representative Democracy*, New York: Free Press.
Halley, Janet E. 1993: *Reasoning about Sodomy. Act and Identity in and after Bowers v. Hardwick*, 79 VA L. Rev. 1721.
Hamby, Alonzo L. 1995: *Man of the People. A Life of Harry S. Truman*, New York/Oxford: Oxford UP.
Howard, John R. 1999: *The Shifting Wind. The Supreme Court and Civil Rights from Reconstruction to Brown*, Albany: State University of New York Press.
Kaplan, Morris B. 1997: *Sexual Justice. Democratic Citizenship and the Politics of Desire*, New York/London: Routledge.
Kluger, Richard 1975: *Simple Justice. The History of Brown v. Board of Education and Black America's Struggle for Equality*, New York: Vintage Books.
Laponce, Jean A. 1991: "Minorities, protection of," in: Vernon Bogdanor (ed.), *The Blackwell Encyclopaedia of Political Science*, Oxford/Cambridge, MA: Blackwell, 371-372.
Miller, Merle 1974: *Plain Speaking. An Oral Biography of Harry S. Truman*, New York: Berkley Publishing Corp.
Myers, Steven Lee 1999: "Gay Group's Study Finds Military Harassment Rising," in: *New York Times*, March 15.
Myrdal, Gunnar 1944: *An American Dilemma. The Negro Problem and Modern Democracy*, New York: Pantheon Books.
O'Connor, Karen 1992: "Gender," in: Kermit L. Hall (ed.), *The Oxford Companion to the Supreme Court of the United States*, New York/Oxford: Oxford UP, 328-335.
Papadopoulos, Mark E. 1997: *Inkblot Jurisprudence. Romer v. Evans as a Great Defeat for the Gay Rights Movement*, 7 Cornell J. of L. & Public Policy 165.

Rawls, John 1971: *A Theory of Justice*, Cambridge, MA: Harvard UP.
Richards, David A.J. 1998: *Women, Gays, and the Constitution. The Grounds for Feminism and Gay Rights in Culture and Law*, Chicago/London: University of Chicago Press.
Riddick, Winston/Riddick, Patricia 1996: *Overview of the United States Supreme Court Affirmative Action Decisions in Race and Gender Cases: 1980-1995*, 23 S. U.L. Rev. 107.
Rogers, Jerald W. 1997: *Romer v. Evans. Heightened Scrutiny Has Found a Rational Basis – Is the Court Tacitly Recognizing Quasi-Suspect Status for Gays, Lesbians, and Bisexuals?* 45 Kan. L. Rev. 953.
Rose, Arnold 1968: "Minorities," in: David L. Sills (ed.), *International Encyclopedia of the Social Sciences*, vol. 10, New York/London: Macmillan, 365-371.
Rosen, Jeffrey 1996: *The Color-Blind Court*, 45 Am. U.L. Rev. 791.
Rothstein, Melissa 1997: *The Defense of Marriage Act and Federalism. A States' Rights Argument in Defense of Same-Sex Marriages*, 31 Fam. L.Q. 571.
Schmitt, Eric 1999: "Gay Rights Advocates Plan to Press Clinton to Undo Policy of 'Don't Ask, Don't Tell'," in: *New York Times*, December 25.
Schwartz, Bernard 1993: *A History of the Supreme Court*, New York/Oxford: Oxford UP.
Sechting, Stefan 1998: *Affirmative Action und Frauenförderung*, Osnabrück: Universitätsverlag Rasch.
Seymour, Stephanie K. 1998: "Women as Constitutional Equals: The Burger Court's Overdue Evolution," in: Bernard Schwartz (ed.), *The Burger Court. Counter-Revolution or Confirmation?* New York: Oxford UP, 66-82.
Shuki-Kunze, Jennie R. 1998: *The 'Defenseless' Marriage Act. The Constitutionality of the Defense of Marriage Act as an Extension of Congressional Power Under the Full Faith and Credit Clause*, 48 Case W. Res. L. Rev. 351.
Sohn, Louis B. (ed.) 1986: *International Organization and Integration. Annotated Basic Documents of International Organizations and Arrangements. Student Edition*, Dordrecht/Boston/Lancaster: Nijhoff.
Spaeth, Harold J./Segal, Jeffrey A. 1999: *Majority Rule or Minority Will. Adherence to Precedent on the U.S. Supreme Court*, Cambridge: Cambridge UP.
Thernstrom, Abigail M. 1987: *Whose Votes Count? Affirmative Action and Minority Voting Rights*, Cambridge, MA/London: Harvard UP.
Warren, Earl 1977: *The Memoirs of Chief Justice Earl Warren*, Garden City, NY: Doubleday.

Baker v. Vermont, no. 98-032.
Rice v. Cayetano, no. 98-818.
Slaughterhouse Cases, 16 Wall. (83 U.S.) 36 (1873).
Texas v. Johnson, 491 U.S. 397 (1989).
United States v. Carolene Products Co., 304 U.S. 144 (1938).
Wisconsin v. Mitchell, 508 U.S. 476 (1993).

Canada – A Pioneer in the Management of Constitutional Politics in a Multi-national Society

Peter H. Russell

It is Canada's fate to have become a pioneer in managing a very challenging type of constitutional politics. This is the constitutional politics of a democratic political community among whose people there are very different senses of national allegiance and identity. In such a society the big background issue of constitutional politics always is: can these people or peoples constitute a political community?

Canada's engagement in this kind of constitutional politics has come about not through rational choice or abstract philosophy. We have stumbled into this situation without fully realizing what we were doing. Even now many Canadians, perhaps even a majority – especially in "English Canada" and among new immigrants –, would not accept my characterization of Canada as a multi-national society. They yearn for a Canada with a single sense of national identity. In effect, they yearn for a different Canada than the one in which they find themselves. Indeed, their very sense of unease about our disunity is an important element in Canada's constitutional restlessness.

In large measure we Canadians stumbled into the situation we find ourselves in through incomplete conquests. In the eighteenth century, the British did not complete their conquest of New France by expelling the Canadiens as they had earlier done with the Acadians. Nor did they carry through with a program of forced assimilation of French Catholics into their English/Protestant culture. Within 15 years of the conquest they recognized the conquered people's religion and civil law. The British did not do this out of any profound philosophical commitment to political or cultural pluralism. They did it mainly as a strategy for securing the loyalty of the Canadiens at a time when the Empire was threatened with rebellion in the American colonies to the south. Nonetheless it was a decisive move towards a deeply pluralist Canada and Empire.

The absence of any commitment to cultural pluralism was evident again in the nineteenth century when British constitutionalists responded to rebellions in their two Canadian provinces. Lord Durham's plan was to assimilate the French Canadians into the English culture which he believed would soon dominate a reunited Canada. But the Québécois defeated this effort by surviving with their own sense of identity and forcing a federal constitutional solution with a province in which they as a majority would have énough political power to secure the essential elements of their distinct society.

The other incomplete conquest concerns the Indigenous peoples. In the seventeenth and eighteenth centuries the British (like the French) for military and commercial reasons entered into treaty-like agreements with Aboriginal nations. The Royal Proclamation of 1763 which set out British policy for governing the lands ceded by France at the end of the Seven Years War recognized the Indian nations' possession of territory outside the settled British colonies and laid down that settlement in this territory could take place only on lands that were sold or ceded by the Indians to the Crown. The Royal Proclamation, though often ignored in the nineteenth and twentieth centuries, survives as part of Canada's constitutional law. In 1982 its primacy was acknowledged in section 25 of the new Canadian Charter of Rights and Freedoms.

In Canada as in the United States once the settlers clearly had the upper hand militarily and demographically, treaty-like relations with Indigenous peoples gave way to colonial domination. Still there is an important difference between the two countries. In Canada right up into the twentieth century, treaties were the principal means for acquiring new lands from the Indians for settlement and economic development in much of Ontario, the western prairies, north-eastern British Columbia and part of the Northwest Territories. While the practical impact of these treaties was massive dispossession, nonetheless they did entail recognition by the incoming settler state of the Aboriginal signatories' nationhood and their collective ownership of traditional lands. The United States also made hundreds of treaties with Indian nations and through Chief Justice John Marshall's jurisprudence accorded Indian peoples the status of "domestic, dependent nations." However, soon after the Civil War, Congress abolished all future treaty-making. The American west was won from the Indians through brutal warfare rather than duplicitous treaties.

The continuity of treaty relationships with Aboriginal peoples in Canada has had important consequences for the present day. In the 1960s and 70s, a resurgence of Aboriginal nationalism induced the federal government to abandon its program of assimilation and resume the process of making agreements with native peoples who continue to occupy their traditional lands. Taking advantage of the constitutional restructuring brought on by Québec nationalism, Aboriginal peoples were able to have their rights, including treaty rights, recognized in the Constitution Act of 1982. Federal and provincial governments in Canada now recognize Aboriginal peoples as "First Nations" and are engaged, all across the country, in a process of negotiating self-government agreements with them, as well as with the Métis nation and Inuit peoples.

It is the persistence over centuries of the Québécois and the Indigenous peoples of Canada in insisting on their recognition as distinct peoples or nations that obliges Canada, if it is to survive with its present borders and population, to manage the constitutional affairs of a multi-national community. Let us be clear that what is at issue here is not simply a multi-cultural state but a multi-national state. Virtually every state in the world is in fact multi-cultural and acknowledges this, in varying degrees, in its laws and policies. Canada goes much further with multi-culturalism than most, extending financial support and encouragement to many ethnic minorities besides French-speaking Canadians and Aboriginal peoples. Functioning as a multi-national political community means something much more difficult and problematic than multi-culturalism. It means, in the Canadian case, acknowledging that two groups, French Canadians and Indigenous peoples, are not just cultural minorities but political societies with the special rights of homeland peoples to maintain political jurisdictions in which they can ensure their survival as distinct peoples.

Most of the Canadian citizens who belong to these "nations within" have a dual sense of national identity. In varying degrees most Aboriginal Canadians and French-speaking Québecers identify with Canada as well as with their own historic nations – though they may be reluctant to recognize Canada as "their nation." Alongside them, the majority of Canadians acknowledge Canada as their nation – their only nation – and in varying degrees despair of accommodating the "nations within." Managing the constitutional affairs of a population with such conflicting and incoherent notions of national identity is not just Canada's challenge but the challenge of many areas in the world today where some kind of national autonomy within a larger political community is the main alternative to the splintering of states or international conflict. That is why Canada's fortunes in dealing with this challenge bear watching.

Throughout its first century the Canadian federation had very few constitutional affairs to manage. The Confederation Constitution was based on an agreement between English and French Canadian politicians laden with ambiguity and conflicting expectations about the future of the federation. Indigenous peoples were included only as mute subjects of the new central government. Constitutional sovereignty – the power to amend the constitutional text – remained in the hands of the British Parliament. The federation grew and its structure evolved without any grand attempts to settle or accommodate constitutional differences. The main developments were the strengthening of provincial rights, a very strong commitment to a federal ethic, the confining of French Canada primarily to Québec, and concerted efforts by the federal government, despite the treaty process, to assimilate native peoples into what was fervently believed to be the superior culture of the Europeans.

Canadians did not become embroiled in constitutional politics until after World War II when federal politicians – French as well as English – moved by a sense of Canadian nationalism became determined to terminate Canada's constitutional colonialism and "patriate" the country's Constitution. They then confronted the unresolved ambiguities and differences about the nature of Canada as a political community. For transferring the power to amend the Constitution from Britain to Canada meant deciding who or what in Canada – which government or governments, which people or peoples – would be constitutionally sovereign. By the mid-1960s it was becoming clear that this grand issue – a mega issue in constitutional politics if ever there was one – would not be easy to resolve. A secular nationalism was also now moving many French Québecers to insist that patriation, the fulfillment of Canadian nationhood, should take place only if the position of Québec as the homeland of a nation within Canada was more strongly and explicity secured in the Canadian Constitution. The result, of course, of this collision of nationalisms and constitutional visions was an entire generation of very heavy constitutional politics – what I have called "mega constitutional politics."

Fear not – I am not about to take you through the many chapters of this seemingly endless constitutional struggle – the Victoria Charter, Trudeau's initiatives, the 1980 Québec referendum, Patriation, the conferences with Aboriginal peoples, Meech Lake, the Charlottetown Accord, the 1995 Québec referendum and all of that. If you want details, there are many books written about all of these events, including one of my own (Russell 1993). (Indeed, I am in no position to complain about the struggle as I have truly dined out on it – in Canada and around the world). But I do wish to reflect on its outcome, and what we can learn from the experience about constitutionalism in societies that are deeply divided in a multi-national sense.

The first thing to observe is that after a generation of constitutional wrangling Canadians are no closer to resolving explicitly in formal constitutional terms the big issues that divide them. Important constitutional changes were made in 1982 – patriation, a constitutional bill of rights and constitutional recognition of Aboriginal rights. But Prime Minister Trudeau's government forced these changes through over the opposition of Québec's provincial government and most of Canada's Aboriginal leaders. This led to the subsequent constitutional efforts – the inconclusive First Ministers' Conferences with Aboriginal leaders, the defeat of the Meech Lake Accord designed to accommodate Québec and the referendum defeat of the Charlottetown Accord designed to accommodate everyone. The miracle is not that this latter effort failed but that it came so close to succeeding!

At the end of all this, many observers of our constitutional scene would conclude that the Canadian political community is more deeply divided than it was at the beginning of this constitutional struggle. In the light of the nearly 50-50 split in the 1995 Québec referendum, the same might be said of

Québec as a political community. And, as the Nisga'a Treaty with its provision for an Aboriginal nation to exercise a real share of law-making sovereignty in Canada runs into stiff opposition among non-Aboriginal Canadians, there is no sign of a clear consensus on the future of Aboriginal peoples in Canada. The one point on which Canadians are now constitutionally united is their exhaustion with contesting constitutional issues. It is this feeling of constitutional exhaustion that may in the end persuade Québec sovereignists not to proceed with yet another referendum. These failed efforts at reaching a constitutional consensus in Canada did succeed in changing one important feature of Canada's constitutional culture: they democratized it. Making the written Constitution the most important political issue in the country for a generation, talking about the Constitution as ideally a vision of our society, a mirror in which all Canadians can see themselves, a document inscribing what we are all about – all of this convinced the Canadian public that they must have a crucial say in making any important changes in the Constitution. Political elites may still play the lead role in negotiating and drafting constitutional proposals – that much of consociational democracy remains intact. But proposals for fundamental constitutional change to be legitimate in Canada they must now be ratified by the people voting in referendums.

This democratization of Canada's constitutional process has not been written into the country's Constitution – though it has been incorporated into the constitutional systems of Québec, the three western-most provinces and several Aboriginal nations. Nonetheless, I believe that for major constitutional changes in the structure of our federal institutions or the structure of the federation, in the status of Indigenous peoples, or in the Charter of Rights and Freedoms, a Canadian wide referendum would be a political imperative for all. For this reason Bruce Ryder and I in a paper on "Ratifying a Post-referendum Agreement on Quebec Sovereignty" (Ryder/Russell 1997) argued that, if after a sovereignist win in a Québec referendum, federal, provincial and Aboriginal leaders negotiated an agreement on a fundamental change in Québec's constitutional status, their agreement would have to be submitted to a Canada-wide referendum.

At a very abstract philosophical level, a compelling case can be made for this democratization of the constitutional process: in a constitutional democracy, after all, shouldn't the people be sovereign and have the final say on their highest law, the Constitution? The trouble with applying this simple principle of popular sovereignty to a multi-national society like Canada is the absence of an agreement on who the sovereign people are or on how that will can be identified. Québec sovereignists would say the people of Québec are sovereign and a majority of them express the people's will. This view is repudiated by federalists within and outside Québec, many of whom would argue that some majority of Canadians – simple or extraordinary – is sovereign in Canada. Most Aboriginal people do not believe their nations ever surrendered their sovereignty – though they might have difficulty agreeing on how that sovereignty is expressed in the present context.

Thus in the Canadian case – and I would submit in other multi-national communities – that first step in the Lockean social contract whereby all consent to form a single sovereign people to be governed by an agreed upon political authority has not and may never be taken. In a setting such as this attempts at grand constitutional settlements are much more likely to exacerbate than to resolve societal conflict.

The recipe for managing constitutional affairs that this analysis yields is not one of constitutional immobilisme. One of the worst myths haunting Canada's constitutional affairs is that the only alternative to a grand resolution of constitutional issues is a constitutional deep-freeze. Through the 1990s since the demise of the Charlottetown Accord important changes have been taking place in the operation of our constitution. Changes in the roles and responsibilities of government in our federal system have occurred without formal constitutional amendment. Some of this was consolidated in a political agreement on the Social Union (see Lazar/McLean: this volume). The parties to this agreement were the federal government and all of the Canadian provinces except Québec. In this agreement, the provinces for the first time acknowledge the legitimacy of the federal government using its spending power to support initiatives in areas of exclusive provincial jurisdiction, and in exchange the federal government agrees to launch such shared-cost or block-funded programs only with the agreement of a majority of provincial governments.

Québec's non-participation in the Social Union agreement demonstrates the strength and limitation of this kind of change. In effect it underlines Québec's special status in the Canadian federation without requiring that Canadians agree on explicit recognition of this special status in the constitutional text – an agreement that would probably be impossible to secure.

Progress has also been made in reforming Aborginal relations. The Royal Commission on Aboriginal Peoples – the first collaborative inquiry in world history of indigenous and non-indigenous people into the past, present and future of their mutual relationship – has mapped out the path to a post-colonial relationship through treaty-like agreements on land and governance. Through such an agreement, Nunavut, the homeland of the Eastern Arctic Inuit, is now up and running as a new self-governing territory of Canada. Treaty negotiations on land and governance issues are currently under way at approximately 80 different "tables" in every part of Canada. The Supreme Court of Canada's 1997 decision in *Delgamuukw* confirming Aboriginal peoples' ownership and control of their traditional, unsurrendered lands gave strong legal backing to this modern treaty process.

Popular support for this process of recognizing Aboriginal nations as self-governing nations within Canada is, however, shaky. Many non-Aboriginal commentators in the popular media are shocked to learn that under the Nisga'a Agreement the Nisga'a people besides being citizens of Canada will be recognized as citizens of the Nisga'a nation and that the Nisga'a government will have supreme law-making authority on matters such as their own constitution, language and culture, the education of their children and the management of the 10% of their traditional lands and resources recognized in the Agreement as belonging to them. Similar provisions are contained in other agreements now being negotiated across the country. The Nisga'a people have ratified the agreement and a very unpopular British Columbian government has pushed it through the British Columbia legislature. It is now before the federal parliament which must also approve it before it becomes law. The Chrétien government having been a party to the treaty and with a majority in the House of Commons will ensure its safe passage, but not without an acrimonious political debate. If, as the opposition urged, the Nisga'a Agreement had been put to a referendum in B.C., it would very likely have been rejected. The Nisga'a agreement, the product of over twenty years of negotiations, is inevitably a compromise. It is bitterly attacked by native critics as giving up too much land and self-government, just as many non-Aboriginal Canadians question it for going too far the other way. In constitutional referendum campaigns fought through the mass media nay-sayers have an easier time standing on the high ground of pure principle and scare-mongering about change than do the defenders of grubby compromise.

Thus we Canadians limp along adjusting constitutional relationships in our multi-national political community without definitively settling the question of who or what we are, and without any clear popular consensus on the nature of the country expressed in the text of our constitution. The lesson we may have taught ourselves, and perhaps other deeply divided political communities, is that it is best not to try reaching a grand and explicit popular agreement on fundamental constitutional principles. As a number of our constitutional commentators have observed, abeyance and avoidance of intractable abstract questions such as the locus of sovereignty and the identity of the nation are conditions of constitutional peace in Canada. Of course, there are some who do not want peace. The most militant of these are the Québec sovereignists. They, by definition, do not accept that sovereignty should be shared. And despite constitutional exhaustion, they may yet force the issue. If they do have another referendum, and if they win it (whatever "winning" means), I am not sure what the final outcome will be – a totally independent Québec, a Québec in some new partnership relation with Canada or the status quo. However, I am fairly certain of one thing which is that in a newly configured Canada or an independent Québec with its present borders, as in Canada as it now is, sovereignty will in fact be shared among peoples, and there will once again be a need to practice the quiet and delicate constitutional arts of sharing sovereignty in a multi-national society.

References

Russell, Peter H. [2]1993: *Constitutional Odyssey. Can Canadians Be a Sovereign People?* Toronto: University of Toronto Press.
Ryder, Bruce/Russell, Peter H. 1997: "Ratifying a Post-referendum Agreement on Quebec Sovereignty," in: *The Secession Papers*, Toronto: C. D. Howe Institute.

III. Constitutional Jurisprudence – Does it Stimulate or Prevent Reform?

Change is a Sometimes Thing: Constitutional Jurisprudence in the United States

Martin Edelman

Virtually from the beginning, controversy has surrounded the role of the Supreme Court within the American political system. Once the Court asserted its authority to declare the acts of other governmental agencies null and void for violating the Constitution (*Marbury v. Madison* 1803), the Court could not conceal its policy-making functions. That, in turn, provoked the continuing debate about the legitimacy of the Court's role. More recently, however, scholars have begun systematically to explore the Court's capabilities to influence public policy formulation. Given the inevitable policy effects of judicial decisions, scholars have sought the conditions under which judicial decisions produce political and social change. The aim here is to suggest the factors which support or limit the Supreme Court's ability to promote change through its constitutional decisions.

I.

Ideally, a written constitution should help resolve certain fundamental political issues. It should incorporate a national consensus about a society's basic values and the structure of its government. A constitution elevates those matters above the ordinary political realm. In this sense a written constitution has both a legal and a political significance. Legally, it embodies the highest norms of the State. State organs, including the judiciary, are expected to give those norms priority in arriving at their decisions. Politically, a constitution sets parameters on public policy and enumerates the human rights to be protected. Not only does a constitution authorize, limit, structure, and allocate political power, but it also performs an aspirational function. As a statement of a nation's values, it helps to educate the citizenry while it simultaneously serves as guideline for the political elite. In sum, a constitution encapsulates the nature of a polity (Murphy/Fleming/Barber [2]1995: 3-7).

Written constitutions by themselves, however, rarely resolve important political/social issues. Because the core message of a constitutional text is framed in broad, general principles, few, if any conclusive answers are provided.[1] A constitution's entrenched values can supply the basis for contesting virtually any issue that a nation confronts. Resolving conflict about and among those basic values is left to the constitution's implementers and interpreters. Once the courts are successfully able to assert their authority to become the interpreters of the constitution (*Marbury v. Madison* 1803), and especially when the courts are able to claim the authority to be the ultimate, authoritative, constitutional interpreters (*Cooper v. Aaron* 1958; *United States v. Nixon* 1974; *Boerne v. Flores* 1997), they become important "players" in the political process. That has certainly been the situation in the United States. As Tocqueville (1835: I, 290) noted about the first modern nation with a written constitution, "[s]carcely any political question arises in the United States that is not resolved, sooner or later into a judicial question."

The legalization of political conflict helps to bring it within bounds; it does not end the conflict. For the boundaries at any given moment are established by particular conceptions of the basic principles, expressed in general language, that are entrenched in the document. People with differing political interests are quite likely to place different meanings on the same text.[2] Therefore, the operating rules of the game at any given moment are themselves ultimately contestable and changeable. The operative understanding of the constitutional text at any given time is, after all, only one possible interpretative conception of broader, general values (Dworkin 1985).

It is within this complex political and interpretive context that we must assess constitutional jurisprudence in the United States. More specifically, the question here is: to what extent can courts promote change?[3] Not surprisingly, the answer to be gleaned from the American experience is highly contextual: it depends upon the substantive nature of a judicial decision and how that decision is perceived by the other political actors in the system.

In a famous article, Robert Dahl (1958) attempted an appraisal of the Supreme Court as a policy-maker within the American political system.

---

1 Note James Madison's trenchant comment on this point: "When the Almighty himself condescends to address mankind in their own language, His meaning, luminous as it must be, is rendered dim and doubtful by the cloudy medium through which it is communicated" (Madison/Hamilton/Jay [1788] 1987: 245).

2 Thomas Hobbes expressed this point in his usual trenchant manner: "All laws, written and unwritten, have need of interpretation. The unwritten law of nature, though it be easy to such, as without partiality and passion, make use of their natural reason, and therefor leaves the violators thereof without excuse; *yet considering there be very few, perhaps none, that in some cases are not blinded by self-love, or some other passion*; it is now become of all laws the most obscure, and has consequently the greatest need of able interpreters. The written laws, if they be short, are easily misinterpreted, from the divers significations of a word, or two: if long, they be more obscure by the divers significations of many words" (Hobbes [1651] 1957: 180).

3 Note that I refer to "change" rather than "reform," since not all changes entail an improvement as is implied by the word reform.

While Dahl's account must be modified in light of subsequent criticism (Casper 1976), it nonetheless remains a highly fruitful starting point. Hence, I suggest examining the American Supreme Court's ability to promote change in the following categories:

1. When the Court promotes policies which are consistent with those favored by the dominant political consensus of the time, its ability to promote change is at its highest.
2. When the Court promotes policies which are opposed by the dominant political consensus of the time, its ability to promote change is at its lowest.
3. When the Court promotes policies which are marginal to the concerns of the dominant consensus of the time, it will most likely be able to promote change *unless* those policies energize the emergence of a new consensus opposed to the Court's policies.

I.1.

When the American Supreme Court acts in conjunction with the elected political leadership, it is usually difficult, if not impossible, to assess the Court's role in promoting change. Petitions to the Supreme Court ask the Justices to evaluate the constitutionality of policies already propounded by, and most frequently implemented by, other agencies in the political system. When the Court supports actions that alter the status quo, it is ratifying changes promoted by other actors. In a democracy, changes initiated by the elected agencies of government are presumed to be supported by a general public consensus. In this circumstance, the Court is performing an important function. As the "guardian of the Constitution"[4] and the values embodied therein, the Supreme Court legitimizes policies by declaring that those actions pass constitutional muster (Black 1960). Examples of such moments were the Court's belated legitimization of New Deal regulation of the economy,[5] and the establishment of the administrative state.[6] In such instances,

4 Alexander Hamilton: "This independence of the judges is equally requisite to guard the Constitution [...]" (Madison/Hamilton/Jay [1778] 1987: 440); James Madison thought that the federal courts "would consider themselves in a peculiar manner 'the guardians' of [the rights enumerated in the Bill of Rights]" when he urged Congress to adopt those Amendments (*Annals of Congress* 1: 439 [8 June 1789]).

5 *N.L.R.B. v. Jones & Laughlin Steel Corp.*, 301 U.S. 1 (1937) [legitimizing Congress' use of the Commerce Clause; reversing *Schechter Poultry Corp. v. United States*, 295 U.S. 495 (1935), and *Carter v. Carter Coal Co.*, 298 U.S. 238 (1936)]; *Steward Machine Co. v. Davis*, 301 U.S. 548 (1937) [legitimizing Congress' use of the Tax Clause; reversing *United States v. Butler*, 297 U.S. 1 (1937)]; *West Coast Hotel v. Parrish*, 300 U.S. 144 (1937) [sustaining State regulations from challenges under the Due Process Clause; reversing *Adkins v. Children's Hospital*, 261 U.S. 525 (1925)].

the Court may put certain conflicts to rest. Nonetheless, it is usually difficult to attribute change to the Supreme Court's legitimization of policies advanced by other governmental agencies.

There have been a few occasions, however, when the Supreme Court has advanced policies for which there was only a latent consensus. Determined minorities favoring the status quo had used their strategic positions to prevent the agencies accountable to the public through the electoral processes from promoting change. In those circumstances, Supreme Court decisions have *sometimes* produced significant change.

Two significant changes were successfully advanced by the Supreme Court during the tenure of Chief Justice Earl Warren. The "reapportionment revolution" altered the way American State legislatures and the United States House of Representatives were elected. In a series of 1964 decisions, the Court insisted that election districts conform to a new constitutional standard: "one person, one vote; one vote, one value; in relatively equal population districts" (*Wesberry v. Sanders* 1964; *Reynolds v. Sims* 1964; *Lucas v. Forty-Fourth General Assembly of Colorado* 1964).

Before then, State legislatures had refused to reapportion themselves periodically. When they had been required to change Congressional districts as a result of population shifts revealed by each decennial census, they had invariably favored the interests and areas already solidly entrenched in the legislatures. Many legislatures had not even been reapportioned to take account of such a long-term trend as urbanization. It was an American equivalent of the Eighteenth Century "rotten borough" system in England. An appeal to the electoral political process to cure this particular vice was an exercise in pure futility: the very politicians and interests who benefitted from the status quo had a stranglehold on the electoral process. The majority who would benefit from change was caught in a legislative strait jacket (Clark 1962).

Gross malapportionment distorted the significance of the franchise. The right to vote is at the core of all theories of democracy; majority rule is considered to be the keystone of a democratic political system (Pennock 1979). Limiting the effectiveness of popular political participation transforms democracy's basic institution – the electoral process – into a meaningless ritual. Protecting and nourishing the democratic political process itself was the basic rationale which justified and ultimately sustained judicial intervention.

Moreover, by insisting that representative bodies conform to the "one person, one vote" standard, the Court sought to maintain the legitimacy of American electoral institutions in terms of their origins. Equality is central to the natural rights theory enshrined in the American political tradition.[7] That

---

6 Compare *Yakus v. United States*, 321 U.S. 414 (1944) with *Panama Refining Co. v. Ryan*, 293 U.S. 388 (1935).

7 "We hold these truths to be self-evident, that all men are created equal [...]:" *The*

same tradition makes voting central to the American notion of self-government.[8] The exercise of the franchise is a principal means of protecting and advancing a person's interest. It is also the constitutionally sanctioned method for an individual citizen to participate in decisions affecting her life. Within the American culture, unequal access to the electoral process erodes the legitimacy of its central institutions (Ely 1980; Edelman 1984).

Both political self-interest and the values embedded in the American political tradition provided the widespread support for the Supreme Court's "reapportionment revolution." To the extent that they were aware of the gross malapportionment in State legislatures and in the House of Representatives, a majority of the attentive public opposed rule by an unrepresentative minority. Most Americans, however, had been blithely unaware that their representative institutions did not conform to an equality standard like the "one person, one vote; one vote, one value" standard. When they realized the extent of the prevailing institutionalized departure from a voting equality standard, they widely supported the Supreme Court's decisions. Thus, the politicians and groups who sought to reverse the "reapportionment revolution" could not muster the necessary public support to revert to the status quo ante (Edelman 1984: 144). In sum, where the public is ignorant of certain conditions, and the politicians refuse to deal with them, Court decisions can sometimes affect issues that otherwise might have remained unaddressed (Monti 1980).

The Warren Court is even more famous for its desegregation decisions. In *Brown v. Board of Education* (1954), a unanimous Supreme Court declared that the segregation of children in public schools solely on the basis of race deprived them of equal educational opportunities, even if the racially separate facilities were equal. The Court held that because racially segregated schools deprived students of the opportunity to learn by association with their fellow citizens, and because these conditions were likely to generate feelings of inferiority and superiority solely on the basis of race, separate educational facilities were inherently unequal. As such, they violated the Equal Protection Clause of the Fourteenth Amendment. In subsequent cases, the Court extended *Brown* to other segregation laws. Governmental practices which had created a system *legally* segregating black citizens from white were invalidated. Henceforth, race was a "suspect category;" the separation of American citizens on the basis of their race was subjected to strict judicial scrutiny. To withstand strict judicial scrutiny, governmental action would have to advance a compelling governmental interest by the least restrictive means available. That judicial test was invariably fatal to legally imposed racial segregation.

Declaration of Independence, 1776.

8 "We the People of the United States [...]:" Preamble, *The Constitution of the United States*, 1787; "[...] that government of the people, by the people, for the people, shall not perish from the earth:" Abraham Lincoln, *The Gettysburg Address*, 1863.

The (white) political leadership of the Southern states reacted to the *Brown* decision by proclaiming their defiance. Some Southerners even revived the pre-Civil War doctrine of state nullification: they asserted that the *Desegregation* decisions were "null, void, and of no force and effect." Outside some regions in the border states and in the District of Columbia, there was no effort to comply with the *Desegregation* decision. Rather, the Southern politicians followed the lead of Harry Byrd, the senior U.S. Senator from Virginia, who organized a policy of "massive resistance" to desegregation. In 1956, 101 Congressmen and Senators issued the "Southern Manifesto" which denounced *Brown* and which pledged to "use all lawful means to bring about a reversal of [that] decision which is contrary to the Constitution" (Kluger 1975: 949-950). At the time, the Southern Democratic-Republican Coalition controlled Congress. In addition, President Dwight Eisenhower refused to lend his personal and institutional support to the Court decision (Rosenberg 1991: 76). For three long years, the Supreme Court was the only national institution actively promoting the equal citizenship of black Americans.

Yet, survey after survey indicated that the vast bulk of the American people were fully supportive of the *Brown* decision and its progeny. A governmentally imposed apartheid system, even in one section of the country, was simply incompatible with the basic American belief in equality (Myrdal 1944). Political leaders who favored desegregation were able to utilize this widespread tacit consensus to sustain the change introduced by the Court. The efforts to reverse *Brown* were rebuffed. Gradually, very gradually, desegregation became the actual, operative law of the land. In 1957, then Senate Majority Leader Lyndon Johnson was able to push through the first national civil rights legislation since Reconstruction had ended in 1876. Still later, then President Lyndon Johnson was able to break the back of legal segregation in the United States when he had Congress enact the 1964 Civil Rights Act and the 1965 Voting Rights Act. Once again, the Supreme Court had taken the lead in changing American society. In certain situations, then, the Court has the capacity to call forth the aspirations of the American people, to remind them of their constitutional duty, and to use that mobilized public consensus to change public policy (Bickel 1962: 26).

I.2.

"The impact of *Brown* and other desegregation cases on American constitutional law and society extended far beyond matters of race. Propelled by the decision, courts began to strike down [...] differences in official treatment based on sex, alienage, length of residence, illegitimacy of birth, and sometimes (but less often than one would wish) ability to pay."

Archibald Cox made that assessment in 1987. Twelve years later, it is clear that, at least as to issues of economic inequality, Professor Cox was too sanguine. The Supreme Court was unable to help American society address the issue of poverty.

Economic egalitarianism was indeed the thrust of many Warren Court decisions. In a 1966 case invalidating a Virginia law which had required the payment of a poll tax in order to vote, the Court said: "Wealth, like race, creed, or color is not germane to one's ability to participate intelligently in the electoral process. *Lines drawn on the basis of wealth or property, like those of race, are traditionally disfavored*" (*Harper v. Virginia State Board of Elections* 1966: 668; emphasis added). As early as 1970, Alexander Bickel called attention to the Court's efforts to lead American society to a more egalitarian democracy. He also subjected them to scathing criticism. Such issues, Professor Bickel argued, should be resolved by the elected agencies of government (Bickel 1970). In the event, those institutions, reflecting the electoral majority's reluctance to redistribute wealth in American society – a redistribution that would undoubtedly come at some expense to those groups and individuals who comprise the actual electorate – resisted the Court's efforts. The same forces which frustrated President Johnson's "war on poverty" defeated the Supreme Court.

To be sure, it was not a total defeat. Within the judicial system, an area subject to its supervision, the Warren Court was able to introduce some measure of equality. After *Gideon v. Wainwright* (1963), indigents must be supplied with counsel at public expense in all serious criminal cases, whether federal or state. Similarly, the Court required the government to furnish lawyers and transcripts for at least one appeal (*Griffin v. Illinois* 1956; *Douglas v. California* 1963). Yet legal services for the poor have never been adequately funded, so the poor still do not, in practice, receive equal treatment within the judicial system. The same pattern of indifference to the plight of poorer Americans is evident in governmental policies dealing with a woman's right to an abortion. After the Supreme Court had interpreted the Constitution as protecting that right (*Roe v. Wade* 1973) (to be discussed more fully below), most legislatures and the Congress refused to fund access to abortions for indigent women (*Maher v. Roe* 1977; *Harris v. McRae* 1980). Nor were state legislators and members of Congress inspired by Warren Court decisions to fund welfare programs sufficiently to lift indigent Americans from mere subsistence to a level approximating the Government's definition of poverty income (*Dandridge v. Williams* 1970).

The clearest example of the Warren Court's inability to promote economic egalitarianism is in the area of education. In *Brown*, Chief Justice Warren had written for the unanimous Court:

"Today, education is perhaps the most important function of state and local governments. Compulsory school attendance laws and the great expenditures for education both demonstrate our recognition of the importance of education to our democratic society. It is required in the performance of our most basic public responsibilities, even service in the armed forces. It is the very foundation of good citizenship. Today it is a principal instrument in awakening the child to cultural values, in preparing him for later professional training, and in helping him to adjust normally to his environment. In these days it is doubtful that any child may reasonably be expected to succeed in life if he is denied the opportunity of an education. *Such an opportunity, where the state has undertaken to provide it, is a right which must be available to all on equal terms.*" (493: emphasis added)

Responding to this language, in the early 1970s, state courts and lower federal courts began to hold state educational systems to an increasingly egalitarian funding standard (*Milliken v. Green* 1972; *Serrano v. Priest* 1971; *Van Dusartz v. Hatfield* 1971). Those opinions argued that education was a fundamental right and that unequal funding plans were therefore unconstitutional. Despite the fact that there was a clear correlation between funding levels and student success in schools, those decisions were met with energetic opposition by state and local officials who were unwilling to upset the district-based systems which favored the middle and upper classes. Republican President Richard Nixon also responded to that constituency. His appointments to the Supreme Court formed the majority which rejected the proposition that "wealth or property [...] are traditionally disfavored" categories under the U.S. Constitution and thereby refused to subject classifications based upon wealth to strict judicial scrutiny. Since the 1973 *San Antonio School District v. Rodriguez* decision, the impetus for court-led change in this area has all but disappeared (Henig et. al 1999).[9]

As Alexander Hamilton noted at the outset of the American constitutional system, the "judiciary has no influence over [...] the purse; no direction [...] of the wealth of the society [...]" (Madison/Hamilton/Jay [1788] 1987: 437). The Supreme Court has little leverage to compel the expenditure of funds. When the Court cannot mobilize popular support for its policies, it cannot promote change. This is particularly true when it fails to tap into an American ideal of sufficient strength to override an existing, broadly-based consensus (Frug 1978).

I.3.

Many cases which are decided by the United States Supreme Court are marginal to the values embraced by the existing public consensus. Certain values

9 The New Jersey Supreme Court based its decision in *Robinson v. Cahill*, 62 N.J. 473 (1973) on the state constitution, as opposed to the Equal Protection Clause of the 14th Amendment of the U.S. Constitution, so it still retains some vitality. The yearly budget battles, however, have yet to produce substantially equal funding for students in all New Jersey school districts.

cannot even fairly be said to be latent within that consensus. The values which are significant to the groups comprising that consensus cannot possibly include all issues confronting a nation of 250 million people. And the diversity of the American population ensures that no consensus approaches unanimity. In the United States, marginal groups have historically sought redress through the courts when their values and interests have not been satisfied or recognized by the institutions more responsive to the electoral majority. Minority group access, in fact, has frequently been used to justify judicial review (Ely 1980; Choper 1980). So we must examine those situations in which the Court promotes policies which are not central to the dominant consensus of the time.

Marginality, however, does not invariably mean societally unimportant. In fact, since we are examining the Court's role in promoting societal change, the policies involved in this section must be significant. It is simply that, for a variety of reasons, most groups did not fully consider the issue until after the Court announced its decisions.

Such was the case with religion in the public schools in the early 1960s. At the outset of the Republic, education had been a private matter. Most usually, children (boys, really) were educated in denominational schools. In the course of the 19th Century, education gradually became a public responsibility. During this transition, practices of the dominant religious groups' schools were carried over to the public schools. Conflicts developed as the religious diversity of the American people increased, especially in urban areas. Religious minorities resented their children being subjected to the religious beliefs of the majority. Yet, until the Supreme Court acted, the public focus, like that of the Kennedy Administration, was elsewhere: the Cold War, desegregation, and economic issues.

In 1962 and 1963, the Court held that the No Establishment Clause of the First Amendment prohibited prayers and religious exercises in the curriculum of public schools (*Engel v. Vitale* 1962; *Abington School District v. Schempp* 1963). The decisions were roundly criticized by political and religious leaders. The Court was accused of taking God out of the classroom and thereby imposing an atheistic ethic upon American school children. Yet after more than three and a half decades, proponents of school prayers have not been able to secure the support necessary to change the Court's interpretation and to allow public schools to revert to previous practices.

The initial attempts to reverse this Court-induced change was to have Congress adopt a constitutional amendment authorizing school prayers. The efforts foundered on the sheer size of the country and the religious diversity of the American people. On reflection, many religious leaders realized that either *their own* members would comprise the minority subjected to "alien" beliefs in different areas of the country, or, alternately, that their children would confront generalized "prayers" devoid of religious substance. No proposed constitutional amendment attained the two-thirds majority in each house of Congress needed to send it on to the states for further consideration (Keynes 1989: 174-205).

Subsequently, opponents of the Court's policy tried a variety of measures to reverse it at the state level. They tried to rally support around the idea that the posting of the Ten Commandments in classrooms would help promote moral values. To the Court, however, it was an obvious attempt to advance religion (*Stone v. Graham* 1980). Similarly, proponents of religion in the public schools tried to introduce a moment of silence for contemplation or prayer. Since the law specifically mentioned prayer, the Court held it unconstitutional (*Wallace v. Jaffre* 1985). The Court also held unconstitutional the efforts by fundamentalist Christians, largely concentrated in the rural areas of the South and Midwest, to proscribe the teaching of Darwin's theory of evolution (*Epperson v. Arkansas* 1983). Again, the efforts within the states to reverse the Court foundered on the size of the United States and the diversity of its population. The system worked as Madison had predicted: "A religious sect may degenerate into a political faction in a part of the [Union]: but the variety of sects dispersed over the entire face of it must secure the national councils from any dangers from that source" (Madison/Hamilton/Jay [1788] 1987: 122-128).

Religion, now as in the past, is an important factor in American society. Efforts to restore prayers and comparable religious practices to the public schools, however, were marginal to the dominant consensus at the time of the Supreme Court decisions. Either the very diversity of religious groups precluded the development of consensus, or the particular practice was deemed too trivial for the majority of the public to be aroused. Current controversies involving religion focus on government financial aid to religious education. That issue is important to many Catholics, Jews, Muslims, and Protestants. The potential for a broad-based coalition plus the high cost of private education in all parts of the country ensures the continued national saliency of this issue. That the Supreme Court has not removed *all* religion-state issues from the American political agenda should not blind us to what it *has* accomplished in the controversial area of religion-government relations. In the United States, prayers and similar religious practices have generally disappeared from the curriculum of the public schools.[10]

Religious beliefs were certainly prime factors in the widespread opposition to the Supreme Court's decision that the Constitution protected a woman's right to terminate her pregnancy. Prior to *Roe v. Wade* (1973), pro-choice groups were focused on state laws proscribing or greatly restricting

10 In a few rural areas, geographic insulation combined with the religious homogeneity of the population, still permits exceptions to the national policy proclaimed by the Court (see Beaney/Beiser 1964 for an early study of this phenomenon).

access to abortion.[11] Those campaigns, because they were state-by-state efforts, never generated national momentum and did not provoke a national reaction. *Roe* changed all that. Abortion ceased to be marginal to the national political dialogue and for a time became *the* central issue.

Roe ignited a firestorm of controversy. Members of Congress introduced numerous constitutional amendments, funding restrictions, and various other statutory measures to limit the effects of the Court's abortion decisions. In the states, pro-life (anti-abortion) groups sought similar remedies: "In [1973], immediately following *Roe*, for instance, some 260 abortion-related bills were introduced in state legislatures, and 39 passed. By 1974 another 19 out of 189 bills were enacted" (Craig/O'Brien 1993: 77). Nonetheless, pro-life forces were unable to energize a new national consensus opposed to the Court's policy that the Constitution protected a woman's right of access to abortion.

In fact, public opinion polls showed that the public, like the Court, did not favor an absolute right of abortion but did support pro-choice policies (Craig/O'Brien 1993: 245-277). Despite the defeat of the Equal Rights Amendment to the Constitution,[12] women were increasingly gaining acceptance as equals in all aspects of American life. Moreover, American society as a whole was becoming more "rights-oriented." There was an increased acceptance of individual autonomy – now including women – as the central value of American society (Bellah et al. 1985). Together, these shifts in the underlying beliefs of the majority of Americans meant that the opponents of *Roe* could never mobilize the support needed to overturn that decision.

The abortion struggle culminated with the 1992 Supreme Court decision *Planned Parenthood v. Casey*. Three Justices, appointed by anti-abortion Presidents Ronald Reagan and George Bush, reaffirmed what they called the "essence" of the constitutional right of abortion while at the same time permitting some state restrictions. Central to the joint opinion of Justices Sandra Day O'Connor, Anthony Kennedy and David Souter was the statement that

"for two decades of economic and social developments, people have organized intimate relationships and made choices that define their views of themselves and their places in society, in reliance on the availability of abortion in the event that contraception should fail. The ability of women to participate equally in the economic and social life of the Nation has been facilitated by their ability to control their reproductive lives." (*Planned Parenthood v. Casey* 1992: 856)

---

11 Four states and the District of Columbia permitted an abortion for any reason, 13 states permitted abortion to protect a woman's physical and mental health, one state to preserve the woman's life and in the case of rape, 29 states to preserve a woman's life, and three states prohibited all abortions (Craig/O'Brien 1993: 75).

12 Congress had submitted the ERA to the states in 1972. By 1978, it was clear that the ERA would not be ratified by two thirds of the states within the requisite seven years, so the deadline was extended for another 5 years. The ERA died on 30 June 1982 still lacking the support of 3 more states.

There have been no significant abortion cases since *Casey*. Even state efforts have abated. Despite the occasional sound and fury, a woman's constitutional right of access to abortion has become part of American life. Thus a constitutional decision by the Supreme Court creates a new default position in the policy process. The decision can shift the balance of power among societal groups. The Court's policy can only be overturned by the mobilization of significant forces.

The Supreme Court, however, does not always have a free hand to deal with marginal issues. At times, a line of Court decisions has not only generated a backlash sufficient to move the issue to the center of the national political agenda, but also to mobilize an opposition sufficiently strong to reverse the policy. Affirmative action is one such policy.

The Supreme Court's desegregation policies were widely supported in all regions of the country except the South. When it became apparent that President Johnson and Congress were finally ready to help end racial segregation, the Court began to ratchet up its standard. In 1964, it announced that the "time for mere 'deliberate speed' [had] run out" (*Griffin v. School Bd. of Prince Edward County* 1964: 234). In 1968, the Court held that desegregation – i.e., simply ending past segregative practices – was no longer sufficient. Government agencies which had legally enforced racial segregation now had "the affirmative duty to take whatever steps might be necessary to convert to a unitary system in which racial discrimination would be eliminated root and branch" (*Green v. County School Bd. of New Kent County* 1968: 437-438). The Supreme Court policy had moved from *desegregation* (ending racial segregation) to promoting racial *integration.*

The Court's integration policies met with considerable resistance. Integration imposed considerably more change on the white majority than desegregation. As long as the Court was able to connect its rulings to the rectification of past governmental segregative acts, integration was grudgingly accepted. No one could deny that legally mandated segregation had *some* impact on existing segregation patterns even if the precise causal connection could not be specified. The legitimacy of the Court's approach was difficult to counter. Thus Charlotte-Mecklenburg, where segregation had been required by North Carolina law, was ordered to integrate its entire school system. The fact that much of the segregation was attributable to housing patterns common to all American urban areas did not limit the scope of the integration order (*Swann v. Charlotte-Mecklenburg Bd. of Education* 1971). Similarly, the Denver, Colorado school authorities had deliberately tried to confine racial minorities to certain inner city districts. Had a totally colorblind policy been in effect, only those areas and the surrounding districts would have been integrated, yet the Court ordered an integration plan covering the entire city (*Keyes v. Denver School District #1* 1973). But there was an obvious limit to this rectification approach. Not all racial discrimination in the United States could be connected to governmental acts of racial segregation. Most racial discrimination stemmed from private acts.

Throughout the 1960s white opposition to court-imposed integration orders increased. Congress attempted to limit court-ordered school busing decrees (Keynes 1989: 207-244). That same reaction fueled the 1968 presidential campaigns of both George Wallace (Carter 1995) and Richard Nixon (Phillips 1969). While the Nixon appointments to the Supreme Court insisted that Congress lacked the authority to restrict remedial court orders enforcing a constitutional right (*Swann v. Charlotte-Mecklenburg Bd. of Education* 1971: 15-18), they helped create the judicial majority which restricted Court orders to remedying past governmental acts of segregation (*Milliken v. Bradley* 1974).

Taking their cue from the Supreme Court, federal and state governments and large corporations had originally sought to end racial segregation and discrimination in education, housing, and employment. They had promoted a wide range of affirmative action programs that included aggressive recruiting and remedial training programs; programs which set numerical goals and guidelines; and others which contained minority set-asides quotas specifying the exact numbers of minority members to be recruited and hired (Glazer 1975). These affirmative action programs triggered heated political controversies. For the Supreme Court, they posed the issue of whether the Equal Protection Clause of the 14th Amendment *permitted* agencies responsible to the electoral processes to utilize racial classifications to pursue integration. Supporters of affirmative action argued that in order to get beyond racism, it is necessary to first take account of race. That is, in order to treat some persons equally we must treat them differently. The supporters of affirmative action argued that it would be perverse to let the Equal Protection Clause perpetuate racial supremacy (Blackmun 1978). The opponents argued that it was wrong to disadvantage the current white population who may not have engaged in racial discrimination and to favor those members of minority groups who may not have actually been victims of discrimination. All persons, white as well as black, the opponents of affirmative action argued, were entitled to the same equal protection of the law (Powell 1978).

As a matter of constitutional interpretation, the Supreme Court originally supported the argument of the opponents of affirmative action that no racial classification could be benign, but as a matter of public policy, it frequently sustained programs designed to alleviate racial disparities (*Regents, University of California v. Bakke* 1978; *United Steel Workers of America v. Weber* 1979; *Fullilove v. Klutznik* 1980). Gradually, however, the addition of the judicial appointments of Presidents Ronald Reagan and George Bush led to a Court majority unwilling to sustain affirmative action programs except those clearly designed to remedy government acts of racial segregation (*Aderand Constructors v. Pena* 1995).

In the early 1960s, affirmative action was a policy that affected only white Southerners. By the 1980s and 1990s, affirmative action was no longer a marginal issue in national politics. It was a salient, meaningful threat to a majority of white Americans. As a result, it was Court policy that changed, not American society. In short, the Supreme Court's ability to promote change is bound by the beliefs and norms of the political culture, and decisions which stray too far from those values are likely to be severely criticized and reversed (Rosenberg 1991: 11).

II.

The Supreme Court was the national institution most responsible for instituting the revolution in race relations. As Justice Potter Stewart noted, the Court had proclaimed that segregation was "invalid simply because [the U.S.] Constitution presupposes that men are created equal, and that therefore racial differences cannot provide a valid basis for governmental action" (Stewart 1963: 317). The Court subsequently led the fight that ended legally enforced segregation. It also supported and helped sustain the civil rights movement (Kalven 1965). But despite some initial successes, when the Court sought to encourage the emergence of a racially integrated society via the utilization of affirmative action programs, it failed. The public consensus which had supported the end of legal segregation could not be led by the Court to support policies which threatened the majority's accustomed place in society.

Thus there are limits to Court-induced change in the American democracy. When the Supreme Court promotes policies that are consistent with those favored by the dominant political consensus of the time, the Court's ability to promote change is at its highest. That was the situation with both its reapportionment and desegregation decisions. When the Court promotes policies that are opposed by the dominant majority of the time, the Court's ability to promote change is at its lowest. That was the situation with the Court's effort to lead the country towards more economic egalitarism. When the Court promotes policies that are marginal to the dominant consensus of the time, the Court will most likely be able to promote change (as was the case with prayers in the public schools) *unless* those policies energize a new consensus opposed to the Court's policies (as was the case with affirmative action).

The Justices, of course, do not have the benefit of historical hindsight. When they first confront important issues, they frequently have no certain knowledge as to how their decisions will be received by the groups comprising the dominant public consensus.[13] In such situations, when the Court acts, there *may be* a latent consensus or an issue *may remain* marginal to dominant public consensus. The Justices must make their assessments independent of how the public will react to their decisions (Murphy 1964: 196). They must take a chance.

In the institutional scheme of American democracy, the Court's uncertainty is not necessarily a bad thing. It may encourage the justices "to do the right thing," to interpret the Constitution and the laws as they honestly believe best. Personally, they have nothing to lose. The Constitution secures their position for life and American history has guaranteed the power of their institution.[14] Sometimes the Court's efforts will be rebuffed. Sometimes the Supreme Court will be able to promote change. In any event, the Supreme Court decisions will become part of the national dialogue (Casper 1976; Jacobsohn 1977).

---

13 In an attempt to isolate the Supreme Court's impact that was the situation in all the policy areas discussed in this paper.

14 If as popular a President as Franklin D. Roosevelt, fresh from his 1936 landslide re-election and enjoying overwhelming party majorities in each house of Congress, could not, in the depth of the Great Depression, rearrange the power of the Supreme Court that was frustrating his policies, the Justices need not fear.

References

Beaney, William/Beiser, Edward 1964: "Prayer and Politics: *Engel* and *Schempp* in the Political Process," in: *Journal of Public Law* 2, 475-503.

Bellah, Robert et al. 1985: *Habits of the Heart*, Berkeley: University of California Press.

Bickel, Alexander 1962: *The Least Dangerous Branch. The Supreme Court at the Bar of Politics*, Indianapolis: Bobbs-Merrill.

—— 1970: *The Supreme Court and the Idea of Progress*, New York: Harper Torchbooks.

Black, Charles 1960: *The People and the Court*, New York: Macmillan.

Blackmun, Harry 1978: *Regents, University of California v. Bakke*, 438 U.S. 265, 402-408.

Carter, Dan 1995: *The Politics of Rage. Wallace, The Origins of the New Conservatism, and the Transformation of American Politics*, New York: Simon and Schuster.

Casper, Jonathan 1976: "The Supreme Court and National Policy-Making," in: *American Political Science Review* 70, 50-63.

Choper, Jesse H. 1980: *Judicial Review and the National Political Process*, Chicago: University of Chicago Press.

Clark, Tom 1962: *Baker v. Carr*, 369 U.S. 186, 251-266.

Cox, Archibald 1987: *The Court and the Constitution*, Boston: Houghton, Mifflin.

Craig, Barbara Hinkson/O'Brien, David 1993: *Abortion and American Politics*, Chatham, NJ: Chatham House Publishers.

Dahl, Robert 1958: "Decision-Making in a Democracy: The Supreme Court as National Policy-Maker," in: *Journal of Public Law* 6, 279-295.

Dworkin, Ronald 1985: *A Matter of Principle*, Cambridge: Harvard University Press.

Edelman, Martin 1984: *Democratic Theories and the Constitution*, Albany: State University of New York Press.

Ely, John H. 1980: *Democracy and Distrust*, Cambridge: Harvard University Press.

Frug, Gerald 1978: "The Judicial Power of the Purse," in: *University of Pennsylvania Law Review* 126, 715-798.

Glazer, Nathan 1975: *Affirmative Discrimination. Ethnic Inequality and Public Policy*, New York: Basic Books.

Henig, Jeffrey R. et al. 1999: *The Color of School Reform. Race, Politics, and the Challenge of Urban Education*, Princeton: Princeton UP.

Hobbes, Thomas [1651] ed. by Michael Oakshott 1957: *Leviathan*, Oxford: Basil Blackwell.

Jacobsohn, Gary 1977: *Pragmatism, Statesmanship and the Supreme Court*, Ithaca, NY: Cornell UP.

Kalven, Harry, Jr. 1965: *The Negro and the First Amendment*, Columbus: Ohio State University Press.

Keynes, Edward, with Randall K. Miller 1989: *The Court vs. Congress*, Durham, NC: Duke UP.

Kluger, Richard 1975: *Simple Justice*, New York: Alfred A. Knopf.
Madison, James/Hamilton, Alexander/Jay, John [1788] ed. by Isaac Kramnick 1987: *The Federalist Papers*, London: Penguin Books.
Monti, Daniel 1980: "Administrative Foxes in Educational Chicken Coops," in: *Law & Policy Quarterly* 2: 233-255.
Murphy, Walter F. 1964: *Elements of Judicial Strategy*, Chicago: University of Chicago Press.
——/Fleming, James E./Barber, Sotirios A. [2]1995: *American Constitutional Interpretation*, Westbury, NY: Foundation Press.
Myrdal, Gunnar 1944: *An American Dilemma*, New York: Harper & Bros.
Pennock, J. Roland 1979: *Democratic Political Theory*, Princeton: Princeton UP.
Phillips, Kevin 1969: *The Emerging Republican Majority*, New Rochelle, NY: Arlington House.
Powell, Lewis 1978: *Regents, University of California v. Bakke*, 438 U.S. 265, 269-325.
Rosenberg, Gerald N. 1991: *Hollow Hope. Can Courts Bring about Social Change?* Chicago: University of Chicago Press.
Stewart, Potter 1963: *Abington School District v. Schempp*, 374 U.S. 203, 308-320.
Tocqueville, Alexis de [1835] 1954: *Democracy in America*, New York: Vintage Books.

Abington School District v. Schempp, 374 U.S. 203 (1963).
Adarand Constructors v. Pena, 515 U.S. 200 (1995).
Boerne v. Flores, 521 U.S. 520 (1997).
Brown v. Board of Education, 347 U.S. 483 (1954).
Cooper v. Aaron, 358 U.S. 1 (1955).
Dandridge v. Williams, 397 U.S. 471 (1970).
Douglas v. California, 372 U.S. 353 (1963).
Engel v. Vitale, 370 U.S. 421 (1962).
Epperson v. Arkansas, 393 U.S. 97 (1968).
Fullilove v. Klutznik, 448 U.S. 448 (1980).
Gideon v. Wainwright, 372 U.S. 335 (1963).
Green v. School Board of New Kent County, 391 U.S. 430 (1968).
Griffin v. Illinois, 351 U.S. 12 (1956).
Griffin v. School Board of Prince Edward County, 377 U.S. 218 (1964).
Harper v. Virginia State Board of Elections, 383 U.S. 663 (1966).
Harris v. McRae, 448 U.S. 297 (1980).
Keyes v. Denver School District #1, 413 U.S. 189 (1973).
Lucas v. Forty-Fourth General Assembly of Colorado, 377 U.S. 713 (1964).
Maher v. Roe, 432 U.S. 464 (1977).
Milliken v. Bradley, 418 U.S. 717 (1974).
Milliken v. Green, 389 Mich. 1 (1972).
Planned Parenthood v. Casey, 505 U.S. 833 (1992).
Reynolds v. Sims, 377 U.S. 533 (1964).
Roe v. Wade, 410 U.S. 113 (1973).
Serrano v. Priest, 5 Cal 3d 584 (1971).
Stone v. Graham, 449 U.S. 39 (1980).
Swann v. Charlotte-Mecklenberg Board of Education, 402 U.S. 1 (1971).

United States v. Nixon, 418 U.S. 683 (1974).
United Steel Workers v. Weber, 443 U.S. 193 (1979).
Van Dusantz v. Hatfield, 334 F. Supp. 870 (D.C. Minn 1971)
Wallace v. Jaffre, 472 U.S. 38 (1985).
Wesberry v. Sanders, 376 U.S. 1 (1964).

The Canadian Charter of Rights and Freedoms: Product and Catalyst of Socio-Political Change in Canada

Martin Thunert

"The adoption of the Charter is undoubtedly the most significant event in the evolution of Canadian political culture in the twentieth century." (Laforest 1995: 125)

I. Introduction

Until the mid-1980s, political and social change was not a judicially driven affair in Canada. Within their respective areas of jurisdiction, the federal and provincial political systems worked in a perfectly majoritarian fashion, as they were supposed to do in the Westminster system. In Parliament or in the legislatures it often did not require more than 40% of the electorate to form a majority government which was then quite uninhibited when it introduced change in its area of jurisdiction. In 1969, for example, it was quite easy for a majority Liberal government under Pierre Trudeau to "force" official bilingualism on federal agencies in the Canadian West, where the Liberal Party had only a weak basis and bilingualism was rather unpopular. Different governments of Québec were quite free to introduce legislation that was explicitly designed to favour French over English as the language of work in the province. Some of the landmark changes in Canadian political history such as the creation of the postwar welfare state with the introduction of medicare, pension plans and unemployment benefits, the Official Languages Act, the policy on multiculturalism, wage-and-price controls in the 1970s, the decision to negotiate and ratify a free trade arrangement with the U.S., or the goods and services tax were fashioned in the parliamentary channels of majoritarian democracy with little or no judicial input. Even Canada's most notorious political struggle, the battle for or against Québec sovereignty, was up until the 1990s fought in parliaments and commissions of inquiry, in election campaigns, referendums and the media, but rarely in the courts.

Enter the Canadian Charter of Rights and Freedoms. The Charter was entrenched into Canada's constitution nearly two decades ago. It has changed traditional Canadian liberal democracy forever. This paper attempts to partially evaluate some of its consequences for Canadian society. I shall argue against a growing body of literature which claims that the Charter is an "alien" document that was superimposed on a country with a traditional political culture of deference and consensus by a small liberal elite. In contrast I argue that the Charter is at the same time a product as well as a catalyst of social and political change in the northern part of the North American continent.

II. The Canadian Charter of Rights and Freedoms: A Short Overview

The substantive clauses of the Charter of Rights and Freedoms were the results of late-modern institution making. The core of the Charter consists of classic individual negative rights. In contrast to the American Bill of Rights, these clauses were not written in the philosophical style of the European enlightenment, but in late 20th century Franco-Anglo legal prose. The Charter's core sections deal with fundamental freedoms (section 2), democratic rights (sections 3-5), mobility rights (section 6), legal rights (sections 7-14), and equality rights (section 15).The second major component of the Charter is a number of peculiar Canadian clauses such as a uniquely Canadian response to the problem of linguistic group rights (sections 16-23). Two other important sections of the Charter pay tribute to the Canadian tradition of parliamentary supremacy: section 1 makes all of the rights and freedoms in the Charter subject to "such reasonable limits prescribed by law as can be demonstrably justified in a free and democratic society." Section 33, the so-called "notwithstanding" or "legislative override" clause, provides that federal or provincial legislation in conflict with the fundamental freedoms or the legal rights guaranteed by the Charter may operate for a period of at least five years (notwithstanding Charter rights) if Parliament or a provincial legislature expressly declare so. The third ingredient, which gave the Charter a distinctly modern or postmodern image, are special affirmative action provisions (section 15 [2]), the guarantee of gender equality, and a multicultural interpretation clause (section 27).

To understand why the Charter itself is a product of the social transformation of Canada after the late 1960s and to explain the current controversies around the Charter and the jurisprudence it has created, a short analysis of the document's history is necessary.

III. The Charter as a Product of Canada's Social Transformation between the 1960s and the 1980s

1. The Historical Development

A Charter of Rights was not entrenched into Canada's patriated constitution in 1982 to mark the end of a period of authoritarian rule. Neither was it introduced to end a period of unchecked elective parliamentary dictatorship. On the contrary, a discourse about rights, their constitutional status and protection came to Canada despite a comparatively benign historical record in the protection of human rights when compared not to utopian visions, but to the dismal human rights records of many other nations. Unlike Britain, modern Canada has never been a country without a written constitution. The long-prevailing doctrine of parliamentary supremacy was always a muted one as it did only apply to specific jurisdictions (one federal and ten provincial jurisdictions) and it was always checked by a – however weak – judicial branch, first by the Judicial Committee of the Privy Council in London, after 1945 by the Supreme Court of Canada. Parliamentary supremacy was in full force, however, when a government backed by a parliamentary majority in the House of Commons or in a provincial legislature acted within its proper jurisdiction. Despite the majoritarian character of the Westminster system of government, Canada's political culture was characterized by an absence of strongly ideological parties and of deep social cleavages. Rather, Canadian politics was noted for a decision-making culture of (elite) accommodation, negotiation and consent.

Inevitably, before looking at the impact of constitutional jurisprudence in the area of basic rights and freedoms, one has to address the question why a discourse about rights and their constitutional protection became so important in postwar Canada in the first place. The causes for this development are manifold. Undoubtedly, the Charter has origins in important socio-legal developments, both on the international as well as on the domestic level. Internationally, the Universal Declaration of Human Rights, adopted by the United Nations in 1948, as well as the general trend towards the "constitutionalization of the world" are indispensable explanatory variables for an understanding of the Canadian constitutional experiment. Domestically, the Charter was also a result of two important sociological developments salient in post-war Canadian society: one is the demographic "de-Britainization" of Canada caused by vigorous "third force" immigration after World War II, the other the new assertiveness of French Canadians after 1960 in combination with the so-called "self-consciousness explosion" of hitherto marginalized societal groups after the late 1960s.

In sum, the Charter represents the culmination of a growing rights consciousness in Canada and elsewhere triggered by experiences such as the Holocaust, European totalitarianism, and home-made violations of civil liberties against Japanese Canadians during the war and under the Duplessis regime in Québec. A feeling grew among political and intellectual elites that the traditional British-Canadian approach of protecting rights in a low key fashion through statutes, the common law and a liberal consensus was no longer true to the reality of a country where the British share of the population rapidly declined. Subsequent legal reforms such as the enactment of the 1960 (Canadian) Bill of Rights did not fundamentally change the British-Canadian regime of rights protection, because the Bill was only a federal statute. Neither did it cover rights violations by the provinces nor did it give rights any constitutional protection. It was thus an even weaker instrument than the American Bill of Rights was before the American Civil War. In the Canada of the 1950s, these legal shortcomings, which were not perceived as such by most political actors, failed to create anything resembling a social movement for an entrenched catalogue of rights. The sparkle that was needed to light a broader public debate about citizens' rights was (a) the self-consciousness wave of the late 1960s and early 1970s, when women, lifestyle groups, ethnic and "third force" Canadians claimed recognition for their newly developed political identities and their demands like access to abortion, non-discrimination, public funding for parochial schools, etc., and (b) the discovery of "rights issues" as a powerful political weapon in the hands of the federal government against the decentralizing forces in Canadian constitutionalism – especially against Québec nationalism. Unlike in other western countries, where the welfare state had been a truly nationalizing force, Canadian welfare state policies had resulted in a more decentralized state and had failed to remedy the regional fragmentation of the nation-state. The entrenchment of a distinctively Canadian Charter of Rights was seen as the next best hope by the federal Trudeau government to fight the forces of political centrifugalism and as an integrative tool to modernize Canadian democracy on a national scale. While most politicians and academic advisers emphasized institutional reform of federalism, Prime Minister Pierre Trudeau could be assured of widespread public support and media coverage when in the 1970s and early 1980s he sold a proposed catalogue of entrenched rights – what was later to become the Charter – as a "people's package" to create a counterweight to the dull song of repeated provincial demands for more jurisdictional power.

2. *The Political Purposes behind the Charter*

As a policy initiative, the basic rationale for Trudeau's Charter strategy was to urge these centrifugal forces into a constitutional debate about national citizenship – a discussion that had little to do with the provinces' own federalism/division of powers agenda. To achieve its ultimate success by becoming the law of the land, Trudeau's Charter-strategy had yet to be linked to the social self-consciousness movements mentioned earlier. Despite its popularity in the media and in opinion polls throughout the late 1970s, the Charter proposals remained a clever governmental initiative with little active political support until the constitutional bargaining forum shifted from intergovernmental conferences to debate within Parliament and its committees early in 1980 (see Banting/Simeon 1985:17). In the public constitutional hearings held in the winter of 1980/81, the Charter was overwhelmingly accepted and demanded by interest groups, social movements and rights-conscious individuals searching for the political recognition of their multiple identities. As the core of a "citizens' constitution" (Alan Cairns), the Charter's legitimacy resided in its capacity to give constitutional recognition to identities beyond territory and region. From the perspective of political psychology, the Charter debates around the 1980/81 parliamentary constitutional hearings mark an important change in the constitutional culture of Canada. For the first time in constitutional politics were the political demands of women, native people, ethnic and "visible-minority" Canadians, the handicapped and others phrased as constitutional rights competing for recognition and consideration with the long-established rights of French and English language groups and with both levels of government.

With the Charter, Trudeau and his supporters hoped to develop a common idea of national citizenship. A genuine Canadian personality, that of the "Charter Canadian," had to be manufactured. However, as Alan Cairns has shown, "Charter Canadians" do not necessarily pledge allegiance to the Charter in its entirety, but often limit their support to specific clauses in that document pertaining to their special interest. Charter support is highly segmented into a non-territorial pluralism composed of women's groups (support sections 15 and 28) and language minorities (endorse section 23); multicultural Canadians stand behind section 27, members of visible minorities and other seekers of equality line up behind anti-discriminatory clauses and traditional civil liberties. With the advent of the Charter, the constitutional constituency in Canada was no longer restricted to governments and to a network of legal scholars. Indeed one might argue that the constitutional stakes of governments representing territorial units and majorities have been severely weakened. Henceforth, the Charter has driven a wedge between those who see themselves mainly represented by territorial political bodies – mainly the Québécois – and those who consider themselves represented as citizens of Canada by functional modes: women, the handicapped, ethnic minorities, lifestyle minorities, etc. The Charter was designed and has become a catalyst for redrawing the boundaries of political community in Canada.

IV. Canada's Public Philosophies and the Charter

What makes it difficult for an outside observer of Canadian constitutional politics to make sense of a growing body of literature is the highly normative character of most arguments within the debate on the Charter of Rights: "Whether one likes the Charter will depend in part on whether one thinks judicial power is likely to further one's political agenda" (Knopf/Morton 1992: 8). As one summarizer of the Charter debate wrote some years ago, there is much "left- and right-wing Charterphobia in Canada" (Sigurdson 1993). The following sections attempt to cut through this ideological jungle and to provide (a) an overview of the main positions in the Charter debate, followed (b) by a short impact assessment of the first one and a half decades under the Charter on four analytical levels: institutional, jurisprudential, political and cultural.

Some of the Charter's liberal drafters and defenders believe that liberal constitutionalism has still not gone far enough, and that a more empowering jurisprudence is necessary (see Axworthy/Trudeau 1990). From the beginning, the Charter has been criticized as a framework of liberal individual rights imposed on a country with both a Tory (order and good government) and a socialist (communitarian and cooperative) political and cultural tradition, and thus not entirely comfortable with a rhetoric about the primacy of liberal rights. Opposition to the Charter comes from a somewhat strange alliance of Tory conservatives, socialists, feminist and post-modern thinkers and practitioners. In contrast to liberal defenders of the Charter, these critics are sceptical about its potential as a means for progressive or desirable social transformation. While the right-wing version of this criticism primarily anticipates and fears an erosion of law and order and predicts the ungovernability of an increasingly rights-seeking entitlement society, the left-wing or communitarian critique laments the loss of community attachment and alienation in a society where negative liberty triumphs over participatory rights, and important policy questions are litigated in terms of rights instead of being discussed as questions of substantive justice (see Taylor in Cairns/Williams1985: 183-229). These critics argue that the Charter entails mostly negative rights and thus curtails positive state action – especially in the name of the disadvantaged.

The most articulate voices among conservative Charter critics are two Alberta-based political scientists, F.L. Morton and Rainer Knopff (see Knopff/Morton 1992), as well as an Ottawa-based think tank, the Centre for Renewal in Public Policy. Among the intellectual critics of the left, political philosopher Charles Taylor represents the communitarian objections to a Charter regime in Canada (see Taylor 1993), while law professor Michael Mandel is the most orthodox socialist Charter-basher (see Mandel 1994).

But there is a third current of Charter interpretation which sees the Charter as a perfect expression of Canada's philosophy of diversity and pluralism. Political scientists like David Elton (1989) or the legal scholar Noel Lyon (1987) have pointed to the uniqueness of the Charter as a document containing negative as well as positive rights. Human freedom, the argument goes, is often advanced by positive state action, and the Charter recognizes this, unlike the American Bill of Rights. The singling out of designated groups for protection makes the Charter more than a purely individualist document.

From the early 1980s, the Charter has become a catalyst of identity politics in Canada. The content of the Charter is not unresponsive to such concerns, as sections 1 and 33 as well as minority language education rights and the affirmative action provision of section 15 (2) illustrate.

V. The Charter: A Short Impact Assessment

1. Institutional Impact

Since 1982, Canada has had a rigid constitution that is very hard to change – possibly only by referendum, but at the very least by more than a two-thirds majority – and a strong regime of judicial review. The traditional Canadian institutional logic of parliamentary supremacy – within the confines of federalism – was replaced by the principle of constitutional supremacy. The power of Canadian legislatures to fundamentally change the course of politics as they pleased was clearly diminished. In terms of cross-national institutional comparison, Canada is among the four democracies worldwide whose regime of judicial review has been rated as "very high" (see Lijphart 1999). The Canadian regime of judicial review is second only to that of Germany, the United States and possibly India. The impact of judicial review depends only partly on its formal existence and much more on the vigour and frequency of its use by the courts, especially supreme or constitutional courts. Therefore, the most important institutional change must be seen in the newly assumed constitutional review role of the Supreme Court of Canada.

Compared to its counterpart in Washington, D.C., the Canadian Supreme Court played a rather muted role in the Canadian political system until the mid-1980s. The only exception to this rule were some rulings in federalism issues, with which the Supreme Court of Canada and its predecessor, the Judicial Committee of the Privy Council, became agents of change for brief periods. Even after 1960, when Canada introduced a Bill of Rights that only applied to the federal level of government, it was understood that the Supreme Court would not dare to substantively alter laws and orders passed by the electorally legitimized branches of government. In more than 20 years between the early 1960s and the early 1980s, the Court struck down only one obscure section of the Indian Act. Otherwise it practised an extreme form of judicial self-restraint, judicial deference to democratically legitimized decisions. As a consequence of its new role, judicial appointments to Canada's highest court have become more important and perhaps more politicized.

2. *Jurisprudential Consequences*

The nine Supreme Court Justices did not continue to treat the Charter of Rights as a toothless tiger in the tradition of the statutory Bill Of Rights. Over the past one and a half decades, a consensus on the Court has emerged according to which the Justices have an explicit constitutional mandate to strike down any legislation if it violates the Charter. Although this is not a consensus about judicial activism, the broad application of the Charter has inevitably brought an American debate about the nature of judicial review to Canada. The reality of the Charter as a third pillar of the Constitution has shifted the academic and political debate away from the discussion of the desirability of judicial review as such to the conflict between judicial activism and self-restraint. The most important arena of debate about judicial review is the bench itself; the "demonstration" clause of section 1 of the Charter compels the Justices to indulge in such an internal debate. In its landmark section 1 case, *Regina v. Oakes*, the Supreme Court sent a clear message to the political arena that the burden of proof to demonstrate the reasonableness of legislation in conflict with the Charter is on the plaintiff – i.e., the rights-curbing instance, government – rather than on the defendant. Moreover, the Supreme Court of Canada has not adopted the (American) concept of non-justiciable political questions.

During the first decade of the Charter regime (1982-1992), Charter claimants won in 33% of the Supreme Court decisions, or in 65 out of 181 cases. 14 cases remained inconclusive. In comparison, the success rate for rights claimants under the Canadian Bill of Rights (1960-1982) was only 15%. But statistics offer only a very superficial picture. The vast majority of Charter cases decided under Chief Justices Laskin and Dickson (until 1989)

Table 1: Outcomes of the First Decade of Supreme Court Decisions on the Charter of Rights and Freedoms

Year	Claimant Loses	Claimant Wins	% Wins
1984	1	3	75
1985	3	6	60
1986	8	3	27
1987	16	6	26
1988	16	7	30
1989	16	8	31
1990	25	15	35
1991	14	11	38
1992	17	6	23
Total	116	65	33

Source: Compiled from Morton/Russell/Riddell 1994.

belonged to the field of criminal justice (see Morton 1987; Monahan 1987). A high success rate of Charter-based claims in the early years seemed to indicate that the traditional emphasis on crime control as the basic rationale of the criminal justice and law enforcement system in Canada has yielded to an American-style due process approach (see Morton 1987; Lipset 1990). Clearly, the first phase of Charter interpretation (until 1989) was characterized by judicial activism, by a mode of interpretation that is called "independent interpretivism" – i.e., independent, substantive interpretations –, as well as by an alliance with interest groups. In the eyes of its critics (see Knopff/Morton 1992), the Court became too detached from the forces of electoral politics by bolstering an alliance with interest groups which have turned to courts for reforms that could not be won using ordinary legislative politics. This alliance of interest groups has been dubbed the "Court Party" by critics and "Charter Canadians" by more sympathetic observers. Most of these groups revolve around cleavages that are rather non-traditional – i.e. non-economic, but middle-class oriented and post-material.

During phase 2, which has lasted from 1990 until today, the high court Charter interpretation became much more inconsistent. There is hardly any consensual jurisprudence: Justices are torn between legal formalism and realist social analysis. Decisions reflect combinations of four modes of interpretation:

- textualism-originalism – adhere to the founders' will;
- deference-restraint – defer to the judgement of the elected branches;
- independent interpretivism – independent, substantive interpretations;
- democracy reinforcement – protect the democratic process.

The 1990s have brought fragmented decision-making and jurisprudential fragmentation. But one pattern emerges: the Court remains activist in legal rights, but has become a lot more cautious in interpreting substantive rights, such as equality rights. Statistically, the Court did not use the Charter to strike down exclusively or mainly provincial legislation. However, important provincial – and especially Québec – legislation which had high priority on provincial political agendas was among the major victims of Charter-based constitutional review. Thus it seems to be fair to conclude that through its interpretation of the Charter, the Supreme Court tends to strengthen an individualistic rights-based vision of national political community and thus has weakened the capacity of regional and local majorities – especially in Québec – to deviate from national standards. Despite the invoking of the notorious "notwithstanding clause" (section 33), the Charter-based rulings on Québec's language and education laws have contributed to alienating a substantial segment of the French-speaking Québécois from an already fragile belief in a political future within Canada.

3. Political Consequences

One of the most important impacts of the Charter – irrespective of the constitutional jurisprudence flowing from it – was the framing of new constitutional identities. I would argue that the Charter has proved an innovative political force, simply because it complemented existing constitutional identities which were primarily territorially based with cross-cutting political identities. Without any doubt, the Charter has broadened the political opportunity structure for social and political movements by providing another important point of access to the decision-making process of an otherwise closed and executive-driven Westminster system. Therefore, the Charter was particularly welcomed by those forces in Canadian politics which do not feel adequately represented by a political system favoring territorially organized interests. It was met with reservation by advocates of traditional parliamentary party politics as well as by those representing entrenched and relatively homogenous regional majorities. But one should refrain from taking the "constitutional fashioning of communities" argument too far: It is simply untrue that neither individual nor collective actors used litigation and the courts to further their social interests before the arrival of the Charter. Before 1982, the courts were endowed with less powerful weapons to adjucate rights-based claims of citizens, organized interests and social movements. This does not mean, however, that some of the new movements exist just because of the Charter. It is equally untrue that without the Charter, there would be no gay movement employing legal strategies to advance its causes. What did indeed change after the Charter became part of the constitution were not the movements or their strategies, but their prospects for success.

The "traditionalist-conservative school" of Charter critics argues that the Charter of Rights has opened new avenues for organized interests seeking to influence the policy-making process in their favour. With the Charter and its many enumerated provisions – e.g., for equality rights – it has become possible for these interests to circumvent the institutions and processes of majoritarian parliamentary democracy and to utilize the courts as instruments of social change benefitting special interests. On the other hand, it is precisely organized interests, such as advocates of organized labor, the poor and even business associations, which complain that the Charter has done little to ameliorate social inequalities or to protect individual property rights. Defenders of the economically weak or disadvantaged are among the harshest critics of the Charter, because the Charter does not include clauses needed to defend collective economic or social rights. While it is true that the Charter is silent on economic and social issues, it is equally true that this provides the courts with considerable discretionary power to either limit or advance "progressive" economic causes.

The critical legal studies school has argued that the false promise of Charter politics has a demobilizing effect on social movements. Instead of engaging in grassroots mobilization and traditional lobbying efforts, many worthy left-wing causes devote considerable resources and political energy to litigation and legal strategies. On the other hand, women's groups and liberal feminists outside Québec were and still are the staunchest supporters of a Charter regime in Canada. They see the Charter as an institution that challenges an allegedly reactionary, male-dominated regime of executive federalism and parliamentary supremacy. Thanks to the Charter, policies of gender equality are no longer one policy option among many, but have become a constitutionally mandated obligation. By relying mostly on the Charter as an instrument of progressive social change in gender relations and sexual politics, the Canadian women's movement has run the risk to cast an essentially political controversy in the technicalities and abstractions of legal rhetoric about what constitutes "equality."

4. *Cultural Consequences*

The big cultural question behind the Charter and its impact on the value system of Canadian society is how much a regime of entrenched constitutional rights strengthens the value of liberty and weakens values like community and authority. In the past, the value systems of Canada and the United States displayed fundamental differences, despite the gradual disappearance of structural differences between the two neighbouring countries (see Lipset 1990). The sub-field of legal culture may serve as an example to illustrate Lipset's point: a different frontier experience explains different approaches to law and order in both societies. While the U.S. have always been following a "due process" model of emphasizing the rights of the accused, the Canadian approach to criminal law favours "crime-control." It prefers the rights of the community over the rights of the individual if they are in conflict. In general, Lipset concludes, Canadians were traditionally more inclined to show deference toward police and authority than Americans. If the Supreme Court interpretation of the Charter is moving away from a more deferential "crime-control" model, to what extent is the Canadian public following this trend? A detailed survey of public attitudes toward the Charter and civil liberties (see Sniderman et al. 1996) sheds an interesting light on the development of Canadian value systems. When Canadians were asked how far they were prepared to go in tolerating opinions and behaviour of fellow citizens with a quite opposite view of the world, political and legal elites were prepared to grant more liberty of expression to dissenters than the general public. While Sniderman et al. consistently found deep cleavages between elites and the mass in support of civil liberties, they could find no marked differences in the responses of English and French Canadians. Moreover, the cleavage pattern between elites and the public is consistent with American surveys on attitudes toward fundamental freedoms. Another result, however, seems to confirm the often mentioned "state bias" of Canadian political culture, which is at the heart of Lipset's writings. The same elites who showed a high degree of support for dissenting views and manifestations were also more inclined to accept the rights of governments to interfere with the private sphere of the citizen (wire tapping, etc.) than the general public, which is less inclined to accept the reason of state as an excuse for such measures. Yet, even this result is compatible with American findings.

The empirical findings of Sniderman et al. indicate that the contemporary Canadian perception of this tension between liberty on the one side and community and authority on the other contains elements of continuity and change. Canadians – both elites and the public – seem to respect liberty and a sense of community at the same time. They choose, or so it seems, to live with a built-in tension between the right of the citizen to a maximum of personal freedom and the right of governments to uphold an orderly society. The research data does not permit the conclusion that Canadian political culture has yet embarked on a path to the worship of unrestrained individualism. With respect to the anglophone-francophone cleavage, the points of similarity in the attitudes of members of the two language groups by far outweigh differences. Regarding basic political attitudes, the authors conclude that "the notion of Québec as a distinct society does not fit the results of our study" (Sniderman et al. 1988: 15). There are, however, significant differences among elites with respect to government rights, differences that largely depend on ideology and occupation. Members and supporters of the Conservative and Reform parties and executive elites are more willing to accept state interference with civil liberties than members of the NDP or of the legal profession. The Charter Survey shows that community is still an important and salient value in forming the opinion of Canadians toward individual and government rights. On the other hand, American and Canadian as well as French and English Canadian attitudes seem to converge into a more North American political culture: in both countries and all regions, the value differences underlying many political issues are at the centre of political discussion.

VI. Conclusion: Constitutional Jurisprudence and the Policy-Making Environment

Increased sensitivity with regard to Charter issues can have a beneficial effect on policy-making, as policy-making will have to take Charter rights seriously. It has already proved difficult for the political powers to promote policy objectives that may conflict with enumerated protected rights or to invoke the notwithstanding clause. However, parliamentary supremacy will not be completely replaced by a "Charter regime," because Charter compliance of policies can take different shapes and follow different avenues. The Charter does not mandate specific policy choices, but it protects citizens in the last resort against illiberal policy choices. However, the legislative and executive branches will no longer be able to define by themselves which limitations on rights can be justified in a free and democratic society. This is the sole prerogative of the courts, especially of the Supreme Court of Canada. Policy choices will be subjected to rights-based considerations as well as to public-interest considerations. This may result in some undesirable effects, which can be witnessed in other countries with an even stronger regime of judicial review, such as Germany. Rights talk will sometimes prompt elected politicians to avoid difficult and controversial policy choices by delegating them to the courts on the grounds that they involve issues of fundamental rights which have to be resolved in the legal arena. Politicians will find it politically expedient to shift the blame for unpopular no-win decisions to the courts. However, case studies by authors such as Janet Hiebert (1996) have shown that the Charter does indeed structure the terms of official and unofficial political discourse. Policy-makers anticipate rights-based criticism and they act accordingly. Most political representatives are not intimidated by the Charter discourse and most do not shy away from advocating policy positions against which Charter-based criticism can be expected. Section 1 of the Charter is an encouragement to justify customary practices in violation of Charter principles by referring to the "reasonable limits" provision.

The Charter has not washed away Canada's political tradition of belief in order, good government and cooperative community. But it has added constitutional legalism as a further important dimension to the universe of Canada's public philosophies. The Charter has changed Canada less in substantive than in procedural and institutional terms by giving a new prominence to courts – notably, the Supreme Court of Canada – and by emphasizing a legal and sometimes even legalistic approach to politics and policy-making. The Charter has neither completely stopped legislative reform efforts nor has it always prevented judicially mandated reform impulses. Charter-based constitutional jurisprudence is less of a chief instrument of social change than many of its supporters hope, but it is not the dangerous tool against democratic politics feared by some of its critics either. Nearly 20 years into the Charter's regime, constitutional jurisprudence should be considered a normal institution of Canadian political life, sometimes upsetting, sometimes comforting, at times ahead of public opinion, at others behind legislative initiative, but nothing extraordinary and no case for long-lasting debates. And nothing that should greatly worry us.

Postscript: The Charter, Constitutional Reform and National Unity

The Charter has been at the heart of the debate about Canada's future over the past twenty years, because it has become an extremely unifying force in Canada outside Québec (COQ) and a separating force as far as the issue of national unity is concerned. Québecers are not a people collectively opposed to fundamental rights and freedoms. Various surveys (see Sniderman et al. 1996; Thunert 1992) have demonstrated that the Québécois are even more liberal with regard to issues that are of utmost importance for a civil rights-based society. For Québécois it is more acceptable to have their children taught by homosexual teachers than for Canadians in the Maritimes and Ontario; they are more liberal with regard to film censorship, etc. What they deny, however, is the right of people outside Québec to determine the contents, the application and the interpretation of a catalogue of basic rights pertaining to the social and political life in Québec.

Québec and the rest of Canada have embarked on a collision course for the past decade, because the Charter has brought to the forefront a deep disagreement about what should constitute the basis of a liberal society like Canada. For a majority of Canadians outside Québec and a minority within the province this basis is one of a "procedural republic," a neutral state that guarantees fair procedures to ensure nationwide equality of opportunity and life-chances, as well as a broad range of individual rights, and that – above all – prevents discrimination on any basis. For a majority of Québecers the pursuit of a collective, substantive goal – the flourishing of the French language and culture – is prior to the rules of procedural fairness. In terms of political philosophy, Québec derives policies and constitutional arrangements from an axiomatic collective good, whereas the Charter of Rights establishes a regime that enables people to choose from several conceptions of the good including a menu of two official languages equal in status. The key Supreme Court decisions on Québec's language legislation, the long and unsuccessful mega-constitutional debate on the meaning of the distinct-society clause in the failed Meech Lake and Charlottetown Accords, and the criticism against the use of the "notwithstanding clause" have convinced many Québecers that the Charter – section 33 notwithstanding – imposes procedural liberalism on Québec and thus constitutes a threat to a society organized around a collective purpose. Conversely, the procedural outlook embodied in the Charter of Rights cannot tolerate that segments of society are restricted in choosing between several conceptions of the good life. While a multicultural Canada outside Québec is unable to agree on substantive conceptions of the good, most Québecers, or so it seems, cannot afford to live by all the procedural norms of the Charter.

On issues other than language legislation or those pertaining to Québec cultural sovereignty, the Charter has proved a unifying force. In important Charter decisions, nearly all of them originating in the rest of Canada, alignments over issues such as abortion, strikes and picket lines, pornography, citizenship, etc. are constantly changing and non-territorial in nature. Prolifers are pitted against pro-choicers, unionized workers against small businessmen, libertarians against supporters of the state, etc. In Canada outside Québec, the Charter has become a third – and for some, the most important – pillar of the constitution, the epitomization of Charter patriotism in Charles Taylor's words (see Taylor 1993) or "Grundrechtspatriotismus" in my own terminology (see Thunert 1992).

References

Axworthy, Thomas S. 1986: "Colliding Visions: The Debate over the Charter of Rights and Freedoms 1980-81," in: Weiler/Elliott (eds.), 13-26.

——/Trudeau, Pierre E. (eds.) 1990: *Towards a Just Society. The Trudeau Years*, Markham, Ont.: Viking Books.

Banting, Keith/Hoberg, George/Simeon, Richard (eds.) 1997: *Degrees of Freedom. Canada and the United States in a Changing World*, Montreal/Kingston: McGill-Queen's UP.

——/Simeon, Richard (eds.) 1983: *And No One Cheered. Federalism, Democracy and the Constitution Act*, Toronto: Methuen.

——/—— (eds.) 1985: *Redesigning the State. The Politics of Constitutional Change*, Toronto: University of Toronto Press.

Batemann, Thomas M.J. 1998: "Rights Application Doctrine and the Clash of Constitutionalisms in Canada," in: *Canadian Jorunal of Political Science* 31, 1, 5-29.

Bayefsky, Anne F. 1989: *Canada's Constitution Act 1982 & Amendments. A Documentary History*, 2 vol., Toronto: McGraw-Hill Ryerson.

——/Eberts, Mary 1985: *Equality Rights and the Canadian Charter of Rights and Freedoms*, Toronto: Carswell.

Bernier, Ivan/Lajoie, Andrée (eds.) 1985: *The Supreme Court of Canada as an Instrument of Political Change*, Toronto: University of Toronto Press.

Bothe, Michael 1986: "La protection des droits fondamentaux au Canada," in: *Jahrbuch des Öffentlichen Rechts der Gegenwart* 35, 267-289.

Bryden, Philip/Davis, Steven/Russell, John 1994: *Protecting Rights and Freedoms. Essays on the Charter's Place in Canada's Political, Legal and Intellectual Life*, Toronto: University of Toronto Press.

Cairns, Alan/Williams, Cynthia (eds.) 1985: *Constitutionalism, Citizenship and Society in Canada*, Toronto: University of Toronto Press.

Canada 1984: *Constitution of Canada, Office Consolidation, 1867-1982*, Ottawa: Supply and Services.

Dobrowolsky, Alexandra 1998: "Of 'Special Interest': Interest, Identity and Feminist Constitutional Activism in Canada," in: *Canadian Journal of Political Science* 31, 1, 707-742.

Eisenberg, Avigail 1994: "The Politics of Individual and Group Difference in Canadian Jurisprudence," *Canadian Journal of Political Science* 27, 3-22.

Elkins, David J. 1989: "Facing our Destiny: Rights and Canadian Distinctiveness," in: *Canadian Journal of Political Science* 32, 4, 699-716.

Greene, Ian 1989: *The Charter of Rights*, Toronto: Lorimer.

Hiebert, Janet 1996: *Limiting Rights. The Dilemma of Judicial Review*, Montreal/Kingston: McGill-Queen's UP.

Hutchinson, Alan 1995: *Waiting for Coraf. A Critique of Law and Rights*, Toronto: University of Toronto Press.

Knopff, Rainer 1998: "Populism and the Politics of Rights: The Dual Attack on Representative Democracy," in: *Canadian Journal of Political Science* 31, 4, 683-706.

——/Morton, F.L. 1992: *Charter Politics*, Scarborough: Nelson.

Laforest, Guy 1995: *Trudeau and the End of the Canadian Dream*, Montreal/Kingston: McGill-Queen's UP.

Lijphart, Arend 1999: *Patterns of Democracy. Government Forms and Performance in Thirty-Six Countries*, New Haven: Yale UP.

Lipset, Seymour M. 1990: *Continental Divide. The Values and Institutions of the United States and Canada*, New York: Routledge.

Lyon, Noel 1987: "Group Rights in the New Canada," paper prepared for the conference on Canadian Law and Legal Literature: The Commonwealth Perspective, May 29-30, 1987, Duke University (Durham, NC).

Mandel, Michael 1994: *The Charter and the Legalization of Politics in Canada*, Toronto: Wall Thompson.

Manfredi, Christopher 1993: *Judicial Power and the Charter: Canada and the Paradox of Liberal Constitutionalism*, Toronto: McClelland & Stewart.

Monahan, Patrick 1987: *Politics and the Constitution. The Charter, Federalism and the Supreme Court of Canada*, Agincourt, Ont.: Carswell.

Morton, F.L./Russell, Peter H./Riddell, Troy 1994: "The Canadian Charter of Rights and Freedoms: A Descriptive Analysis of the First Decade, 1982-1992," paper presented at the 16th World Congress of the International Political Science Association, August 21-25, 1994 (Berlin).

Petter, Andrew 1987: "Immaculate Deception: The Charter's Hidden Agenda," in: *45 Advocate*, 857-869.

Riddell, Troy/Morton, F.L. 1998: "Reasonable Limits, Distinct Society and the Canada Clause: Interpretive Clauses and Competition for Constitutional Advantage," in: *Canadian Journal of Political Science* 31, 3, 435-465.

Russell, Peter H. 1983: "The Political Purposes of the Canadian Charter of Rights and Freedoms" in: *Canadian Bar Review* 61, 30-54.

—— 1986: "Overcoming Legal Formalism: The Treatment of the Constitution, the Courts and Judicial Behaviour in Canadian Political Science," in: *Canadian Journal of Law and Society* 1, 5-33.

—— 1988: "Canada's Charter of Rights and Freedoms: A Political Report," in: *Public Law*, Autumn, 385-401.

—— 1989: "The Supreme Court and the Charter: A Question of Legitimacy," in: Shugarman/Whitaker (eds.), 225-240.

Seidle, F. Leslie (ed.) 1993: *Equity and Community. The Charter, Interest Advocacy and Representation*, Montreal: IRPP.

Shugarman, David P./Whitaker, Reg (eds.)1989: *Federalism and Political Community. Essays in Honour of Donald Smiley*, Peterborough, Ont.: Broadview Press.

Sigurdson, Richard 1993: "Left- and Right-Wing Charterphobia in Canada: A Critque of the Critics," in: *International Journal of Canadian Studies* 7-8, 95-116.

Smith, Lynn (ed.) 1986: *Righting the Balance. Canada's New Equality Rights*, Saskatoon: The Canadian Human Rights Reporter, Inc.

Smith, Miriam 1998: "Social Movements and Equality Seeking: The Case of Gay Liberation in Canada," in: *Canadian Journal of Political Science* 31, 2, 285-309.

Sniderman, Paul et al. 1996: *The Clash of Rights. Liberty, Equality, and Legitimacy in Pluralist Democracy*, New Haven: Yale UP.

Strayer, Barry L. 1988a: *The Canadian Constitution and the Courts. The Function and Scope of Judicial Review*, Toronto: Buttersworth.

—— 1988b: "Life under the Canadian Charter: Adjusting the Balance between Legislatures and Courts," in: *Public Law*, Autumn, 347-369.

Taylor, Charles 1993: *Reconciling the Solitudes. Essays on Canadian Federalism and Nationalism*, Montreal/Kingston: McGill-Queen's UP.

Thunert, Martin 1992: *Grundrechtspatriotismus in Kanada? Zur politischen Integrationsfunktion der Canadian Charter of Rights and Freedoms*, Bochum: Brockmeyer.

Trudeau, Pierre E. 1990: "The Values of A Just Society," in: Axworthy/Trudeau (eds.), 357-385.

Weiler, Joseph M./Elliott, Robin M. (eds.) 1986: *Litigating the Values of a Nation. The Canadian Charter of Rights and Freedoms*, Toronto: Carswell.

Zimmermann, Bettina 1992: *Kanadische Verfassungsinstitutionen im Wandel: Unitarisierung durch Grundrechtsschutz*, Berlin: Duncker & Humblot.

Conclusion

Roland Sturm

For most citizens in democratic societies the existence of a constitution which gives legitimacy to their national political systems and guarantees human rights is one of the few undisputed fundamental prerequisites of democracy. Debates on constitutional questions in the established and, by post-cold war standards, "old" democracies – i.e., in the United States and Canada – do remind us, however, of the fact that constitutions have to be flexible and above all, have to respond adequately to pressures for change which stem from various sources, national as well as international ones. In the United States the problem of "relegitimizing government" (Brinkley 1997) has even provoked the question "whether the American political system has in fact failed as an experiment in democracy" (Polsby 1997: 161). In Canada we find similar doubts about fundamental constitutional principles. The literature is full of alarmist titles such as "Kanada in der Krise" (Schultze/Schneider 1997) (no question mark), "The Unmaking of Canada" as "hidden theme in Canadian history since 1945" (Chodos/Murphy/Hamovitch 1991) or "The Collapse of Canada?" (Weaver 1992).

Is there really a constitutional crisis in Canada and the United States, or are we just observing the usual difficulties of constitutional adjustment? How should the dynamic of constitutional change be analysed, and what does it mean when the constitution, which provides the glue for society because it embodies a social consensus on rules and values, undergoes reform?

Research in the field of comparative politics has so far only started to deal with constitutional politics and the special characteristics of policy-making in the context of challenges to constitutions which range in their radicalism from evolution to revolution. The theoretical approaches presented by Rainer-Olaf Schultze and Petra Dobner convincingly show that on the one hand we do need further comparative research, but also that on the other hand this kind of new research should build on available insights which might help to structure and guide new research.

There can be no doubt that Georg Jellinek's classical definition of the state as the unity of territoriality, sovereignty and a people has lost some of its relevance today. If a constitution can only be conceptualised as an in-between between a people and its state, it has to accept that it looses control.

For North American nations, in contrast to European members of the EU, the mismatch of constitutional reach and sovereignty is less dramatic, but it still is a reality. With free trade and NAFTA in international politics, for example, but also with regard to the definition of competing rights to sovereignty of states in the United States and provinces in Canada, more fundamental problems of constitutional uncertainty and limitations to constitutional rule-making on the national level have arrived here, too. A special and even greater challenge of this kind is the claim of a considerable number of Québecers to be a people separate from the rest of Canada, which has as one consequence the inability of Canadians to come to all-Canadian constitutional compromises.

But it is still true that what we observe in North America are not only efforts of constitution-making, but – maybe of even greater relevance today, at least in the United States – efforts to revise the existing constitutions either formally or informally. As Rainer-Olaf Schultze reminds us, constitutional change has to be judged and debated in its historical context. We need to identify the interests, goals, options and constraints of constitutional change. All this together may open up the window of opportunity for redefining the rules and in some extreme cases also the values which a society would like to see as binding. The efforts in this volume to fathom constitutional reform are firmly set in this framework. Instead of speculating about the chances of political disintegration of North American societies and polities the authors concentrate on the much more relevant micro-analysis of the role of constitutions. In Canada and the United States they observe frictions in the functioning of institutions, in the federal systems, in budgetary politics, and with regard to the integration of minorities. Very often, and Canada and the United States are no exceptions to this rule, constitutional change is the result of judicial activism. In both countries the Supreme Court both arbitrates constitutional disputes and by way of its interpretation of the constitution is itself an influential factor for constitutional reform.

R. Kent Weaver shows that constitutional reform agendas in Canada and the United States had more differences than similarities both because of their social context and because of the differences of interest of political decision-makers. Institutional differences between Canada and the United States explain why constitutional reform in Canada has been concentrated on constitutional "rounds" initiated by federal governments whereas in the United States the role of Congress in the political system and the diffusion of power allows multiple interests and coalitions of decision-makers to shape the agenda of institutional reform more permanently. Institutional differences between Canada (Westminster parliamentary system) and the United States (presidential political system) do, however, only restrict, but not exclude the possibility of crossborder learning with regard to constitutional politics. This can be shown, for example, for the case of Senate reform in Canada.

In both Canada and the United States the list of items which make it to the agenda of constitutional reform is impressive, the outcome of constitutional politics is, however, much more modest. When one looks for reasons for the limited success of constitutional reform proposals, the Canada-U.S. comparison shows that the courts in the United States have had a much more active role in defending the status quo than in Canada. Constitutional reform in Canada is confronted with the difficult, some say impossible, task of consensus building in Canadian society.

In the Canadian debate, constitutional reform in the strict sense of the word – i.e., the adjustment of existing institutions and not their replacement – is often connected with an evaluation of the Westminster model of government, and especially with the problem of a reconciliation of federalism and parliamentary sovereignty. A broader, inclusion-oriented approach geared towards both constitution-making and constitutional revisions, the so-called politics of mega-constitutional change, dominated the political agenda of the eighties and early nineties, and for a while seemed to make debates on old-style constitutional reform superfluous. Today this approach is on the political backburner. It did not solve the big constitutional problems and created additional ones. And today we know that it is still worthwhile for students of constitutional reform to have a closer look at the traditional centres of power in the political system, Parliament and the cabinet.

Numerous reform efforts in Parliament have not overcome the traditional adversarialism of parliamentary exchange and have also not led to a strengthened role of the MPs vis-à-vis the federal government, although Canada has a more developed and theoretically more efficient committee system than the British Parliament. A consensus on the need for reform of the Second Chamber of Parliament, the Senate, is at the heart of many reform proposals, both piecemeal and radical ones. So far the final test has been avoided whether a reformed Senate would really challenge the very core of Canada's Westminster system, parliamentary sovereignty. Steffen Schneider argues that "Senate reform proposals were a badly conceived attempt to balance competing interests and ultimately incompatible constitutional perspectives."

Although it has many critics, prime-ministerial government in Canada is unchallenged. The control of the Prime Minister over his or her cabinet and its procedures has, if anything, been strengthened in the eighties and nineties. The imperatives of expenditure control and lean government (as much as this is possible in a country which has to have a regionally balanced cabinet membership) have legitimised this development. There remains an extreme mismatch between the wealth of reform proposals for the machinery of government and the remarkable resistance to change it displays.

Outside the world of politics in Ottawa and Washington, D.C., there exists the universe of federalism and its different expressions in Canada and the United States. This includes differences in the way national constitutions bind together the units of federation and the national centre. The tricky task for constitutions in countries such as Canada and the United States, which give a priori state/provincial governments a relatively small role in national politics, is to find and define a way of managing federal-subnational relations efficiently and in a way that creates sufficient social consensus which is, as Roland Sturm argues, "the glue which holds federal systems together and which finds its expression in a federal constitution."

A prime mover in this respect has been the Supreme Court in the United States. From the New Deal period to the early 1970s it had contributed to the advance of federal power at the expense of state power. The Rehnquist Court has started very successfully to reverse this trend and has rediscovered federalism, although one should, as Timothy Conlan shows, not overstate this case, at least for the time being. There are doctrinal limits, traditions of cooperative federalism, political limits and philosophical constraints which prevent the Rehnquist Court from going to extremes. The Rehnquist Court sees itself above all as "stabilizer of the federal-state balance of power" (Conlan).

With regard to reforms of Canadian federalism Harvey Lazar and John McLean identify top-down informal change as the only efficient strategy at present. The efforts of political elites to create a new constitutional consensus in a process of top-down formal constitutional reform found their expression in the failed attempts of several rounds of constitutional legislation which did not succeed in mobilising the necessary democratic majorities. Bottom-up formal constitutional reform initiated by provincial legislatures has failed to command legitimacy Canada-wide. Bottom-up informal constitutional reform has concentrated on the strengthening of individual rights (Charter of Rights and Freedoms) and has been supported by judicial review. It has, however, come into conflict with the federal principle because of the erosion of autonomy of provincial governments it implies. This is particularly true for Québec, the only province which did not agree to the Constitution Act of 1982.

Top-down informal constitutional reform finds its expression in political and administrative agreements between federal and provincial governments. Most of them do not in a strict sense affect the constitution, but still have far-reaching consequences for the Canadian polity. They include fiscal federalism, the social and economic union, and intergovernmental and environmental development. The paradox which evolved here is that the reformed Canadian federalism is "both more collaborative and more disentangled" (Lazar/McLean). Because the Québec government sometimes decides not to sign the above-mentioned administrative agreements, the asymmetry in Canadian federalism has increased. In the long run non-constitutional reform of this kind is a weak substitute for constitution-making; it may buy time for the Canadian federation, but it will not solve its problems.

In political disputes between federal and state or provincial governments funding always plays a prominent role. Budgeting in itself is an issue of controversy among constitution-makers. Markus Müller shows that in the case of the U.S. we can observe a step-by-step process of budgetary reform that has complicated the rules of budget-making in which both the executive branch and Congress are involved today to such an extent that rule-making has to be used to force the institutions to come to results. Rule-making itself is an exercise which can be and was challenged for its legality at the Supreme Court. Even bipartisan reform projects such as the line item veto have failed this test. Beyond institutional struggles between the President and Congress lies, however, more – namely, the "small government doctrine," the conviction that the federal government has to be forced to stop its irresponsible spending and taxing habits.

Much more than budgeting in the United States, Canadian budgeting is a balance act of federal and provincial interests. One of the largest categories of spending in the federal budget is the grants or transfers made to the provinces under a number of programmes. The justification for this is the federal spending power doctrine which assumes that the federal Parliament has the power to authorize the spending of money whenever and however it wishes. Allan Maslove finds that the "system of intergovernmental grants that has developed in Canada over several decades is an imaginative response to fiscal and program challenges that have developed." But he also argues that these arrangements "have been characterised by confusion and blurred lines of responsibility." There is a built-in tension between the wish of federal governments to control outcomes of their financial initiatives, especially in the field of social policies, and the preference of provincial governments for more unconditional resources.

The constitutional cohesion in Canada and the United States is not only challenged by the need to accomodate subnational pressures. The constitutions of both countries also have to cope with the realities of multicultural societies, and have to adjust themselves accordingly. In the United States, the decisions of the Supreme Court are central to this process of adjustment. Michael Dreyer argues that gender rights cases "seem to be pretty much settled by now," whereas "affirmative action, reapportionment and the meaning of equality for the black minority are as much open for interpretation as ever. And waiting around the corner are the issues of equal rights for gays and lesbians in areas like marriage law, armed services, employment, and a host of other problems."

For Canada it can be said that multiculturalism was both a product and an aim of constitutional reforms. This goes way beyond the Québec question and institution-building in mega-constitutional rounds. The stalemate with regard to the latter is characterised by Peter Russell with the sentence: "The one point on which Canadians are now constitutionally united is their exhaustion with contesting constitutional issues." For Canada's society a new development is certainly the recognition of Aboriginal nations as self-governing nations within Canada. Such a step is, of course, not the grand solution to all constitutional problems or problems of minority rights, and is not planned to be. To quote Peter Russell again: "abeyance and avoidance of intractable abstract questions such as the locus of sovereignty and the identity of the nation are conditions of constitutional peace in Canada."

In both Canada and the United States many, though not all, controversial constitutional problems end up as court cases. This gives the U.S. Supreme Court the possibility to mould the constitutional agenda, but, as Martin Edelman argues for the case of the U.S., not with the same degree of efficiency under all circumstances. Only "when the Court promotes policies which are marginal to the concerns of the dominant consensus of the time," will it with the greatest degree of efficiency "be able to promote change," unless these policies energize the emergence of a new consensus in society which opposes the Court's policies. Supreme Court decisions in constitutional matters are bound by the beliefs and norms of political culture, and decisions which stray too far from these values are likely to be severely criticised in public discourse and revised. As for Canada, Martin Thunert argues that the insertion of a Charter of Rights and Freedoms into that country's constitution has greatly strengthened the role of the courts – especially the Supreme Court –, and has been both "product and catalyst of socio-political change." Against the Charter's left and right-wing critics, he demonstrates the rather unspectacular consequences of this constitutional reform, which modified Canadian political life without radically altering political tradition or power balances.

There is a limit for constitutional experiments with regard to the jurisdiction of Supreme Courts in North America, but also with regard to constitutional engineering by institutional reformers, or to what can be achieved by the recourse to the people in referenda.

References

Brinkley, Alan 1997: "Relegitimizing Government," in: Alan Brinkley/Nelson W. Polsby/Kathleen M. Sullivan (eds.), *New Federalist Papers. Essays in Defense of the Constitution*, New York/London: Norton, 123-136.

Chodos, Robert/Murphy, Rae/Hamovitch, Eric 1991: *The Unmaking of Canada. The Hidden Theme in Canadian History Since 1945*, Toronto: James Lorimer.

Polsby, Nelson W. 1997: "Constitutional Angst: Does American Democracy Work?, in: Alan Brinkley/Nelson W. Polsby/Kathleen M. Sullivan (eds.), *New Federalist Papers. Essays in Defense of the Constitution*, New York/London: Norton, 159-179.

Schultze, Rainer-Olaf/Schneider, Steffen (eds.) 1997: *Kanada in der Krise. Analysen zum Verfassungs-, Wirtschafts- und Parteiensystemwandel seit den 80er Jahren*, Bochum: Brockmeyer.

Weaver, R. Kent (ed.) 1992: *The Collapse of Canada?*, Washington, D.C.: Brookings Institution.

Contributors

Timothy J. **Conlan**, Ph.D., received his education at the University of Chicago and Harvard University (Cambridge, Massachusetts). He is Associate Professor at George Mason University (Fairfax, Virginia), where he has taught since 1987, after two years at Georgetown University (Washington, D.C.). From 1977 to 1985 he was research fellow, analyst and senior analyst at the Advisory Commission on Intergovernmental Relations, and from 1985 to 1986 he was Assistant Staff Director of the U.S. Senate Subcommittee on Intergovernmental Relations. Specializing in American federalism and in the politics of state and tax policy making, Professor Conlan has published numerous articles, book chapters and research monographs on these topics, as well as two books: *New Federalism: Intergovernmental Reform from Nixon to Reagan* (Washington, D.C.: Brookings Institution 1988), and *Taxing Choices: The Politics of Tax Reform* (with Margaret T. Wrightson and David R. Beam, Washington, D.C.: Congressional Quarterly Press 1990).

Dr. Petra **Dobner** studied medicine, political science and philosophy at the Free University of Berlin. From 1994 to 1999, she was a lecturer at the Chair for Political Theory of the University of Potsdam, where she received her doctorate with a thesis on "Konstitutionalismus als Politikform. Zu den Effekten staatlicher Transformation auf die Verfassung als Institution" in 1999 (to be published by Nomos, Baden-Baden, in the fall of 2000). She has now started work on a *Habilitation* project entitled "Sozialpolitik und Sozialtheorie. Zur Übersetzung der Vorstellungen vom guten Leben in Konzeptionen sozialer Politik." Recent and forthcoming publications include "Zum Staatsbürgerschafts-Diskurs," in: *Widerspruch* 19, 37 (1999), 185-191; "'Fasse wacker meinen Zipfel! Hier ist so ein Mittelgipfel...' Bauernschlau der Mittelbau?" in: Erhard Stölting/Uwe Schimank (eds.), *Krise der Universität*, Opladen: Westdeutscher Verlag (2000, forthcoming); and "'Soziales Verhältnis' und 'politische Form': Kommentare zur aktuellen Staatsdebatte," in: *Berliner Debatte/Initial* 3 (2000, forthcoming).

Dr. Michael **Dreyer** is Assistant Professor of Political Science at Friedrich Schiller University, Jena. He received his education mainly at Christian-Albrechts University, Kiel, where he took his degrees. He is currently in the finishing stage of a *Habilitation* project on the political thought of Hugo Preuss. Research interests include German and American political theory, federalism, and the U.S. Supreme Court. Publications on these topics include *Föderalismus als ordnungspolitisches und normatives Prinzip: Das föderative Denken der Deutschen im 19. Jahrhundert* (Frankfurt/M. 1987); *Die deutsche Diskussion um die Kriegsschuldfrage 1918/19* (with Oliver Lembcke; Berlin 1993); and a forthcoming volume on *Emanuel Lasker – Schach, Philosophie, Wissenschaft* (ed. with Ulrich Sieg). Related articles include "German Roots of the Theory of Pluralism," in: *Constitutional Political Economy* 4, 1 (1993); "Recht und Politik: Die Geschichte des amerikanischen Supreme Courts," in: *Historische Mitteilungen* 7 (1994); and "The State in Decline? The Nation State on Its Way to the Virtual State?" in: Klaus Dicke/Karl Schmitt (eds.), *Transformation and Integration in Europe* (Berlin 1998).

Martin **Edelman**, Ph.D., is Professor of Political Science at the Rockefeller College of Public Affairs and Policy of the University at Albany, New York. He has been a visiting professor at the University of Liverpool (England), at Tel Aviv University (Israel), and at Beijing University (China). He has served on the Executive Committee of the International Political Science Association's Research Committee on Comparative Judicial Studies since 1979, and was the chair/convenor 1991-1997. Professor Edelman is the author of *Democratic Theories and the Constitution* (1984) and *Courts, Politics, and Culture in Israel* (1994), as well as articles and chapters on American constitutional law and Israeli courts in professional publications.

Harvey **Lazar**, Ph.D., was educated at McGill University, the University of British Columbia and the London School of Economics and Political Science. Dr. Lazar is currently the Director of the Institute of Intergovernmental Relations at Queen's University, Kingston (Canada). Previously, he had a long career in the Canadian Public Service, including assignments as Deputy Chairman of the Economic Council of Canada (1986-1992) and Senior Assistant Deputy Minister, Strategic Policy, Human Resources Development Canada (1992-1995). Dr. Lazar has overseen and/or contributed to a number of major research reports during his years in Public Service, on such diverse topics as retirement income policy, social policy, labour market development, financial institutions and foreign investment policy. His current work focuses on the Canadian social union, trends in labour market policy, Canadian and comparative federalism, and the changing nature of the social contract in Western democracies in the face of globalization. His most recent publications include *Canada: The State of the Federation 1997. Non-Constitutional Renewal; Canada: The State of the Federation 1998/99. How Canadians Connect* (with T. McIntosh); "The Future of the Welfare State," in: *Interna-*

tional Social Security Review 51, 3 (1998); and "Civil Society and Federalism in Canada," in: Jutta Kramer/Hans-Peter Schneider (eds.), *Federalism and Civil Societies* (1999).

Allan **Maslove**, Ph. D., is a Professor in the School of Public Administration at Carleton University in Ottawa, Canada. An economist specializing in public finance, Dr. Maslove is a graduate of the Universities of Manitoba (Canada) and Minnesota (United States). In 1980-81, Dr. Maslove was a visiting professor at the University of California at Berkeley. He was Director of the Carleton School of Public Administration from 1981 to 1987. In 1987-88 he was a Scholar-in-Residence at the Institute for Research in Public Policy. In July 1997, he was appointed as the first Dean of the new Faculty of Public Affairs and Management at Carleton University. Dr. Maslove is the author or editor of more than 15 books and has written numerous articles in the areas of public policy and public finance. His main areas of work have been in taxation, budgetary policy and federal-provincial fiscal relations with a particular focus on the financing of Canadian health care. He has also written on the financing of and fiscal arrangements for Indian government, and has served as an advisor to a First Nation on self-government negotiations. He has been a consultant to agencies and departments of all levels of government and to Royal Commissions (including the Macdonald Commission and the Royal Commission on Aboriginal Peoples).

John **McLean** is a Research Associate of the Institute for Intergovernmental Relations and a Ph.D. candidate in the Department of Political Studies at Queen's University. His areas of research include Canadian and comparative federalism and constitutional law and politics in Canada and Australia. His current research projects focus on recent attempts to reform the Canadian Social Union and the effects of the Charter of Rights on Canadian politics.

Markus M. **Müller**, M.A., is Project Coordinator at the *Sozialwissenschaftliches Forschungsinstitut*, University of Erlangen-Nuremberg. His research interests are in the fields of German and comparative politics (United States, United Kingdom), political economy, and constitutional governance. His publications include *Haushaltsausgleich durch Verfassungspolitik? Die Diskussion um ein Balanced Budget Amendment in den USA* (Berlin: Logos 1997); *Public Deficits: A Comparison of Their Political and Economic Consequences in Britain, Canada, Germany and the United States* (with Roland Sturm; Harlow: Longman 1999); and "Ein neuer regulativer Staat in Deutschland? Die neuere Theory of the Regulatory State und ihre Anwendbarkeit in der deutschen Staatswissenschaft", in: *Staatswissenschaften und Staatspraxis* 4 (1998), 507-534 (with Roland Sturm).

Peter H. **Russell** is a Professor Emeritus of the Department of Political Science, University of Toronto (Canada). He is an expert in political theory,

Canadian and comparative constitutional law and judicial processes, and has written or edited numerous journal articles, book chapters and books on this topic, including *The Judiciary in Canada: The Third Branch of Government* (Toronto: McGraw-Hill Ryerson 1987); *Federalism and the Charter. Leading Constitutional Decisions: A New Edition* (with Rainer Knopff/Ted Morton; Ottawa: Carleton UP 1989); and *Constitutional Odyssey: Can Canadians Be a Sovereign People?* (Toronto: University of Toronto Press 1992). His most recent publication is an edited volume on *The Future of Social Democracy: Views of Leaders from Around the World* (Toronto: University of Toronto Press 1999).

Steffen **Schneider**, M.A., studied at the University of Munich, Laval University (Québec, Canada), the University of British Columbia (Vancouver, Canada), and the University of Augsburg. He is a Research Associate of the Institute for Canadian Studies and a Ph.D. candidate/lecturer in political science at the University of Augsburg. His research interests are in the fields of comparative (American, Canadian, German) government, policy analysis, and the political economy of urban development. His publications include *Staat und regionale Entwicklung*, a study of Québec industrial policy (Bochum: Brockmeyer 1994), *Kanada in der Krise* (ed. with Rainer-Olaf Schultze; Bochum: Brockmeyer 1997), a volume devoted to recent trends in Canadian politics, as well as journal articles and book chapters on a range of topics, including forthcoming texts on Canadian foreign policy and German labour market policy.

Prof. Dr. Rainer-Olaf **Schultze** studied political science, history and Romance languages at the University of Heidelberg and Harvard University. He is a Professor of Political Science and Managing Director of the Institute for Canadian Studies at the University of Augsburg, as well as Chairman of the Board of the *Stiftung für Kanada-Studien* (Foundation for Canadian Studies in the German-speaking Countries). Specializing in comparative political analysis and political sociology with a focus on interest representation, political behavior and federalism in European and North American democracies, Dr. Schultze is currently a member of the Parliamentary Commission on Federalism Reform of the Bavarian *Landtag*. He is co-editor of the 7-volume *Lexikon der Politik* (Munich: Beck 1992-1998); other recent publications include various journal articles and book chapters on elections and federalism in Germany and Canada, as well as *Kanada in der Krise* (ed. with Steffen Schneider; Bochum: Brockmeyer 1997).

Prof. Dr. Roland **Sturm** received his education at the Free University of Berlin, the University of Heidelberg, Sheffield University (United Kingdom), and Stanford University (Palo Alto, California). He is a Professor of Political Science and Head of the Institute of Political Science, University of Erlangen-Nuremberg. His research interests are in the fields of German and comparative politics, comparative public policy, political economy, and the politics of the European Union. Recent publications include *Public Deficits: A Comparative Study of Their Economic and Political Consequences in Britain, Canada, Germany and the United States* (with Markus M. Müller; London/New York: Longman 1999); *The Return of Labour – A Turning Point in British Politics?* (ed. with Hans Kastendiek/Richard Stinshoff; Berlin/Bodenheim: Philo 1999); *Hinter den Kulissen von Regierungsbündnissen* (ed. with Sabine Kropp; Baden-Baden: Nomos 1999); *The Information Society and the Regions in Europe* (ed. with Georg Weinmann; Baden-Baden: Nomos 2000); *Föderalismus* (Berlin: Landeszentrale für politische Bildung 2000); *Regulierung und Deregulierung im wirtschaftlichen Transformationsprozess* (ed. with Gabriele Dautermann/Jürgen Dieringer/Markus M. Müller/Jana Volákova; Opladen: Leske & Budrich 2000).

Dr. habil. **Martin Thunert** studied political science, philosophy and public law at the Universities of Tübingen and Glasgow (Scotland), and received his M.A. from Goethe University, Frankfurt. After graduate work at Queen's University and McGill University (Montreal, Canada), he received his doctorate in political science from the University of Augsburg with a thesis on the political role of the Canadian Charter of Rights and Freedoms in 1991, published as *Grundrechtspatriotismus in Kanada? Zur politischen Integrationsfunktion der Canadian Charter of Rights and Freedoms* (Bochum: Brockmeyer). He has taught comparative politics at the University of Hamburg since 1992. His areas of research are the politics of industrialized democracies, comparative institutions, political culture, think tanks and other advisory bodies. Dr. Thunert's current projects are a comparative study on the role of think tanks and an introduction to American politics. His most recent publication in English is "Players beyond Borders? German Think Tanks as Catalysts of Internationalization," in: *Global Society* 2 (April 2000).

R. Kent **Weaver**, Ph.D., received his education at Haverford College and Harvard University. He has been a Senior Fellow in the Governmental Studies Program at the Brookings Institution since 1987. His major fields of interest are American and comparative social policy, comparative political institutions, Canadian politics, and the politics of expertise. Moreover, Dr. Weaver is an adjunct professor at the Nitze School of Advanced International Studies of Johns Hopkins University, where he teaches a course in Canadian politics. Prior to being appointed a Senior Fellow at Brookings, he was a Research Associate in the Governmental Studies Program between 1983 and 1987. Before coming to Brookings, he was a member of the Political Science Department at the Ohio State University from 1981 to 1983. Dr. Weaver has written articles for scholarly journals and contributed chapters to edited volumes on a variety of topics, including "Deficits and Devolution in the 104th Congress" and "Social Indicators as Policy Triggers." He is the author of

Ending Welfare As We Know It (Brookings 2000); *Automatic Government: The Politics of Indexation* (Brookings 1988); and *The Politics of Industrial Change* (Brookings 1985). He is also the co-author and editor of several books, including *Looking Before We Leap: Social Science and Welfare Reform* (Brookings 1992) and *Think Tanks and Civil Societies* (Trans Action Publishers 2000). Weaver is currently writing a book on what the United States can learn from the experiences of other advanced industrial countries in pension reform, and co-editing a volume on alternative sources of policy advice for governments and another volume comparing the capacity of the U.S. and Canadian governments to impose losses on politically powerful groups in society.

Program of the Conference on Constitutional Reform and Constitutional Jurisprudence in Canada and the United States, University of Augsburg, Germany, October 22-23, 1999

22 Oct., 1999

8:45-9:15 Welcome: Gunther Gottlieb (*Prorektor*, University of Augsburg)

Constitutional Reform – Theoretical and Historical Perspectives

9:30-11:15 Peter Russell (University of Toronto, Toronto): *Canada – A Pioneer in the Management of Constitutional Politics in a Multi-National Society*

Petra Dobner (University of Potsdam, Potsdam): *Constitutionalism and the Transformation of the State*

Constitutional Governance – Policy Issues

1. Institutional Change in the Legislative and Executive Branch

11:30-13:15 Steffen Schneider (University of Augsburg, Augsburg): *Constitutional Reform and Parliamentary Government in Canada: Shifting Away from the Westminster-Model?*

R. Kent Weaver (Brookings Institution, Washington DC): *Institutional Change and Constitutional Politics – A Theoretical Perspective*

2. Budgeting

15:00-16:45 Allan Maslove (Carleton University, Ottawa): *The Canadian Case*

Markus M. Müller (University of Erlangen-Nuremberg, Erlangen): *Regulation, Taxation or Inaction? Budgetary Politics, Institutional Reform and American "Judicialism"*

23 Oct., 1999

3. Minorities

8:45-10:30 Yasmeen Abu-Laban (University of Alberta, Edmonton): *Reconsidering the Constitution: Minorities and Politics in Canada* (Co-author: Tim Nieguth, University of Alberta, Edmonton)

Michael Dreyer (University of Jena, Jena): *The American Case*

4. Federalism

10:45-12:30 Roland Sturm (University of Erlangen-Nuremberg, Erlangen): *Federalism and Constitutional Politics – A Theoretical Perspective*

Timothy Conlan (George Mason University, Fairfax): *The American Case*

14:00-15:45 Harvey Lazar (Queen's University, Kingston): *The Canadian Case*

Marc Desjardins (Privy Council Office, Ottawa): *The Evolution of Canadian Federalism: Some Recent Developments*

Constitutional Jurisprudence – Does it Stimulate or Prevent Reform Efforts?

16:00-17:45 Martin Edelman (SUNY, Albany): *Change is a Sometimes Thing: Constitutional Jurisprudence in the United States*

Martin Thunert (University of Hamburg, Hamburg): *The Canadian Case*

17:45-18:15 Concluding Discussion

SPRINGER NATURE

<u>GPSR Compliance</u>

The European Union's (EU) General Product Safety Regulation (GPSR) is a set of rules that requires consumer products to be safe and our obligations to ensure this.

If you have any concerns about our products, you can contact us on ProductSafety@springernature.com

In case Publisher is established outside the EU, the EU authorized representative is:

Springer Nature Customer Service Center GmbH
Europaplatz 3
69115 Heidelberg, Germany

Kolibri 360 GmbH
Ferdinand-Jühlke-Straße 7
99095 Erfurt, Deutschland
produktsicherheit@kolibri360.de